Disturbing Bodies

The SAR seminar from which this book resulted was made possible with the generous support of the Paloheimo Foundation.

School for Advanced Research
Advanced Seminar Series

Disturbing Bodies

Contributors

Serrin Boys
Florida Gulf Coast University

Zoë Crossland
Columbia University

Luis Fondebrider
Argentine Forensic Anthropology Team

Pamela L. Geller
University of Miami

Rosemary A. Joyce
University of California, Berkeley

Debra L. Martin
University of Nevada, Las Vegas

Isaias Rojas-Perez
Rutgers University

Tim Thompson
Teesside University

Hugh Tuller
Joint POW/MIA Accounting Command, Central Identification Laboratory

Heather Walsh-Haney
Florida Gulf Coast University

Disturbing Bodies

Perspectives on Forensic Anthropology

Edited by Zoë Crossland and Rosemary A. Joyce

SAR PRESS

School for Advanced Research Press

Santa Fe

School for Advanced Research Press
Post Office Box 2188
Santa Fe, New Mexico 87504-2188
www.sarpress.org

Managing Editor: Sarah Soliz
Editorial Assistant: Ellen Goldberg
Designer and Production Manager: Cynthia Dyer
Manuscript Editor: Merryl Sloane
Proofreader: Michelle Coughlin
Indexer: Margaret Moore Booker
Printer: Versa Press

Library of Congress Cataloging-in-Publication Data

Disturbing bodies : perspectives on forensic anthropology / edited by Zoë Crossland and Rosemary A. Joyce.
pages cm. — (Advanced seminar series)
Includes bibliographical references and index.
ISBN 978-1-938645-55-6 (alk. paper)
1. Forensic anthropology. I. Crossland, Zoë. II. Joyce, Rosemary A., 1956-
GN69.8.D57 2015
599.9—dc23
2015007971

Manufactured in the United States of America
Library of Congress Catalog Card Number 2015007971
International Standard Book Number 978-1-938645-55-6
First edition 2015.

Cover illustration: Maureen Schaefer working in cemetery near Zvornik, © Ivan Sebalj.

The School for Advanced Research (SAR) promotes the furthering of scholarship on—and public understanding of—human culture, behavior, and evolution. SAR Press publishes cutting-edge scholarly and general-interest books that encourage critical thinking and present new perspectives on topics of interest to all humans. Contributions by authors reflect their own opinions and viewpoints and do not necessarily express the opinions of SAR Press.

Contents

Disturbing Bodies

1

Anthropological Perspectives on Disturbing Bodies

An Introduction

Zoë Crossland and Rosemary A. Joyce

Although bodies have been exhumed for the purposes of legal inquest for centuries (Hunnisett 1961), the practice of forensic exhumation is relatively recent. Forensic anthropology began in the context of small-scale criminal investigations, and although there were some notable early exhumations of mass graves in the mid-twentieth century (Mant 1987), most of the growth in the field has taken place over the last few decades. The 1990s saw a dramatic increase in the number and scale of exhumations, notably in South America, the former Yugoslavia, and Rwanda. Since then the field has expanded rapidly in terms of both the numbers of anthropologists and archaeologists involved and the numbers of people who are exhumed every year. On a global scale, usually within the framework of investigations into human rights abuses, the dead are increasingly being brought back into the world of the living. Their disinterment often takes place where there is no tradition of exhumation or of preserving the bodies of the dead, and sometimes in ways that are not sanctioned or accepted by relatives or other interested groups. Emotionally charged reactions and responses to the emergent dead reveal the ways in which different understandings of the dead body are unmade and remade through the body's exposure in the grave.

As bodies are revealed, so are the hidden and often incommensurate understandings of the body after death held by different participants. These may include national or ethnic narratives that inform claims to bodies; personal memories and histories maintained by relatives; and the constitution of the corpse as evidence through the performative acts of exhumation, display, and analysis. At the center of this is the work of forensic anthropologists. Although often considered narrowly in terms of its technical and methodological aspects, forensic practice (particularly in the context of human rights investigations) draws upon multiple dimensions of anthropology. As Schmitt (2002:290) says of human rights investigations, "Forensic anthropology and taphonomy of mass graves in this context are more than technical and isolated approaches to evidence collection and remains recovery. Anthropology in all of its facets, including law, cultural patterns, biological diversity, and archaeological interpretation of cultural patterns can and should be brought to bear in the investigation of genocide, war crimes, crimes against humanity, and human rights violations."

Whether working with relatives, analyzing human remains, excavating graves, or thinking about the words that are used to talk about the dead, the day-to-day practices of many forensic anthropologists span subdisciplinary boundaries. (Indeed, the Physical Anthropology Section of the American Academy of Forensic Sciences has changed its name to Anthropology to better capture the wide range of activities carried out by practitioners; Christensen 2014:55.) This becomes especially apparent in the context of exhumation, by its nature a public performance that invites involvement by a wide range of actors. Such excavations have dramatic and persistent social and political consequences, and forensic specialists are caught up in these reactions. In moving between the more public sphere of the excavation site and the interior spaces of the laboratory, archaeologists often have more contact than other forensic specialists with relatives and other interested individuals and groups. Because of the highly visible and sometimes contentious nature of archaeological forensic work, it provides a useful site to think about issues involved in broader forensic anthropological practice. Archaeology is thus the primary focus for this volume, although some chapters encompass issues relevant to forensic anthropology more broadly and do not always separate out forensic archaeology as a distinct field. We offer a range of anthropological perspectives from across the discipline on the work of exhumation and the attendant issues involved.

FORENSIC HISTORIES

A full history of forensic anthropology has yet to be written, but T. Dale Stewart (1978, 1982) and Douglas Ubelaker (1999; Ubelaker and Scammell 1992) have sketched out some of the key moments in the field's history (see also Blau and Ubelaker 2009; Dirkmaat 2012; Márquez-Grant et al.

2012). In the United States forensic anthropologists usually have some understanding of archaeological excavation techniques, but traditionally they have been oriented primarily toward lab-based osteological analysis of the skeleton as part of the legal process. This analysis includes estimating stature, sex, and ancestry; assessing markers of disease or injury in order to build a biological profile of unidentified individuals; and identifying perimortem forms of trauma to the skeleton to help reconstruct how people died. As forensic anthropological investigations expanded around the turn of the twenty-first century, archaeology began to emerge as an important part of forensic work, to such an extent that forensic archaeology is now developing as a field in itself.

Dennis Dirkmaat and colleagues have traced the challenges to the scope of forensic anthropological work in a series of papers that consider the role of archaeology in US forensic practice (Dirkmaat and Adovasio 1997; Dirkmaat and Cabo 2012; Dirkmaat et al. 2008). Forensic archaeology is usually distinguished from forensic physical anthropology in its concentration on the scene of a crime and the use of archaeological techniques, such as excavation, to recover human remains. Forensic archaeologists attend not only to the body in the grave, but also to the wider context of the grave site and associated artifacts. Excavation can contribute evidence of how people died and the context in which their deaths took place. For example, archaeological evidence retrieved from the massacre site at Ovčara, near the Croatian town of Vukovar in the former Yugoslavia, indicated that civilians and hospitalized combatants had been executed in groups at the grave site. In that instance, personal possessions, hospital clothing, and medical equipment were important in demonstrating the status of those killed, and the deposition of bodies and ballistic evidence showed how victims died at the site (Stover 1997; Stover and Peress 1998).

The wider archaeological community has paid little attention to the work being carried out by forensic anthropologists and archaeologists. This is perhaps because, as Connor and Scott (2001:1) have pointed out, archaeology came into forensic investigations as a technique, rather than as a discipline, with archaeological practices transferring into forensic anthropology "independently of the paradigms behind them." In North America, the disparity between the processual emphasis on the search for regularities in human adaptation and the event-focused particularities of forensic archaeology has perhaps also created distance between forensic archaeology and the rest of the archaeological field, although certainly there is much common ground to be found in the concern with taphonomy and depositional processes.

Some of the first accounts to critically reflect on forensic work grew out of an interest with the "contemporary past" (Buchli and Lucas 2001; Crossland 2000; Davenport and Harrison 2011; González-Ruibal 2007; Pearson and Shanks 2001; Renshaw 2007; Weiss 2010). This theoretical space provides a promising arena for continued intellectual exchange. Archaeological studies of clandestine detention centers and other sites of repression in Spain and the countries of Latin America explore the wider context of political violence (Fondebrider, chapter 2, this volume; Fuentes et al. 2009; Funari et al. 2009; González-Ruibal 2011; Zarankin and Funari 2008). This work resonates with growing archaeological interest in the traces of undocumented migrants crossing the border between the United States and Mexico (De León 2012). Another converging theme can be found in ethnographies of archaeological practice, which reflect on the production of knowledge at the trowel's edge (Abu El-Haj 2001; Edgeworth 2006; Hamilakis and Anagnostopoulos 2009).

Forensic anthropologists have also become more interested in exploring the broader dimensions of recent and contemporary violence, whether through the study of skeletal remains or at the site of exhumation (e.g., Gómez López and Patiño Umaña 2007; Komar 2008a, 2008b; Steadman and Haglund 2005). Anthropological explorations of how forms of violence are culturally embedded and historically specific (Appadurai 1998; Uribe 2004) have opened up possibilities for thinking about the violence of the recent past in conversation with forensic observations (see, for example, Ta'ala et al. 2006).

The uniform horror of mass graves can mask very different practices around the disposal of the dead. In the former Yugoslavia the excavation of mass graves was complicated by attempts to hide the evidence of the dead through clandestine exhumation and reburial elsewhere (Pollack 2003; Primorac et al. 1996; Skinner et al. 2002). In Argentina (Olmo 2005) and elsewhere those killed through state-sponsored repression were often buried anonymously in existing cemeteries. In Peru human remains were burned in an effort to disguise the actions of those responsible (Rojas-Perez, chapter 3, this volume). Colombia has seen the development of clandestine cemeteries and mass graves. Rather than being the product of one violent event, these sites have been brought into being through years of repeated use (Gómez López and Patiño Umaña 2007). Elsewhere landscape features, including rivers (Meierhenrich 2009) and caves (Klonowski 2007a), have been used to dispose of bodies. In recording and tracking these differences, forensic work has the potential to contribute to broader debates about contexts of violence, whether structural or interpersonal, from the present or from the more distant past (e.g., Blakely and Harrington 1997; Fiorato et al. 2000; Novak and Kopp 2003).

We hope that conversations within the discipline will open up new avenues for forensic specialists to contribute to ethnographic analyses of contemporary violence and the role of human remains in ongoing conflicts (Petrović-Šteger 2009; Rojas-Perez 2008; Wagner 2008). This volume therefore looks toward a more integrated anthropology of the dead body. This involves embedding archaeological fieldwork and other exhumatory practices in broader relationships and exploring what the rest of anthropology might learn through a more sustained engagement with the questions raised by forensic work.

FORENSIC VARIATIONS

To consider the range and nature of the relationships involved in exhumation, this volume brings together ten scholars involved with anthropological work around the dead: archaeologists, biological anthropologists, and a sociocultural anthropologist, all of whom either work in contexts of forensic exhumation or have interests in mortuary contexts or bioarchaeology. The different chapters explore the values and beliefs that underlie forensic exhumation and the tensions that arise in the practice of forensic archaeological research.

Regular exhumation developed in the 1980s as part of human rights investigations into the disappearances of thousands of people in Argentina in the preceding decades. Luis Fondebrider was involved in establishing the nonprofit, nongovernmental Argentine Forensic Anthropology Team (EAAF) in 1984, under the guidance of American forensic anthropologist Clyde Snow. Established as part of the national inquiry into political violence in Argentina, the EAAF pioneered an interdisciplinary approach and has undertaken investigations throughout the world. In this volume Fondebrider reflects on his experiences as a founding member of the EAAF, including his work training forensic anthropology teams and acting as a consultant for human rights investigations. He argues that the human rights context demands a holistic, anthropologically informed approach that is sensitive to the wider context within which exhumations take place.

In 2001 members of the EAAF visited Peru to assist the newly formed Peruvian Team of Forensic Anthropology (EAAF 2001) and then returned in 2002 to help resolve conflicts that had emerged between Peru's Public Ministry, the Peruvian Truth and Reconciliation Commission, and the Peruvian forensic team. Members of the Peruvian team had a great deal of experience in forensic work and were unhappy with how exhumations were being carried out (EAAF 2002). The EAAF (2002:96–97) observes that such conflicts often emerge in situations of state violence where forensic specialists have to work within the judicial system, and exhumations may be undertaken by people who are untrained in archaeological excavation and osteological analysis. It was in this context that Isaias Rojas-Perez undertook an ethnographic project following the search for remains of those killed at Los Cabitos military base, the center of the state's violent counterinsurgency campaign in the Ayacucho region of the south-central Andes. His chapter explores the frustrations of investigations that at first were unable to find the bodies of the dead. Rojas-Perez asks how the dead can be brought back into being as legal, cultural, and historical subjects in the absence of an individualized and identified body. He notes how archaeological investigations are caught up in state attempts to finalize the past, while at the same time they go beyond the scope of the law narrowly conceived.

The "tension between state making and justice making" that Rojas-Perez outlines has also arisen in other parts of the world, a topic that Hugh Tuller addresses in his contribution. Although forensic anthropological techniques were originally called upon—as the name suggests—in the context of criminal prosecutions, exhumation also has other, nonlegal dimensions. The field of "forensic" anthropology has extended to include a range of more broadly "humanitarian" tasks, and it has taken on an important role in reconstructing and defining memory (Ferrándiz 2006; Renshaw 2007; Sant Cassia 2006). Fondebrider notes the pervasive need to recover the bodies of the dead and the important work of anthropologists in identification and repatriation, aside from the legal work of prosecution. Since the early 1990s, with the implementation of international criminal tribunals to investigate human rights violations in the former Yugoslavia and Rwanda, the judicial and humanitarian excavation of human remains has increased to an unprecedented scale under mandate from the United Nations (Cordner and McKelvie 2002; Heller 2012). Skills developed in investigations of human rights violations in Latin America and elsewhere (e.g., Lõugas 1991; Wright 1995) were drawn upon in developing a framework for the forensic investigation of human rights violations in other places (Haglund et al. 2001; Saunders 2002; Vanezis 1999). The post–Second World War Nuremberg trials, a model for these tribunals, rested largely on documentary evidence and witness testimony (Kirschner and Hannibal 1994). The shift toward using forensic anthropological evidence meant that procedures had to be adapted and new techniques developed for the new contexts of investigation. Tuller's chapter reflects on issues raised by the particular demands and expectations of the tribunal for the former

Yugoslavia. He considers the tension between different demands—of identification of the dead and prosecution of those responsible—and outlines the differences between forensic archaeology and mainstream archaeological research, particularly the different responsibilities of forensic practitioners and potential restrictions on their practice.

There is considerable variation in how forensic anthropology has developed in different parts of the world, which has led to the emergence of localized traditions of practice. In the United States forensic anthropology developed in the context of domestic criminal investigations. Some of the most influential pioneers in forensic anthropology had their training in medical schools and worked in museum contexts, acting as consultants to assess skeletal material for the FBI (Ubelaker 2009:78–79). Today in the United States, anthropologists predominate. They have expanded their work from identification to a variety of tasks, including archaeological investigation. Anthropologists may "assist in missing person searches…estimate postmortem intervals, explain burning patterns of bone, and interpret trauma" (Steadman et al. 2009:351).

Alan G. Morris (2011:3) in a popular text about his experiences in South African forensic anthropology observes that the "practice of forensic anthropology is not the same everywhere…and techniques that work well in Boston may not be applicable in Botswana." The forensic focus in the United States on establishing the race or ancestry of human remains is an example. The assignment of race, which is under debate in the forensic anthropological community (Ousley et al. 2009; Quintyn 2010; Sauer 1992), remains a critical part of the biological profile in the United States. In the United Kingdom, in contrast, Gowland and Thompson (2013:30) report that many physical anthropologists have "abandoned the use of the race concept in teaching physical anthropology." Gowland and Thompson note the commonly recognized methodological problems with "the arbitrary nature of many of the phenotypic divisions used and the poor correlation between traits and geographic location" (30), yet the demand for a racial profile by law enforcement officials remains. In their contribution to this volume Heather Walsh-Haney and Serrin Boys explore the question of racial categories and the biological profiling of the dead in the United States. They outline the expectations around the determination of race in their work with police and medical examiners in Florida. Although the authors work primarily in domestic criminal contexts in the United States, Walsh-Haney also has experience with international criminal and human rights investigations in Guatemala. This encourages her to step back from the particularly American perspective on race to take a wider view.

Another contrast between the United States and the United Kingdom is in the history of how British forensic archaeology developed—independent of anthropology. Forensic archaeology in the United Kingdom has emerged more rapidly, growing out of a broad-based engagement with archaeology as a separate discipline (Cox 2009; Hunter 1999; Hunter et al. 1994). So Tim Thompson in his chapter looks at forensic practice from a theoretical perspective embedded in wider archaeological debates. Thompson, one of a small number of forensic archaeologists in the United Kingdom, works in the university sector and also acts as a forensic consultant for the regional police force in the northeast of the country. Although there is a stronger sense of forensic archaeology as a separate discipline in the United Kingdom, it is only since the 1980s that a forensic archaeological approach has started to coalesce as a separate area of expertise, and it continues to be a small part of domestic forensic investigations (Black 2003; Thompson 2003). A similar situation obtains in South Africa, where study of the human skeleton is usually undertaken in departments of anatomy and can include the use of archaeological techniques to retrieve human remains (L'Abbé and Steyn 2012; Morris 2011). In Australia, there are relatively few instances where archaeology has been used to recover remains domestically (Blau 2004). An awareness of the various histories and modes of practice brought to forensic exhumation by forensic experts from different parts of the world underwrites Thompson's discussion of the ongoing debates about standardization in international forensic investigations.

Archaeology is also an important part of the search for US military and civilian personnel who were lost during conflicts overseas (Holland et al. 2008). Hugh Tuller's work as part of the US Joint POW/MIA Accounting Command's Central Identification Laboratory (JPAC-CIL) has involved excavations and recovery missions in many different parts of the world. The JPAC task force works under the purview of the US Department of Defense and can also be deployed in situations of mass disaster, such as the 2005 Southeast Asian tsunami. Tuller considers the different goals of forensic exhumation and makes the case that archaeologists should be responsible for deciding what information is collected and how, arguing that the fullest possible record should be made regardless of the aim of the exhumation. He contends that forensic archaeology is not simply the search for missing people; rather, practitioners "are interested in broader questions than what the artifact or piece of evidence can provide on its own." In this sense forensic practitioners have more in common with other archaeologists than is often supposed.

OTHER WAYS OF DISTURBING BODIES

This volume brings the six scholars mentioned above, who are actively engaged in work in forensic situations, into conversation with four archaeologists who write on the archaeology of the dead but without the constraints and demands of legal or criminal proceedings. Pamela Geller offers another perspective on the attribution of race to skeletal remains, complementing Walsh-Haney and Boys's more explicitly forensic viewpoint. Geller discusses a collection of human crania labeled as "Seminole," a classification made in the first half of the nineteenth century. She explores the history of the skeletal analyses of the remains of these individuals to draw out the tensions inherent in any attempt to explore complex histories of race and identity through characteristics of the skeleton. She demonstrates both the racially charged and problematic nature of such analysis and the potential it offers for bringing hidden and effaced histories and people into view.

Debra Martin provides another bioarchaeological perspective in her chapter, where she considers why there has been relatively little interchange between bioarchaeology and forensic work, and she points out potential avenues for future conversations in the discipline. Martin's view is from outside forensic archaeology, but her work is closely related in its focus on violence and its effects.

Zoë Crossland and Rosemary Joyce are archaeologists concerned with mortuary and funerary archaeology. Crossland's chapter deals with mass-market texts written by forensic anthropologists from North America. No other part of the anthropological field produces so many popular books aimed at a general audience. This is all the more striking when we consider the small number of active forensic anthropologists. In memoirs and fiction, authors explore the broader resonances and emotional impacts of forensic work, reflections that are not generally found in academic texts. They offer insight into how the field is imagined in the United States by practitioners and the public alike.

In her chapter, Joyce comments on the entire volume: she considers the justifications for disturbing the dead and also inquires into how persons (dead and alive) are produced through archaeological practice. In raising the issue of responsibility to the dead, Joyce foregrounds the question of narration, highlighting the language that is used to talk about the dead in different contexts, a question that Rojas-Perez also touches upon. How do different justifications for disturbing the dead (in forensic practice and in archaeology) underwrite different modes of interacting with them, if at all?

This broadens the question from that of narration to encompass dispositions toward and practices around the dead, as Fondebrider also explores.

The fragmentation of anthropology over the course of the twentieth century can make it difficult to reach across the boundaries between the different parts of the discipline. Subfields have developed their own languages and concerns, and practitioners have different ways of being as anthropologists. During the seminar on which this book is based, we experienced moments when the discussion seemed to move in directions of great interest to some of us and, apparently, less relevance for others. In many ways we experienced the seminar as an ongoing project of translation and explanation as we searched for ways to explore why and how different issues mattered to different participants. Some of these differences also come through in the chapters here, which vary stylistically according to both subfield and author.

We may not wholly share a common vocabulary and rhetorical forms, but there is a large degree of overlap in the concerns that are articulated in this volume. It was salutary to be part of a seminar where all participants made good faith efforts to move out of their disciplinary comfort zones in order to engage in productive cross-field exchanges. The chapters make a strong case for situating forensic anthropology as a critical node in anthropology, where the need for engaged and considered intradisciplinary conversations is being felt.

EXHUMATION IN CULTURAL CONTEXT

The theme of "disturbing bodies" of course has a double meaning, evoking both the work that anthropologists do—the ways in which we disturb the dead—and the ways in which the dead in turn can disturb the living: by their material qualities; through hauntings, dreams, and other forms of presence; and through political claims and challenges often articulated around them (Verdery 1999). Anthropologists spend a great deal of time exhuming and profiling bodies in order to enable the dead to be returned to their families for proper burial, not just for the purposes of prosecution (Burns 1999:204–207; S. Martin 2002; Sassòli and Tougas 2002; Stover and Shigekane 2002). Huge efforts are expended in searching for the dead, as in the former Yugoslavia (Huffine et al. 2001; Klonowski 2007b) and in the continuing search by the United States for soldiers who went missing during conflicts in other parts of the world (Emanovsky and Belcher 2012). There is often a felt need for the physical body to be found in cases of accidental death, murder, and genocide. The expansion of the field of forensic archaeology has prompted study by sociocultural anthropologists and historians of different contexts of exhumation across the world, including in El Salvador (Binford 1996), Guatemala (Sanford 2003a), Cyprus (Sant Cassia 2005), Spain (Ferrándiz 2008, 2009), Vietnam (Kwon 2008), the former Yugoslavia (Wagner 2008), and the former Soviet Union (Paperno 2001; Rév 2005). These accounts explore the wider impact of forensic anthropology as it extends into the terrain of human rights and cultural memory.

Such studies illustrate how forensic excavations for human rights reasons, although assertively scientific and apparently detached from the cultural milieus within which they are made meaningful, are also situated within funerary practices. To locate forensic archaeological practice in the anthropological literature on mortuary rituals is to understand exhumation as a stage in mortuary ritual (Crossland 2000; Froidevaux 2002; Rév 2005; Sant Cassia 2005), a means to transfer the dead body from its liminal location in a temporary grave to a final resting place, where the dead can be reincorporated into society. If the work is successful, the human remains uncovered in forensic excavations will ultimately be reunited with their relatives and undergo the proper funerary rites, once again located in their proper place. Relationships with the living are reestablished through the presence of the body, allowing the proper negotiation of the remains' transfer into the realm of the dead.

Fondebrider asks what happens when a family member tells an anthropologist that he or she knows from a dream where the dead are buried and needs no forensic confirmation, or when relatives cannot recognize the dead in the bones that are returned. It is in these situations, where a sense of contradiction between scientific and local knowledge emerges, that Fondebrider argues that it is important to remember that "before being a forensic anthropologist one is an anthropologist with the benefit of a holistic, more comprehensive approach than the one held by other scientific disciplines, such as medicine or dentistry." Forensic anthropologists have more to offer than techniques for excavating the dead or reading the bones of the body, and their training can help them "walk along this path of contradictions, bridging gaps and reconciling different perspectives."

In viewing archaeological exhumation as part of broader mortuary and funerary practices, shifting and context-specific prohibitions on certain forms of postmortem treatment are made clear: the dead may be exhumed and reburied, but only under certain circumstances. The important role that exhumation can play in reconstructing memory and society underlines the significance of the relationships within which the dead body is situated. In bringing the dead back into view, exhumation sites create radically new contexts for interaction and mourning (Stover and Shigekane 2002). This can be in some conflict with the legal need for excavated evidence (Stover and Shigekane 2004).

Tuller outlines the extemporized nature of the forensic investigations that were part of the International Criminal Tribunal for the former Yugoslavia (ICTY), where new ways of working had to be developed to deal with the enormous number of very recent burials. Tensions quickly emerged between the desire of relatives to recover and identify the dead and the more limited need of the tribunal to find evidence to prosecute those responsible. In 1996 the International Commission on Missing Persons (ICMP) was established with the goal of identifying and repatriating remains exhumed by the ICTY and to continue the process of exhumation. Tuller notes the difficulties in coordinating the work of different organizations and the ways in which different investigative goals can conflict, leaving archaeologists in a difficult position as to how to proceed with the excavation. He reports that there has been debate over the role of the forensic anthropologist in this work, with some arguing that a forensic practitioner's task in such an international investigation should be limited to retrieving evidence for prosecution. Fondebrider makes a strong argument against this position, laying out the case for a more holistic view of forensic work, given the political and historical dimensions of such exhumations.

Thompson outlines examples of different responses to exhumation in different parts of the world. In the former Yugoslavia local workers were excluded from the recovery of bodies in some cases so that international forensic teams would not be seen to favor particular groups, but this frustrated families who were searching for their dead (Petrović-Šteger 2009). In other situations local men were included, to the discomfort of excavation team members who perceived that these workers were not respectful of the dead and may have had some knowledge of the massacre (Brkic 2004; Mitrović 2008). These accounts demonstrate that even though foreign team members are perhaps more easily able to maintain a certain distance from different local interest groups, they remain unavoidably caught up in local politics and in the search by families for their dead. Thompson contrasts this approach with Victoria Sanford's (2003a) account of forensic exhumations in Guatemala, which were undertaken as a community project and where the grave became a location where relatives and survivors could interact with the dead and their traces.

Forensic archaeology is thus deeply culturally and historically embedded, and this is as much the case for the scientific and technical work of excavation as for any more "local" contexts. Crossland (2011:288) observes that archaeological investigation can be a powerful form of post-conflict sense-making that draws some of its symbolic force from "the very act of cordoning off and securing an area of violence and horror...of bringing scientific techniques and practices to bear on a locus of disorder and destruction." Similarly, in his chapter Rojas-Perez notes the faith placed in archaeological techniques as a means to recover the past, and he suggests that the controlled nature of excavation is an important dimension of the truth-making work of archaeology. Rojas-Perez observes that in the investigation at Los Cabitos the archaeologists' search for evidence of mass graves was ineffective at first. He notes the *desánimo,* or "dispiriting," of the archaeologists at their failure to find any entire bodies, despite finding traces of the dead in the form of burnt bone. He suggests that this sentiment reflects their own experiences of Peru's violent past and derives in part from the lack of space to articulate this relationship to the past within a scientific and forensic frame.

The failure of forensic discourse to provide space for the ambiguities of history, of interpretation, and of feeling has been tackled by forensic anthropologists in two key ways. The first is to search for ever-refined methodologies and to create more robust and standardized measures to allow yet more control over the excavation process and its results. Thompson observes in his chapter that most attention is given in the forensic literature on standardization to "dry methodological issues," particularly questions of consistency in methods and their application in different situations, and to standards for forensic training and the assessment of expertise. Techniques for the collection and definition of forensic archaeological evidence vary with the training and background of the archaeologists working on any particular case (Crist 2001; Doretti and Snow 2003; France et al. 1992) and with the particular demands and exigencies of the circumstances on the ground (Hoshower 1998; Skinner 2007; Stover et al. 2003). Grivas and Komar (2008) observe that although some anthropological techniques can be quantified and tested, others are more qualitative and dependent on the careful observation and experience of the forensic expert. Christensen and Crowder (2009) note that this does not make the evidence any less empirical in nature. As Daston and Galison (2007) have outlined, what is at stake is how the "trained judgment" of the expert witness operates and is folded into understandings of scientific objectivity. The search for methodological precision, Thompson suggests, is a way to compensate for the "fuzzy" and qualitative nature of forensic anthropological work, although in so doing it opens up a different set of problems.

The experience of different conditions and expectations for forensic work outside the United States has encouraged more attention to the social and political environment in which investigations take place (e.g., Ferllini, ed. 2007), particularly in the case of highly visible exhumations (Ballbé and Steadman 2008; Cox 2001; Hunter and Simpson 2007; Skinner 2007; Steele 2008). However, even this literature tends to be restricted to explaining legal concerns and describing problems with technical procedures. Fondebrider observes that the tendency is to treat the investigations carried out in the former Yugoslavia as a model for forensic practice elsewhere, with little attention being paid to the historical, cultural, and political specificities of the Balkan exhumations. Thompson notes that relatively little attention has been paid to the work of interpretation and to the implications of standardization for the actors involved. This would involve taking account of the tensions that can emerge at a crime scene, partly because of the difficult and fraught work of exhuming the dead, partly because of the different goals of those involved, and partly because of divergent perceptions of forensic expertise and unrealistic expectations for the work. Reviewing different approaches to exhumation in a range of contexts, Thompson points to some of the different expectations articulated around the dead, and how these may come into conflict with forensic anthropological objectives and assumptions. These are issues that cannot be grappled with through the simple refinement and standardization of methods, instead requiring a wider anthropological lens. The emphasis on methods and on the forensic anthropologist's detachment from the scene of a crime can be counterproductive insofar as it fails to provide avenues to engage with the complexities of exhumation, as Rojas-Perez explores.

Another way in which forensic anthropologists explore questions and issues that cannot be expressed in forensic reports or in articles about techniques and methods is by creating mass media texts, notably fiction and autobiography. Crossland reconnoiters this literary terrain, which is peculiar to English-language forensic anthropology. These texts draw upon a long-standing tradition of detective narratives, revolve around bodily clues and expert decryption, and are situated in a mass of other popular representations of forensic investigation. A key report on forensic science in the United States published by the National Academy of Sciences noted the influence of the police procedural drama *CSI: Crime Scene Investigation* and related television shows (National Research Council 2009:48). At a hearing in the House of Representatives the chair, David Wu, prefaced the proceedings by expressing the hope that they would act to "[bring] reality into better alignment with the high expectations created by our entertainment industry" (5). Although the "*CSI* effect" seems to be more imagined than actual (Cole and Dioso-Villa 2007, 2009), the debate illustrates how public discussion around forensic evidence can create imaginative possibilities for scientific practice. Crossland explores the popular literature on forensic anthropology written by forensic anthropologists themselves as a way of better understanding how forensic anthropological practice is conceptualized in the United States and how, as Walsh-Haney (2011) has observed, it also acts to offset some of the more imaginative fictional portrayals of forensic science.

In many of these popular portrayals, forensic work is positioned as a technical search for truth, which can become complicated by larger social concerns or by the emotional involvement of the protagonist. This view can also inform forensic practice, as Rojas-Perez explores. Emphasizing technique over interpretation, such a perspective entails assumptions about the nature of truth that may be uncontroversial in the context of criminal investigation in the United States, but that can become problematic in other parts of the world. An example is provided by Douglas Ubelaker's assertion in his popular book *Bones* (Ubelaker and Scammell 1992:58) that "there can never be a negative moral consequence to the truth." The experiences of forensic anthropologists working outside the United States reveal how a concept of truth as a unitary and straightforward goal is grounded in a particular cultural milieu. The EAAF, for example, observes on its website that forensic anthropologists should respect family members' wishes in the case of their "total opposition to exhumation." There are diverse ways to the truth, and the refusal by family members of a truth produced through exhumation is respected. The team notes that tribunals and commissions often need only a sample of graves to be excavated, and so forensic practitioners "can often still provide an estimation of the non-exhumed individuals" without needing to disturb the dead.

Problematizing the naturalized understanding of the lived body that underlies biomedicine, Nancy Scheper-Hughes and Margaret Lock (1987:7–8) observe that from the perspective of much Western medicine, social information is seen as extraneous and unnecessary to the treatment of disease, because the real causes are located in biology. Similarly, in forensic anthropology as it has developed in domestic crime investigation in the United States, the social is bracketed off to a large degree. This is reinforced by the lab-based nature of much forensic work, and the perceived need for forensic anthropologists to avoid contact with family members and other interested parties where possible. Textbooks and accounts written for a general audience tend to suggest that the wider social and political context is something to be remembered, lest the anthropologist lose his or her humanity, but not something to actively engage in. Ubelaker observes, "In order to protect the truth every science demands complete objectivity of its practitioners" (Ubelaker and Scammell 1992:58). The privileged access of science to the truth is protected by guarding against subjectivity and the dangers of interference from interested actors. This creates a challenge, and Ubelaker continues, "objectivity is one thing, and aloofness is another" (59). The demands of forensic testimony in the United States encourage a rhetorical privileging of the ability of evidence to stand aside from or "object" to representations about it (Crossland 2009a; also Latour 2000), as well as a search for a quantitative and probabilistic language to express degrees of confidence in forensic evidence (Christensen 2004). Yet the situation becomes more complex when investigations are centered on mass disasters or political violence.

Despite its wide field of influence, the work of forensic anthropology tends to be imagined narrowly by professional organizations in North America. The American Board of Forensic Anthropology (ABFA) asks "What is forensic anthropology?" on its website (http://www.theabfa.org). The response flags the scientific and legal dimensions of the work: "Forensic anthropology is the application of the science of physical or biological anthropology to the legal process. Physical or biological anthropologists who specialize in forensics primarily focus their studies on the human skeleton." Below this, the site gives more detail on "the practice of forensic anthropology," noting that "the analysis of skeletal, badly decomposed, or otherwise unidentified human remains is important in both legal and humanitarian contexts." The website describes how forensic anthropologists not only locate and recover human skeletal remains, but also "assess the age, sex, ancestry, stature, and unique features of a decedent from the skeleton." They often "work in conjunction with forensic pathologists, odontologists, and homicide investigators to identify a decedent, document trauma to the skeleton, and/or estimate the postmortem interval."

The work of forensic anthropology, as it is understood by the ABFA, is circumscribed and tied closely to homicide investigation by the police or to the investigation of human rights abuses. In these descriptions, forensic anthropological work is defined through its methods and through its relationship to other forensic specialists. There is no mention of wider publics or of interactions with relatives and survivors of violence. Equally, the work of writing and of other forms of representation of these methodological interventions is not included in the description, although it is clearly a vibrant and important part of the work of forensic anthropologists (see Crossland, chapter 6, this volume; Komar and Buikstra 2008:15). The US focus on technique and method independent from larger social and political concerns is reiterated in the American Board of Forensic Anthropology's statement of ethics, also available on the board's website (http://www.theabfa.org), which makes no mention of relatives or other interest groups. Heather Walsh-Haney (2011) observes a related lack of attention to ethnographic field interviews on the Scientific Working Group for Forensic Anthropology website (http://www.swganth.org). This absence suggests that forensic anthropology in the United States is still very much conceptualized within the North American framework of domestic criminal police investigations, as Fondebrider explores in his chapter. This is despite the common intervention of North American forensic anthropologists in post-conflict zones across the world and the increasing importance of interaction and communication with the families of the dead in situations of mass disaster and political violence (Sledzik 2012). The work of the New York Medical Examiner's Office in communicating about ongoing work at the World Trade Center site to the families of those killed on September 11, 2001, is a case in point (Mundorf 2003; Rainwater et al. 2012).

The experience of anthropologists who work in the context of mass disasters and human rights investigations abroad has encouraged a broadening of roles and perspectives beyond the scope of laboratory work (Warren et al. 2008). There is a growing recognition of the culturally situated perspectives and training that people bring to any exhumation. Thompson outlines recent developments in the field and argues for considering the different relationships within which forensic work is situated. He suggests that in considering the question of forensic standards and benchmarks "conceivably of greater importance than just standardization are the continued collaborations between workers and interested parties." Tuller concurs that agreed-upon international standards can be counterproductive and suggests that although standards are important, they need to be developed with reference to local contexts and expectations.

Furthermore, Fondebrider maintains that the work of exhumation needs to begin with an awareness and consideration of its location within a range of enmeshed and sometimes irreconcilable projects, including judicial prosecutions, humanitarian assistance, political redefinitions of community and state, economic and infrastructural reorganization, and, perhaps above all, the needs and desires of relatives and survivors. He observes that "what appears as a clear-cut scientific and technical operation may involve complex and ambiguous boundaries, as well as unexpected ethical dilemmas" (2002:886). This speaks to the difficult balance that forensic practitioners have to strike between maintaining the integrity of their investigation and working with families and other interested parties. Fondebrider observed during the SAR seminar that the EAAF may strive to be objective in its investigations and reporting, but its work is not neutral. The team works for the families of the dead and is aligned with them and their interests. Spanish archaeologist Francisco Etxeberría (2012:9) makes the same point, arguing that "objectivity and impartiality should not be confused with neutrality.... No one should be neutral when dealing with Human Rights violations."[1] This starts to unpack some of the complex bundle of historically situated associations that are caught up in the term "objectivity" (Daston and Galison 2007). To disentangle the question of impartiality in excavation and recording from the engaged activism of those who search for the dead is to create a space for ongoing relationships with families and to find room to acknowledge different responses to violence and terror.

THE ESTRANGED AND RELATED DEAD

Fondebrider asks how archaeologists make the shift "from excavating a 700-year-old archaeological site to working in a grave where the corpse is wearing modern clothes or the police are in charge of the process." In her contribution to the volume Rosemary Joyce explores this issue by highlighting the "discursive and experiential dimensions" of archaeological work around the dead. She brings in debates around exhumation and repatriation in the Americas and elsewhere and considers the harm that can be done to the dead and the living through archaeological work. Joyce frames this as a question of the responsibility of the living toward the dead, a perspective shared by historian Antoon De Baets (2004). However, whereas De Baets proposes a comprehensive list of responsibilities that establishes a universal understanding of what is due to the dead, archaeology's more anthropological grounding points to the limitations of such a view, which Adam Rosenblatt (2010) has noted is deeply embedded in a secular Western framework. The chapters in this volume demonstrate the shifting nature of the dead body and indicate the importance of taking full account of the relational composition of human personhood, living or dead, past or present.

How do excavated bodies shift through different categories, moving from being human remains, to people, to objects, to evidence, depending on context and those involved? Joyce suggests that how we talk about human remains can reveal "unexamined assumptions about what kinds of human being merit recognition." This can be seen historically in archaeology's treatment of the dead. Crossland (2009b) has explored how the parallel medical practices of autopsy and dissection allowed postmortem interventions to be framed both as an act of care and as a violent unmaking of the person, and how a similar distinction has played out in archaeological interventions. Whether the dead slip from one status to another depends not only on the goal of postmortem analysis, but also on the way in which it takes place, who is involved, and how access is controlled. This treatment depends primarily on whether the dead are located as part of the community of the living or positioned as estranged from it (Fforde et al. 2002; McGuire 1989; http://www.nps.gov/nagpra/mandates).

The exclusion of some remains from the community of the dead has a long history in legal practice and European Christian traditions around burial in the parish of one's birth (Harding 1989, 1992). The estrangement of some bodies from the living has been at the heart of practices around exhumation and analysis of the dead. It is no coincidence that the claims of indigenous people under the Native American Graves Protection and Repatriation Act (NAGPRA) are defined around a connection of lineal descent, geographic proximity, or cultural affiliation between the tribe and the dead (Bray 2001; Watkins 2001). The most divisive cases, such as Kennewick man (D. Thomas 2002), are those where the relationship between the dead and the living is contested or ambiguous.

In her chapter, Geller takes as her point of departure a group of Seminole skulls collected by Samuel Morton. In the case of the Seminoles, tribal members of African ancestry were disaffiliated from the Seminole Nation of Oklahoma in 2000 on the basis of racialized models of biological descent imported from Europe (TallBear 2003). In the context of this charged history, Geller explores the paradoxes of using Morton's cranial collection to explore the intricacies of race and identity in both the past and the present. She comments on the contrast between the plethora of information available about the Europeans who collected the skulls and the relative obscurity of the individuals whose remains were disinterred, accessioned, labeled, and now rest on the storage shelves of the University of Pennsylvania Museum of Archaeology and Anthropology. The skulls are caught up in the re-creation of biologized racial ideologies that cannot encompass the complexities of Seminole identities in the nineteenth century, particularly the enslavement, alliances, and associations among Native North Americans and African-descended people. Morton did not identify any of the skulls as Black Indians (or "Negroid Indians" in his terms), but cranial analysis based on twentieth-century reference collections suggests evidence of African ancestry in two cases.

What to make of this? How to hold together in the same analytical moment the revelation of possible masked and marginalized racial histories and the violent imposition of racial categories? The biological study of the collection provides a means to write another history, a story of the violence enacted upon individuals whose remains were collected and the ways in which this violence persists in the present. The skulls show evidence of violent trauma and death in battle but also of pernicious "malnourishment, chronic infections, and substandard living conditions," telling a story of traumatic lives and deaths.

Geller suggests that exploring parallels with the assignment of sex might provide a way to start engaging with such complex histories. These problems are particularly salient for forensic anthropologists, who are often asked to translate skeletal morphology into racial categories, as Heather Walsh-Haney and Serrin Boys discuss in their chapter. They consider the issues involved in converting a forensic anthropologist's assessment of the skeleton into apparently "biological" descriptors in order to provide the police and judiciary with language to describe the dead. Walsh-Haney and Boys note that sex tends to be treated in terms of three categories: "male, female, or unknown." As Geller (2009) notes, this is a problematic reduction of the five-point range that is normally used by osteologists to describe different elements of the skeleton, which also fails to capture skeletal variation across and between populations. This work of translation is treacherous. Kemkes-Grottenthaler (2001) discusses many of the issues, including the way in which the assessment of age at death can vary depending on the available bones, the person's particular history, and the population-specific nature of the skeletal markers used to assess sex or race (see Thompson, chapter 4, this volume). For example, the skulls of men exhumed from mass graves in Rwanda showed morphological traits that are usually associated with the skulls of women of European ancestry (Ferllini 1999:296). To shift from the description of a graduated spectrum of osteological morphology to an unknown person's social classification in terms of age, gender, and race is freighted with difficulties, as Walsh-Haney and Boys suggest, not least of which is whether the ascribed social identity was recognized or acknowledged by the person whose remains lie on the analyst's table.

How can we deal with the even more fraught and ambiguous category of race? Walsh-Haney and Boys note that forensic anthropologists recognize race as a charged and noxious social construct that bundles together multiple and shifting physiological traits that may be independent of one another or co-vary in ways that are not well understood. At the same time, race is a culturally salient category in the United States, and law enforcement officials expect the identification of remains in racial terms; to refuse would be to diminish the personhood of the dead and perhaps to lessen the chances of identification. The classifying of skeletons into racialized subjects of the state is work that stabilizes human variation into fixed and static types recognizable in institutional frameworks of governance. This move masks the relational and shifting nature of human identity and physiology. Where does this leave forensic anthropology? Geller notes that one approach is to distinguish between biological race and social race (and perhaps also governmentally recognized race). As Geller explores, this working solution has its own inadequacies, both because it naturalizes biological race and because of the difficulty of reading social and bureaucratic race from the morphological traits of the skeleton (see Albanese and Saunders 2006).

Walsh-Haney and Boys outline another approach that has gained some traction in forensic anthropology: to classify human remains in terms of ancestry rather than race. However, tracing geographical history rather than racial type also has its limits. Simmons and Haglund (2005) note that translating ancestry into a recognized social classification has the same problems as racial typing. They give an example from the United States of a young man whose remains were discovered and assessed as having a mix of European and Native American ancestry. Once identified it was found that he "was a migrant farm worker of Mexican ancestry." They note that his social race category would have been "Hispanic" or "Latino," a linguistic or cultural identity with no clear relationship to skeletal morphology. It is clear that any replacement for current approaches needs to be context-specific, variable, and alive to historical documentation as much as to the skeleton itself. Although ancestry may seem a more neutral and less problematic category than race in the context of the United States, Simmons and Haglund (2005:163–164) observe that in situations of human rights investigations, where massacres may have taken place around the issue of perceived ethnic identity, "the assessment of ancestry can be highly inflammatory." Albanese and Saunders (2006:284) outline how, in many cases, ancestry represents a simple substitution of terms for the older racial typology and leaves the underlying assumptions around race intact.

Walsh-Haney and Boys note that a true shift to ancestry—that is, not a simple remapping of racial categories onto geography—would face difficulties in finding terms that are meaningful for the government agencies that take responsibility for people's lives and deaths. These agencies deal in types and categories that seem to have little room for ambiguity. Walsh-Haney and Boys lay out the inconsistent way in which these different racial and ethnic types are used across different agencies, which demonstrates in itself the fluid nature of human variation even within the scope of these apparently accepted standards. Consistent with these observations, Geller argues for "deracializing biology," moving away from a typologizing approach in which the goal is to place a skull in one or another of the analyst's categories. The tension here is between recognizing that the skeleton bears the traces of its history while also acknowledging that this history is not self-evident and is always interpreted. The question then becomes about the relationships that are involved in making sense of these material traces.

FORENSIC PRACTICE AS A RELATIONAL ARCHAEOLOGY

The forensic archaeological practice developed by the JPAC and by the EAAF starts not with the bodies in the ground but with the living. This is a relational archaeology, which begins by acknowledging the connections between the living and the dead and which proceeds from there. Different circumstances thus give rise to different modes of practice, as evinced by the different relations within which US domestic forensic practice is situated. As Joyce points out, there is nothing inherently wrong with the postmortem circulation of human remains, which is demonstrated by the mobilization of donor organs and, indeed, the curation and peregrination of Christian relics. What matters is the constitution of the relationships that allow or proscribe particular actions, including the relationships between living and dead, and the relationships between different interested groups and archaeologists. Joyce discusses Geoffrey Scarre's (2003, 2006) arguments about how harm may be done to the dead by the living through the enactment of what he terms "relational changes." These might include, for example, spreading falsehoods about the dead that damage their postmortem reputations. Joyce notes the implication that care must be taken in writing history and in our various forms of archaeological representation of the dead.

History is a relational project that connects the signs of the past—bodies, artifacts, texts—with past events and practices through interpreting gestures and representations (after Peirce 1955). This tripartite relationship is recognized in the triple sense of the word "history," which refers simultaneously to what happened in the past, to the traces of the past that persist in the present, and to the narratives that we construct about the past through these traces. To write, speak, or perform history is to reproduce and shift between different configurations of these three elements. As Joyce points out, texts and images are important components of the work of interpretation, and so too are the on-the-ground practices of archaeology. To dig up a body and exhibit it is a form of history making and interpretation just as much as writing a text is.

Such dynamic and unfolding historical relations are demonstrated by Rojas-Perez. He observes that the work of archaeological investigation can be a search for a stable and finished past, but in Peru the violence of state terror is ongoing, and the past continues to reverberate in the present. Here is a moment where terminological and subdisciplinary differences seem to emerge. From the perspective of many archaeologists searching for a record of events that took place some years previously, the past seems definitively finished, even if the effects of violence and terror are still felt. However, from the perspective of the people who have lost their children, spouses, parents, and siblings, such an account of the past remains incomplete precisely because the violence of the past continues to be felt in the present. In Argentina, the pain of this open-endedness was seized upon by some relatives in the 1980s and 1990s as a way to insist on justice. By refusing to acknowledge the remains of the dead that were exhumed, some mothers of Argentina's disappeared rejected the apparent closure that came with the return of their dead (Crossland 2002).

This seems an acknowledgment of a way in which archaeological work can foreclose the past, stabilizing a particular narrative and seeming to fix consensus around a particular set of representations. Yet, as Laurent Olivier (2011:49) has argued, "the space inhabited by the past is not the past itself but the present, and only the present." Some archaeologists (including the authors of this chapter) recognize that archaeological traces exist as signs in the present and can never be separated from this dynamic and living context (cf. Preucel 2006). As such, archaeological evidence is always open to being reconstituted in new and different relationships (Crossland 2013). As Rojas-Perez observes, "The past lingers all over this place of stories." Indeed, the traces that archaeologists deal with are remnants of "processes of violence and state terror that are not entirely situated in the past and that continue to haunt the present." To stabilize a particular view of the past requires work, and work of different sorts depending on what kind of narrative one wishes to construct.

Tuller writes of his experiences in Serbia excavating a mass grave of ethnic Albanian men who had been killed in Kosovo and transported to Serbia for burial. He observes that, as in the Peruvian case documented by Rojas-Perez, great efforts had been made to disguise the killing. Bodies had been burned and moved around with heavy machinery, making it difficult for the forensic anthropologists to assess the number of the dead and to identify the remains. These difficulties led to a series of different estimates of the number of the dead, which circulated in the media. As a result some individuals denied the true scale of the massacre, which caused confusion and more sorrow for the surviving relatives. Here, the history of the site is emergent and in the process of being stabilized by archaeologists. Tuller argues that forensic anthropologists have to balance the need to share the results of their work with families and the wider public, and the responsibility to avoid causing more pain for survivors. Like Fondebrider, he emphasizes the need to keep relatives informed, but also cautions that anthropologists should be careful about what information is released to wider publics.

To realize that the past is knowable only in the context of the present does not mean that the bodies that are exhumed have no reality aside from the narratives that circulate around them. Instead, it is to recognize the ways in which the relationship with the past persists through these bodies and through other traces, including those of memory. To deploy the bodies of the dead as forensic evidence that can be used in a law court, it is necessary not only to maintain rigorous control over the chain of custody, but also to make sure that pertinent relationships established in the past as part of the crime are carefully preserved. This is recognized by those who attempt to efface the traces of past violence, as in Peru and the former Yugoslavia. Efforts made to destroy the material remains of the dead are efforts to obscure the relationship of the bodies to a particular crime at a particular site. This is an acknowledgment of the relationality of history and a recognition that although the events really took place, the past only exists in the present insofar as we can recognize its traces.

One important way in which the past is fixed through archaeological investigation is the destructive nature of the process, as Tuller observes: "A failure to record an observation or collect a piece of evidence may mean that data are lost forever." In losing such evidence, the visibility of the material and human relationships within which the dead were entangled is also lost.

A focus on the apparently static and tangible traces of the dead can sometimes mask the dynamic relationships in which they are still caught up and within which they come to act as signs or evidence in the present. Attempts to construct a finished past, like those Rojas-Perez delineates, parallel attempts to construct a finished and typological racial identity through the traces of the skeleton. In both cases, material traces clearly exist: they present visible and existing patterns that can be described and that can work to fix and stabilize particular narratives. These traces are not self-evident, however, and are always articulated with the events and circumstances of the past, and with the goals and hopes of those who assess these relations in the present.

Acknowledgments

Thanks to the School for Advanced Research for funding the seminar that led to this volume and for providing the beautiful surroundings and wonderful meals that were so conducive to carrying out extended discussions around our topic. Thanks too to all the seminar members for their input into this introduction, and to Victoria Sanford, who joined us in Santa Fe but was unfortunately unable to contribute to the final volume.

Note

1. "Objetividad e imparcialidad que no deben ser confundidas con neutralidad. Ya que, aunque todo pueda ser discuitible, nadie debería ser neutral cuando se trata de vulneraciones de Derechos Humanos." Thanks to Derek Congram for bringing this article to my attention.

2

Forensic Anthropology and the Investigation of Political Violence

Notes from the Field

Luis Fondebrider

This chapter is a reflection on my experience as a member of the Argentine Forensic Anthropology Team (EAAF), which I founded 30 years ago with some colleagues in Argentina (http://www.eaaf.org). In 1984, as Argentina returned to democracy after 8 years of military dictatorship, the investigation of what happened to the thousands of people who disappeared under the military regime was a key component of the transition to democracy (Robben 2000). In that year, I was a student of anthropology at the University of Buenos Aires, and like many young people in those years I was part of a vast movement that demonstrated against the dictatorship and demanded democracy (Catterberg 1991). In that context, a group of students of archaeology, anthropology, and medicine created the EAAF in order to provide an independent alternative to the official forensic system for the relatives of the disappeared (Bernadi and Fondebrider 2007; Snow et al. 1984).

The transition in Argentina from the dictatorship to a democratic government was, from the beginning, marked by the need to know what had happened to the disappeared and to establish who was responsible through fair legal trials. From the early years of the military junta, relatives of the disappeared had organized themselves as the Mothers of the Plaza de Mayo (Asociación de las Madres de Plaza de Mayo 1995; Bousquet

1984; Fisher 1989; Guzman Bouvard 1994). By the end of the military government in 1983, there were 11 human rights organizations pushing the new democratic authorities for investigations. This involvement of civic society gave an enormous initial impulse to the search for the disappeared and for the use of a scientific approach.

At the beginning of 1984, different judges ordered the exhumations of graves in cemeteries where the remains of the disappeared were buried without identification. This task was left in the hands of the state's official forensic doctors. But a problem quickly emerged: they lacked the expertise for recovering human remains. As a result gravediggers ended up exhuming incomplete bodies, inflicting postmortem trauma on the remains, and losing associated evidence, such as projectiles. Despite the long tradition of archaeology in Argentina, no university or academic archaeologist participated in the exhumations, and many remains ended up destroyed or lost in judicial laboratories. This initial situation, dubbed a "horror show" by the media, motivated human rights organizations to search for other, more controlled, and scientific alternatives. This was the origin of the EAAF. However, as I explore below, the work of the EAAF was neither straightforward nor uncontested.

Since the 1980s, about 40 countries that had undergone recent political, ethnic, or religious violence began their various transitions to democracy, simultaneously conducting reviews of their recent past. In addition to Argentina, among the best known are Chile, El Salvador, Guatemala, Peru, and Colombia in Latin America; South Africa, Rwanda, and Sierra Leone in Africa; the former Yugoslavia in Eastern Europe; Cyprus in Western Europe; and East Timor in Asia. A key part of the process of transition to democratic government has been the investigation into the precise details of what happened to the victims of forced disappearances and extrajudicial executions. This has been vital for gaining insight into the truth about the violent acts of the recent past, determining criminal liabilities, and receiving redress. Unfortunately, victims of forced disappearance are not found alive in most cases. When they can be recovered, they are usually found buried in graves or disposed of in rivers, lakes, volcanoes, or the sea.

Finding the remains of the dead and identifying the victims of political, ethnic, or religious violence are particularly sensitive issues, touching upon some of the most painful and distressing feelings for the victims' relatives. These include the earlier uncertainty as to whether their loved ones were dead or alive, the impossibility of burying the dead following their own rites, and the absence of justice. Searching for a living person, a task that involves hope, is very different from looking for the dead, with its terrible certainty (Fondebrider 2012).

Throughout the years, every country that has conducted a review of its past and a search for the victims of forced disappearance has adopted a different mechanism for this process. Most well known are the truth commissions (in Argentina, Chile, Guatemala, El Salvador, Peru, South Africa, East Timor, and Sierra Leone). In other cases the investigation is part of a prosecution of crimes by local or international courts (the former Yugoslavia, Rwanda, Cambodia, and Sierra Leone). Over time, forensic investigations have adapted to their local contexts, taking into account the geographical, political, economic, religious, and ethnic features of the society concerned (see Thompson, chapter 4, this volume).

Despite the variations, my experience in these diverse contexts is that the claims of the victims' relatives are always the same: find out what happened to their loved ones, recover their correctly identified remains, and discover how they died, who should be held liable, and what redress will be made. Unfortunately, these basic and crucial questions are not always answered. Perhaps because those in government are not strongly committed to the search, perhaps because the judiciary is incapable of investigating, or perhaps simply because those involved in the crimes refuse to provide any information, in some cases there is no interest in revealing such information, or there is no effective power to force those responsible to take responsibility for their actions (see Blaauw and Lahteenmäki 2002; Sassòli and Tougas 2002). It is in this context—with some specific variations but within the same general pattern—that most searches for victims of forced disappearance or extrajudicial execution have taken place in the last 30 years. Local nongovernmental organizations, such as those made up of the victims' relatives, are often the first to take to the streets to inquire about their loved ones. In most cases they are the ones who continue the search, regardless of the findings of a truth commission or a government's desire to finalize investigation proceedings.

Science has played a key role in these investigations. Thanks to the application of a range of different disciplines, including medicine, archaeology, anthropology, biology, and dentistry, it has been possible to locate clandestine mass graves, exhume buried bodies using rigorous and systematic methods, and analyze remains in order to identify them and to establish the cause and manner of death (Doretti and Fondebrider 2001; Fondebrider 2002).

FORENSIC ARCHAEOLOGY AND ANTHROPOLOGY: APPLICATION IN DIFFERENT CONTEXTS

As is the case with other scientific disciplines employed in investigating criminal cases, such as medicine, dentistry, and radiology, the methods of forensic archaeology and anthropology vary depending on whether they are applied to domestic criminal cases, mass disasters, or cases of political violence (see overviews in Blau and Ubelaker 2009; Dirkmaat 2012). Even though, from a technical standpoint, the procedures used to determine the biological profile of a set of remains are similar regardless of the case, the context is very different. Probably the most important difference lies in who took a person's life. In "traditional" forensic cases, the perpetrator is normally an individual acting without state support, perhaps killing somebody as a result of a robbery or an accident, or perhaps an individual who commits suicide. In other words, the death is not usually ascribed to political, ethnic, or religious reasons. Where the reasons are political, ethnic, or religious, the majority of murders are usually committed by the state, or in collusion with it, as part of a documented, organized, and often systematic plan (see Ferllini, ed. 2007).

Another significant difference lies in the enormity of the cases and their impact on the population as a whole. Murders in localized, domestic criminal scenarios affect isolated individuals; the killings are condemned by society; and in most cases the state makes use of all its resources (attorneys, judges, police officers, and so on) to further the investigation (Dirkmaat and Adovasio 1997; France et al. 1992; Márquez-Grant et al. 2012; Rainwater et al. 2012). In the context of political, ethnic, or religious violence, the killings are widespread and may involve an entire family, neighborhood, village, or political or ethnic group. The massive scale of these deaths causes terror, disruption, and uncertainty not only among the victims' relatives but among whole sectors of a society.

The forensic expert is also perceived as playing a different role in each scenario. Normally, a forensic scientist works for a governmental body (such as the medical examiner, an institute of legal medicine, or a scientific police department). Therefore, in traditional cases, the forensic expert is not seen as a party to the problem: he or she is not associated with the person who has committed the murder but is regarded as an ally who helps the investigation. In the case of political, ethnic, or religious violence, the situation can be very different. More often than not, no distinction is made between the state apparatus that committed the crimes and the state that, years later, has to investigate them. This situation undermines the credibility of forensic experts, particularly in the eyes of the victims' relatives. It is for this reason, especially in Argentina, Chile, Guatemala, and Peru, that independent forensic teams were created, devoted almost exclusively to cases of this type.

A COMPLEX TRANSITION FROM THE LOCAL TO THE INTERNATIONAL CONTEXT

Before I discuss how forensic anthropology and archaeology fit into this framework, it is important to note that the dividing line between these two disciplines often observed in Anglo-Saxon contexts—for example, in England and, to a lesser degree, in the United States—is often blurred in Latin America, where the term "forensic anthropology" is usually understood as involving both major moments in an investigation: exhumation and the analysis of human remains.

The first time that most of the young archaeologists and anthropologists involved in the forensic field from developed countries—and some of their professors—heard about or became interested in human rights violations, war crimes, and genocides was in the mid-1990s, when the conflict in Bosnia came to an end, or at least gave way to a fragile peace after a five-year dreadful war, as a result of the Dayton Agreement. In 1996, the International Criminal Tribunal for the former Yugoslavia (ICTY) began to fulfill its task of collecting information on crimes of all types committed by the factions involved in the conflict, especially the Serbian armed forces. A crucial part of the task was the opening of mass graves all across Bosnia, where hundreds of bodies had been buried. To perform this task, forensic experts from all disciplines, especially forensic archaeologists, anthropologists, and pathologists, were essential (see Tuller, chapter 5, this volume).

For most of these professionals, the majority of whom were from the United States and the United Kingdom, this was an entirely new world with an altogether different religious and cultural background, and the context was war, hunger, displaced people, the mass rapes of women, and other associated violence. For professionals from Latin American countries, especially Argentina, Peru, Guatemala, and Colombia, although the situation was shocking, it was not very different from their own national contexts, where human rights violations had been or still were an important part of their daily life. In addition, although the technical aspects of the task predominated—excavating graves, recovering bodies in varying conditions, establishing the biological profile of skeletons—the work also involved interacting with stakeholders not usually encountered by most forensic specialists in local, domestic criminal contexts, such as the relatives of victims of forced disappearance or members of military forces. Clearly, most university training does not prepare one for such a task.

In many ways the experience of the anthropologists from Latin America made them better prepared to process these circumstances. The use of forensic anthropology to investigate human rights violations started in Argentina in 1984 under the guidance of Clyde Snow (Snow et al. 1984), extending to Chile, Guatemala, Colombia, and Peru later in the 1980s (Casallas and Piedrahita 2004; İşcan and Olivera 2000; Moscoso Möller 1995; Peccerelli 2007), more than a decade before the mass exhumations in the Balkans. The Argentine team had experienced firsthand the difficulties involved in carrying out such human rights investigations in Argentina, where the lack of understanding of some judges of the role of a forensic anthropologist in the process and the uprising of some members of the army who were resisting prosecutions made the investigations more complex (Crossland 2000). Similarly, the transition from a local context (a single homicide committed by an individual, the finding of one victim's body, the support of the security forces and other human and logistical resources, no contact with the victim's relatives) to an international context (crimes committed by the state, mass graves containing the remains of 30–50 individuals, a postwar climate fraught with poverty, insecurity, hostility to the investigation from the security forces, interaction with relatives, and religious and cultural patterns different from those of the investigators) is far from easy, as Courtney Angela Brkic (2004) has explored.

ONE MODEL, MANY MODELS

There is a tendency to consider the work undertaken in the Balkans in the 1990s as a model to be replicated in other parts of the world where there is a similar need to seek the remains of victims of forced disappearance, as Thompson outlines in this volume. However, as anthropologists, we should be in a better position than physicians and dentists to understand issues related to cultural and religious diversity as well as historical, political, and development processes. For example, to work in a context such as the one in Argentina (with powerful state institutions and victims from urban areas, especially Catholic or Jewish, educated, and middle class) is utterly different from working in South Africa (characterized by a long-standing racial conflict involving a rural and ethnically diverse population, with a potential for inter-ethnic conflict; see Morris 2011). The same distinction holds for the context in which forensic investigations take place. It is fundamentally different to work with the support of the international community (in terms of resources, security, logistics, funds), as has happened in the Balkans and in Iraq, than to work where resources are almost nonexistent and the claims for truth, justice, and reparations from the victims' relatives are seldom heard, as has been the case in Congo, Rwanda, and East Timor, despite declarations and pledges to the contrary.

The cultural and religious dimension is another important aspect to consider, since it undoubtedly affects the task of the forensic anthropologist. Can a grave be opened in a Muslim or Jewish context? Can victims' corpses be touched? What rituals have to be followed before exhumation? What role does a religious leader play in the process? Can women archaeologists participate? How can one explain that identifying remains is a complex task that will not necessarily turn out successfully? Why are blood samples necessary? All of these considerations demand a sensitivity to the local context, some knowledge of local conditions, and a willingness to be open to guidance from local people when carrying out investigations. As yet, little has been written on these topics (although see Skinner 2007 and Wagner 2008).

Another essential aspect to forensic work in the context of human rights violations is the relationship between anthropologists and the victims' relatives, including their local communities and human rights organizations. This is perhaps the most difficult area for those forensic anthropologists who conceive their task as strictly technical and objective in the name of an idealized clinical distance. This is probably the main difference between the two trends that have evolved for the application of forensic anthropology to the investigation of human rights violations. In general, in the United States, Canada, the United Kingdom, Europe, and Australia, forensic anthropological work has tended to focus on technical and scientific dimensions, although there are exceptions to this, such as the investigation of the attack on the World Trade Center on 9/11 (Mundorf 2003) and the interaction of JPAC anthropologists with relatives of the war dead and of those killed in mass disasters (see Tuller, chapter 5, this volume). In contrast, in countries such as Argentina, Chile, Peru, Colombia, and Guatemala, the relationship with the victims' relatives is deemed central and crucial, and it provides the starting point for any investigation.

EXHUMATIONS

Although the investigation process is long and complex, including several phases and stakeholders, exhumation is the iconic activity for investigations of the recent past. Exhumation can quickly have multiple ramifications at the academic, political, psychological, and journalistic levels, to name only a few of the most obvious dimensions. Maybe because it is more public than interviewing a victim's relatives, or because of the impact of finding skeletons and bullets inside a grave for the first time, or because of the profound impression that encounters with the dead leave on the living, exhumations can become a catalytic moment for investigations. Often, the relatives of the disappeared say that to be present during an exhumation and to witness the process allows them for the first time to see positive action being taken and to know something concrete about their loved ones after many years of uncertainty and darkness.

SIMILAR AND DIFFERENT

The opening of graves to exhume the remains of victims of forced disappearance or executions (a relevant distinction in some contexts, constituting the thin dividing line between the uncertainty of a disappearance and the certainty of death) poses questions and gives rise to discussions of different kinds. Some are basically of a political nature: will the opening of a grave open the wounds of the past? Will these actions give rise to a new civil war? At a broader cultural level: what happens to a society in which parents have to bury their children, thus violating the natural order? At a psychological level: what is the impact of being faced with bones 20 years after someone has disappeared, when one's last image of the victim was of a person who was well and alive, with her or his face, clothes, and so on? How can relatives accept that a bone fragment, which sometimes is all that is left, represents their loved one? And for archaeologists, at both technical and emotional levels: how do we shift from excavating a 700-year-old archaeological site to working in a grave where the corpse is wearing modern clothes or the police are in charge of the process? (See Pérez-Sales and Navarro García 2007.)

Distress, uncertainty, pain, anger, a need for closure, and a desire for justice are common feelings mentioned by victims' relatives and other members of societies where investigations aimed at finding disappeared people and exhuming their remains have taken place (S. Martin 2002; Stover and Shigekane 2002). Political and historical contexts also have an impact on investigations, their continuity, the political support given to them, and many other dimensions of the work. Are we, as forensic anthropologists, prepared for this task in this context? Do university studies provide us with the tools necessary to excavate a grave while surrounded by 200 people in a lost town in the midst of the Philippine mountains? Who has taught us to work in a place where exhumations have to be performed under the custody of the army or where the dates for starting or ending the investigation are set by the security forces, as in Colombia? How can we explain to a victim's relative who is watching the exhumation of a grave containing 50 corpses that there are no funds to afford the genetic analysis tests?

These questions, which go beyond matters of methodology and technique, recur in the context of forensic anthropological investigations of human rights violations. It is important that anthropologists incorporate these issues into forensic educational training, or at least practitioners should be aware that when immersed in an environment other than the usual context of their own country or region, they will have to find ways to adapt to the new situation. This is worth emphasizing because most anthropologists who engage in human rights investigations do not come from countries where they are likely to find mass graves or victims of forced disappearance. This means that in traveling to other sites to work, they are thrown into entirely different and more complex contexts than they are used to.

WHAT DOES IT MEAN TO IDENTIFY THE DEAD?

In the forensic field, to identify a body is defined as individualization by the attribution of birth name or other name by matching up two types of information: (a) the biological and physical characteristics of a person when he or she was alive (antemortem data), and (b) the data drawn from the analysis of a skeleton or corpse (postmortem data). This medical-legal definition, commonly accepted by forensic experts worldwide, may pose some difficulties when it is applied to contexts where cultural or religious practices and beliefs play a significant and perhaps conflicting role in determining the treatment of the dead. For example, in most countries of the world, the identification of a corpse is based on one of the following four methods: visual recognition, fingerprints, dental features, genetic features. In the first three cases, but most especially in the case of fingerprints and dentition, an official document (made before death) with verifiable dental records or fingerprints of the suspected victim must be available. But what happens when the relative of a disappeared person says to the forensic expert that she dreamed that her loved one was buried in the graveyard in which work is being conducted, and therefore no forensic analysis is needed for confirmation purposes? Or when a genetic analysis, with all its technical complexity, concludes that a given bone belongs to a given person, but there is nothing visible in the remains enabling the relatives to "see" or "recognize" their loved one (e.g., see Renshaw 2011:130)?

This apparent contradiction between scientific and common knowledge, so to speak, creates problems and challenges for the forensic anthropologist in contexts of political, ethnic, and religious violence. In this scenario of contradictions and opposites, the task of the forensic anthropologist may grow particularly charged. I would emphasize that before being a forensic anthropologist one is an anthropologist with the benefit of a holistic, more comprehensive approach than the one held by other scientific disciplines, such as medicine or dentistry. This approach helps us walk along this path of contradictions, bridging gaps and reconciling different perspectives on the unique phenomenon that is the identification of a human being.

HOW TO INVESTIGATE: LEARNING FROM THE ARGENTINE CASE

For many years, it was thought that the investigative process for these kinds of cases could be modeled on those used for solving an ordinary criminal case or identifying the victims of a mass disaster. As time went by, however, the differences became evident. The situation is vastly different when the murderer is not an individual but the state, with all its administrative, bureaucratic machinery and its ability to make thousands of people disappear. Over time the members of the EAAF came to realize that exhuming remains correctly or conducting anthropological analyses on them is not enough in these contexts. It is also necessary to investigate and understand the organization of the state in relation to these crimes, particularly those carried out by the armed forces, the security forces, and the agencies in charge of administratively "processing" deaths. Identifying people is a much more complex task if this process is not well understood (Tidball-Binz 2006).

How to study such a phenomenon scientifically? What scientific discipline will enable us to formulate working hypotheses to identify a given corpse? How can we recover, analyze, and link together human remains and documents as diverse as a death certificate, a newspaper article, and testimonies of survivors from clandestine detention centers? And how should we go about finding these documents? University schools of medicine, anthropology, and law—to mention the most popular—do not train us for such a job. Although sociocultural anthropologists are used to interviewing different people during their fieldwork, the implications in a forensic context are very different. The purpose of interviews in our work is not to collect material for a scientific paper, but to find the remains of the interviewee's relative. Thus, we developed a multidisciplinary approach and followed a method similar to one used by homicide detectives and also by historians working on the recent past.

The first task was to understand how the Argentine state had operated during the military dictatorship and what documents were available. At the beginning, the purpose was to discover what had happened to the victims of forced disappearance from the moment of their disappearance onward, but over time, we came to understand that it was necessary to investigate the period long before that moment, to find out where they had been activists, what their geographical scope was, who they were in touch with, and so on. This kind of investigation, based on oral and written sources of different types and quality, starts to look like a big puzzle, with scattered pieces gradually fitting in and giving sense to a specific line of investigation. The kind of documents that we consult are varied. Some are of an administrative nature, including official and unclassified documents (cemetery books recording the arrival and burial of corpses, death certificates, licenses for burials, corpses' fingerprints, autopsy reports, and files from military proceedings, among others). These sources need to be complemented with more confidential and classified files, such as intelligence reports from state-run agencies. The analysis of these sources and the linking of the collected data lead to a hypothesis according to which the remains of a specific person are presumed to be buried in a particular grave in a given cemetery. In other words, the preliminary investigation rather than the exhumation is given priority. It might be argued that this is not the traditional task of forensic anthropologists, especially in common crimes or mass disasters. But in cases involving the investigation of human rights violations, this comprehensive and innovative approach has yielded positive results, particularly in terms of the identification of remains and the credibility gained among the victims' relatives.

CONCLUSIONS

Based on my experience with exhumations in search of victims of forced disappearance, I draw the following conclusions:

- The analysis of cases of political violence demands a completely new approach from both the legal and scientific points of view.
- Forensic anthropologists involved in this kind of investigation need to adapt to contexts substantially different from their own. The cultural and religious dimensions of the new contexts and the relationship with the victims' relatives are key components to this approach.
- The exhumation of graves, besides being a technical task, has political, legal, and psychological consequences, which must be understood by the forensic anthropologist.
- The murderers' refusal to provide information; the difficulties in gaining access to relevant documents, especially from intelligence agencies; the dispersed sources; and the short time elapsed—in historical terms—often make a narrowly focused approach unfeasible. Rather, forensic

anthropologists have to work within the given conditions and be flexible and open to finding new areas for exploration (see Rojas-Perez, chapter 3, this volume).

The exhumation and analysis of human remains are links in a broader and more complex network, as this chapter has explained. An open mind and a deep knowledge of the specific repressive regime do not guarantee a good investigation, but they do offer a sound basis from which to start. In this regard, each successful identification enables us to ratify, rectify, or dispute a line of investigation; therefore, assigning an identity to a corpse, beyond its worth in humanitarian and legal terms, has a multiplier effect on the entire process. The chapters in this volume demonstrate some of the complexities of forensic inquiry and show the benefits of a holistic anthropological approach.

3

Unearthing Ongoing Pasts

Forensic Anthropology, State Making, and Justice Making in Postwar Peru

Isaias Rojas-Perez

This chapter focuses on the question of how forensic anthropology—particularly in its intervention at the grave site through archaeological practices—contributes to post-atrocity justice and recovery. Mainstream views situate this contribution squarely in the forensic field. In these views, by recovering unknown bodies from clandestine mass graves and providing hard evidence of atrocities, archaeological practices facilitate post-conflict projects of bringing the dead back into being as legal subjects (victims), cultural subjects (persons to be properly buried and mourned), and historical subjects (persons whose history is not to be forgotten). In so doing, archaeology contributes decisively to the legal, cultural, and political foundations for a new post-conflict democratic order because it enables a crucial condition of possibility for the new order to take shape: a *controlled* recovery of the past. This "technological optimism" about the truth-making capabilities of archaeological practice in contexts of contemporary mass atrocity builds on the modern idea that the world is knowable under certain conditions of logic and procedure. More specifically, it evokes what Valverde (2003), following Carlo Ginzburg's (1989) notion of the evidential paradigm, defines as the "epistemology of the clue"—namely, the idea that a trained and detached observer is able to read the clues and traces left by the past as a means of gaining otherwise inaccessible truths. This view also presupposes that the past as an object of knowledge is stable and fixed (see also Crossland 2009a).

In this chapter I interrogate the technological optimism associated with archaeological practices by looking at the forensic excavation of clandestine mass graves conducted at Los Cabitos—the headquarters of the 1980s and 1990s counterinsurgency campaign in the Peruvian central-southern Andes—between 2005 and 2009. If one truth has emerged from this forensic excavation, it is that the individual missing body is not always recoverable. Most of the human remains recovered in Los Cabitos were ashes and fragments of bones that could not be individualized and identified and hence could not be constituted as legal, cultural, or historical subjects within the institutionalized structures of legal and disciplinary power. The inability to identify specific remains is not unique to the Peruvian case. As Fondebrider suggests in chapter 2 in this volume, forensic anthropologists throughout the world are often confronted, for a number of reasons, with the impossibility of recovering the individual missing body, particularly in contexts of mass violence.

I argue that this "failure" of forensic anthropology to recover the individual missing body brings forth the questions of what kind of object "state terror" is and what it means to have justice served in this context. The continuing unavailability of the individual missing body is not an anachronistic legacy from an arbitrary and violent past but a manifestation of the ongoing presence of the ghosts of state terror in post-conflict state rule. Since the past for the state—in the continuous work of refounding its order—is both finished and unfinished, the past cannot be straightforwardly constituted as a stable object. Nor can forensic experts be neutral and detached, because their "object" of study always already implicates them personally. In making this argument I aim at both problematizing a relation that is often overlooked in the literature of forensic anthropology (namely, the relation between forensic anthropology and the state) and revisiting a relation that, as Fondebrider and Thompson (chapters 2 and 4) note in this volume, has not always been harmonious (namely, the relation between forensic anthropology and the survivors of atrocity). This analytical effort makes sense only if we take as a basic presupposition that while intimately related, there is a fundamental distinction between law and justice (e.g., Agamben 1999; Derrida 1990; Lefebvre 2008; Minow 1998).

I am not an archaeologist or forensic anthropologist but a sociocultural anthropologist, and my argument here draws from my ethnographic doctoral dissertation fieldwork among the Quechua-speaking relatives of the disappeared in Ayacucho, Peru, during the counterinsurgency campaign of the 1980s and 1990s. I conducted short periods of preliminary fieldwork beginning in 2003 and a more extensive period of fieldwork from August 2006 to August 2007, when I accompanied victims' relatives in their participation in forensic exhumations of clandestine mass graves in Los Cabitos. Three questions will serve to center my analysis of the forensic excavations at Los Cabitos. The first is, how has the work undertaken by the Peruvian forensic institutions to bring the (unaccounted-for) dead back into being ended up grounding the post-conflict state's legitimacy rather than establishing post-atrocity justice? Given that the experience of devastating violence and suffering cannot be entirely subsumed in the controlled language and procedures of the law, the second question is, how does the process of the forensic recovery of remnants of state atrocity become a site of contestation where the survivor's voice (embodying the experience of violence and suffering) challenges the expert's voice (embodying the authority of the law and disciplinary power)? The third question is, how do survivors appropriate the outcomes of forensic exhumations to constitute their own forms of mourning and justice without the body as a response to ongoing state terror?

POST-CONFLICT TRUTH-MAKING

On a hot August afternoon in 2006, Santiago, the forensic archaeology legal expert of the Legal Medicine Institute (Instituto de Medicina Legal, IML) in Ayacucho, takes a break from his arduous work to brief the Quechua-speaking mothers of the disappeared about the progress of the forensic excavation in La Hoyada, a dusty and stony narrow depression adjacent to the main barracks of the military base of Los Cabitos.[1] Taking them for a tour around the area, he offers a detailed explanation of the IML's findings and an account of the different phases the forensic investigation has gone through since its beginnings. The mothers listen attentively to the legal expert and, from time to time, interrupt his discourse to add details to the evidence gathered by telling their own stories. In several respects the forensic investigation is simply proving their longtime claims about the atrocities committed in Los Cabitos. Perhaps the time has arrived for some form of justice after more than two decades of denial. In response, Santiago emphasizes repeatedly that the commitment of his team is to find the truth and that their scientifically informed work produces the objectivity and impartiality of such truth. "Nothing is done in secret here," he concludes, "our work is strictly *technical* here" (author's field notes, August 2006).

The forensic archaeology legal expert's assurance of the fairness, transparency, and objectivity of the team's work in search of the truth manifests the shift in the Peruvian state's discursive practices of human rights, which started with the advent of the democratic transition in late 2000. In pledging to a liberal political rule, the new ruling elites sought to establish a clear contrast between the wartime discursive practices of denial, silencing, and impunity and the post-conflict practices of acknowledgment, truth telling, and justice making. Under the international human rights law regime, Peruvian legal institutions reopened criminal investigations into cases of gross human rights violations that the 1995 amnesty law had closed. In this context, the legal institutions also encouraged survivors to participate actively in the legal and forensic procedures in the expectation that this participation would both guarantee the fairness of their work of justice making and allow survivors to gain a certain closure. The Peruvian legal authorities adopted the global humanitarian notion that truth and truth telling have therapeutic powers and asserted that while retributive justice could not perhaps be served in all cases, some form of restitution is always attained by both telling the relatives the truth about what happened to their loved ones and returning the victim's bodies for proper burial (see Rojas-Perez 2010 for more on this new discursive regime).

Forensic sciences, and particularly the newly incorporated discipline of forensic anthropology, emerged as guarantors of this post-conflict promise of justice and restitution. As part of a broader project of transitional justice initiated in early 2001, during the caretaker government of Valentín Paniagua, the legal authorities articulated a project of forensic exhumation aimed at recovering the bodies of the victims of political violence who had been buried in clandestine graves scattered in former war-torn areas of the countryside. In some unprecedented bold steps, the Attorney General's Office (AGO, Fiscalía de la Nación) first established a set of rules and procedures that would govern the forensic exhumation of clandestine mass graves; second, appointed two special prosecutors to conduct the criminal and forensic investigations in the regions most affected by the internal war; and third, entered into an institutional agreement with the Peruvian Truth and Reconciliation Commission (CVR, Comisión de la Verdad y Reconciliación) to conduct joint forensic exhumations. Both the AGO and the CVR recruited archaeologists and anthropologists trained in forensic techniques to participate in their project of transitional justice by providing the technical and scientific expertise needed to obtain the truth.

The first joint exhumation of clandestine mass graves took place in Chuschi, Ayacucho, in March 2002, a highly symbolic act of the (post-conflict) state. Chuschi is the Andean village where the Maoist Shining Path publicly launched its armed struggle in May 1980. Starting a large project of official recovery of the bodies of unknown victims of political violence in the very place where, according to mainstream narratives, the internal war started was clearly meant to proclaim the post-conflict civilizational mission of the state; to manifest the new regime's commitment to break with the violence and arbitrariness of the past; and to show the state's willingness to redeem the suffering of survivors and the relatives of victims through the rational means of the law and forensic sciences. A multidisciplinary task group of prosecutors, forensic experts from the IML, archaeologists and anthropologists from the Peruvian Team of Forensic Anthropology (EPAF, Equipo Peruanno de Anthropología Forense) representing the CVR, and officials from the Ombudsman's Office arrived in the village to carry out this project of bringing victims of atrocious violence back into being as legal subjects, cultural subjects, and historical subjects by means of a controlled recovery of the past.[2]

The CVR and the AGO conducted two more joint exhumations in the Andean villages of Totos and Lucanamarca in late 2002 and early 2003, respectively. In August 2003, at the end of the CVR's mandate, the AGO created a special division of the IML called the Equipo Forense Especializado (Specialized Forensic Team), which has since been in exclusive charge of conducting forensic exhumations of clandestine mass graves in former war-torn areas of the countryside to recover victims of both the guerrilla groups and the Peruvian security forces. Of the more than 2,000 bodies exhumed throughout the Peruvian south-central Andes through late August 2012, only 700 had been duly identified and returned to their families for proper burial. The 1,300 unidentified bodies remain in storage rooms of the IML in Lima and Ayacucho until new data are collected for proper identification (Yuber Alarcon, pers. comm., August 16, 2012).[3] It is my understanding that most of the 700 bodies returned before August 2012 are people allegedly killed by the guerrilla groups, whereas most of the unidentified 1,300 are people killed by the state.

The fact that roughly 65 percent of the bodies exhumed since 2003 are not identified indicates dramatically that in Peru, as elsewhere, the legal and humanitarian goal of bringing the victims of state violence back into being as legal subjects, cultural subjects, and historical subjects is not always attainable. What the numbers do not reveal straightforwardly, however, is that this "failure" does not necessarily speak of technical or epistemological failures but of the kind of problems that forensic anthropology deals with during contemporary investigations of recent experiences of state terror. As the history of the forensic excavation in Los Cabitos suggests, the past is anything but stable and always recoverable in contexts in which the state that investigates and the state that kills are the same. This history shows how survivors of state terror contest some fundamental presuppositions (political, epistemological, and cultural) upon which forensic anthropology bases its intervention and interrogates how forensic anthropologists situate themselves in the highly politically and symbolically charged scenario of the clandestine grave site containing the victims of state terror. In short, the forensic excavation at Los Cabitos allows us to touch on the complex questions of what kind of object state terror is, what it means to have justice served in this context, and how forensic anthropology experts see their relation with the state.

UNEARTHING STATE ATROCITY

The military base of Los Cabitos is located in the northeastern outskirts of the Andean city of Ayacucho, in a desert-like natural fortress surrounded by ravines and steep hillsides that flow into the canyon opened by the Huatatas River. La Hoyada, a dusty and stony large depression, is situated close to the main barracks. The military has always used this area as a shooting and training field. A contemporary first-time visitor unaware of the story of atrocity associated with La Hoyada would find a pleasant atmosphere of bucolic ordinariness. She would see military personnel strolling in the area when not training and peasants of the neighboring *chacras* (plots of land) collecting firewood, prickly pear fruits, and *molle* (*Schinus molle*, Peruvian pepper); grazing their cattle; or simply in transit to their homes located in the surrounding countryside. Except for an abandoned cement tank for oil and the fading remains of recent archaeological excavation trenches, nothing would indicate that during the 1980s La Hoyada housed an extermination camp for the disappeared suspects of terrorism.

At the end of its work in August 2003, the CVR compiled a preliminary list of more than 4,000 people who had been disappeared by the security forces during Peru's 20-year internal war. The CVR established that most of these disappearances took place in the region of Ayacucho between 1983 and 1985—one of the worst periods of the Peruvian state's war against the Maoist Shining Path in the Peruvian south-central Andes. The CVR also concluded that Los Cabitos became during these years a major center for the clandestine detention and disappearance of people labeled as "terrorists" by the security forces (http://www.cverdad.org.pe/ifinal/index.php; for the history of the internal war, see Degregori 1991, 1998; Degregori et al. 1996; Gorriti 1990; Manrique 2002; Poole 1994; Poole and Rénique 1992; Stern 1998).

The most incriminating evidence, however, would come from the forensic investigation the AGO started in La Hoyada in late 2001—that is, before the release of the CVR's final report—in search of clandestine tombs. The first forensic intervention took place in mid-September 2001 with the assistance of personnel from the IML. The investigative team found nine clandestine tombs that had been sacked, and it collected scattered fragments of human bones and circumstantial evidence, such as cartridge cases and shreds of clothing. In December 2002, in a second intervention, the forensic team found the demolished remains of a furnace built of bricks and adobe. In two other interventions, in January and September 2003, the experts found five more clandestine tombs that had also been sacked. However, as important as these initial findings were, they did not constitute conclusive legal evidence to prove two major allegations about Los Cabitos: first, that there were clandestine mass graves in La Hoyada; and, second, that the Peruvian military had built a blast furnace in the area to burn the bodies of its victims. For the prosecutors, a major problem hindering their investigation was that the IML did not have more personnel trained in archaeological theories, methodologies, and techniques.

In 2004, the AGO appointed a special team that included an archaeologist, a sociocultural anthropologist, and a dentist, who were charged with the responsibility of conducting forensic exhumations in the region of Ayacucho. The presence of these experts and particularly of another *perito arqueólogo* (archaeology legal expert) renewed the prosecutors' optimism and confidence in the investigation. This reinforced forensic archaeology team launched a more focused search throughout the entire area of the military barracks, opening dozens of exploratory pits in every possible site where, according to survivors, the Peruvian military had installed dungeons and torture chambers and forced detainees to dig clandestine mass graves. However, all they could find, again, were scattered fragments of human bones and circumstantial evidence, such as cartridge cases and shreds of clothing. They found no clandestine mass grave containing victims' bodies. The initial optimism about the immediate possibility of finding the bodies of the victims started to wither.

By late 2004, the forensic archaeology investigation to find clandestine mass graves containing victims' bodies seemed stalled. Then, a book authored by a leading Peruvian investigative journalist about hitherto unknown crimes committed by the Peruvian military during the counterinsurgency campaign came to the rescue. In one chapter, "La Ladrillera" (Uceda 2004:125–148), the book—based on the testimony of a former leading member of clandestine death squads of the Peruvian army—confirms the existence of clandestine mass graves and blast furnaces to burn the bodies of the killed in La Hoyada and provides details about how the machinery of extermination operated. The book claims that between 1983 and 1984 at least 500 "terrorist" suspects were summarily executed and buried in clandestine mass graves in the area and that in 1985, in an attempt to eliminate the evidence of these crimes, the Peruvian military sacked the clandestine tombs and burned the bodies of at least 300 victims. The implication was that at least 200 bodies remained clandestinely buried somewhere in the area of La Hoyada.

This new piece of evidence reanimated the forensic investigation, which now focused squarely on La Hoyada. If the survivor's voice framed in the grammar of the law had heretofore been an unsuccessful guide to truth, perhaps the perpetrator's voice articulated in a (journalistic) text would be more effective. Adopting the book as a central reference—after entering it as evidence in the criminal investigation—the forensic archaeology investigation resumed in January 2005. The guiding hypothesis was that at least 200 bodies remained buried somewhere in La Hoyada, and following the lead of the book, the forensic experts opened dozens of exploratory trenches. After two weeks of intense work, however, the investigation had not progressed significantly. Similar to previous interventions, all they managed to collect as evidence were dispersed fragments of burnt human bones, shreds of clothing, fragments of burnt bricks, and some debris. At the end of the season, the forensic archaeology investigation appeared trapped in the snares of uncertainty and frustration, and in the face of this new failure abandoning the excavation altogether emerged as a possibility.

This somber scenario of disappointment was transformed with an unexpected intrusion that changed entirely the fate of the investigation. In the afternoon of the last day of work of the season in early 2005, when the disheartened forensic team was packing to leave the site with no clear idea of how, or whether, to continue the archaeological exploration, a drunken man showed up and began to make fun of them in Quechua. The intruder said that they were working in the wrong place and that they should excavate in another area. Out of curiosity, one of the forensic experts followed him to the area he was pointing to. The forensic expert did not want to take the man seriously, first, because he was obviously drunk; and second, because in the area the intruder was pointing to there was no clue indicating the presence of graves. Santiago acknowledges that it was the prosecutor who insisted, against his skepticism, on exploring the area pointed out by the intruder. He vividly remembers that moment: "We opened an excavation trench and then, right before dusk, we luckily found human remains. It was a clandestine tomb in which we later found two individuals, one man and one woman" (author's field notes, August 16, 2006). Stones covered the bodies in the tomb; the people had been blindfolded, and cartridge cases were found associated with them. This evidence indicated that the victims had been executed in that spot and that they probably had to dig their own graves.

After more than three years of inconclusive investigation, this was the beginning of a series of crucial findings that demonstrated categorically, for the first time in Peruvian history, the practices of state terror and systematic atrocity at Los Cabitos. The prosecutor extended the excavation season for two more weeks, and the forensic team recovered 13 more bodies, among them the remains of a teenager dressed in a school uniform. All of the victims had been shot at close range; all of them had been blindfolded; all the tombs had been filled with stones to cover the bodies of the victims; all of the graves showed traces of quicklime, used presumably to accelerate the decomposition of the bodies; and circumstantial evidence, such as cartridge cases, coins, and clothing associated with the bodies, was recovered from all of the tombs. In other words, not only did the forensic anthropology team recover 15 complete bodies, but it also uncovered hard evidence of the use of Los Cabitos as a killing field for suspects of terrorism during the counterinsurgency campaign of the 1980s and 1990s.

The forensic legal expert associates this major discovery with the notion of "luck"; even though said in passing, this seems not to be casually meant. Had the "drunken dude" not intruded, probably they would not have found anything. The man, whose name they do not even remember, accompanied them for several more days—always drunk. They came to know that when he was a child, he witnessed by chance extrajudicial executions and clandestine burials in the area. His family lived in the vicinity of Los Cabitos, and he was in charge of grazing their cattle. At times he reached La Hoyada and, on one of those occasions, he inadvertently observed the military's criminal activities. But soldiers spotted him and detained him for snooping around. When the child was about to be executed as an undesirable witness, a captain acquainted with his family saved him. This captain used to frequently visit the child's house to get some rest and free food. As a result of his intervention, the military released the child, though not before threatening him and his family with death if he said a word about what he saw and the experience he endured. With the word "luck," the archaeologist seems to refer to a chain of chance events that came to facilitate the team's expert work, allowing them to eventually uncover and conclusively document patterns of state atrocity in Peru's recent counterinsurgency campaign.

THE LEGAL EXPERT'S DOUBLE AUTHORITY

In showing how their discipline can contribute to forensic investigations of mass atrocity, some archaeologists have emphasized archaeology's rigorous and scientifically based truth-making capabilities, which make possible a controlled recovery of the past. Saunders (2002), for instance, says that forensic archaeology serves to counter denial, to provide evidence of human rights abuses, to confirm survivors' accounts of atrocity, to uncover the circumstances of the deaths of the victims, to identify the victims, to notify the victims' relatives so that some closure can take place, and to deter future human rights violations by demonstrating that the actions of the past are *always recoverable.* Blau and Skinner (2005), on the other hand, note that both traditional and forensic archaeology are interested in the *controlled* recovery of the past. The goal for both forms of archaeology is to investigate material remains, whether they are objects, corpses, or residues, in order to reconstruct activities of the past. Both are concerned with the understanding, recognition, control, and interpretation of space, site history, and site formation, and the context and attributes of buried features and evidence (artifacts) in a defined area.

This picture of how archaeology can contribute to the forensic investigation of mass atrocity draws on what Valverde (2003:67) calls the "epistemology of the clue." It presupposes that both archaeology and forensic sciences share the belief that real truths, even truths about morality and politics, are those that leave interpretable physical traces in the world (60) and that both share the modernist postulate that the world and others in the world are knowable under certain conditions of logic and procedure. It follows that since both operate on the epistemological assumptions that Ginzburg (1989) defines as the "evidential paradigm"—namely, the idea that seemingly insignificant, but visible, clues and traces provide access to inner and invisible truths—the authority of both the forensic expert and the archaeologist emerges from their ability to read these clues and to produce narratives about otherwise unobservable phenomena. Given that both archaeology and forensic sciences dwell in the same epistemological region, this reasoning suggests that archaeologists may become forensic experts, since they possess the ability to produce knowledge and truth about inaccessible pasts, which is necessary for the work of the law (see Crossland, chapter 6, this volume).

There is yet another crucial presupposition framing the work of archaeology in post-atrocity settings. As post-conflict states predicate their legitimacy on their ability to break with the violence and atrocity of wartime, the central problem for them is how to bring those facts of terror back from the past without letting their noxious effects spill over into the present and poison projects of justice that aim to end suffering and prevent future conflict. Informed by discourses of liberal rule, the mainstream claim states that only a controlled recovery of the facts of terror through the rational means of the law and science guarantees productive access to a toxic past in order to regenerate the present and open up possibilities for the future. The implicit corollary of this presupposition is normative: state terror *must* be treated as a stable object always already situated in the past since the *facts* of terror are located in the past.

Trials or forms of restorative justice, such as truth commissions, have customarily been seen as the best mechanisms for such a controlled recovery of the past. For instance, Martha Minow (1998) argues forcefully that any intervention into the past needs to break the cycles of violence and revenge and that truth commissions are the most appropriate means to that end. François Ost (2005) highlights the role of trials in dealing with atrocity and says that by presenting crimes in the ritualized and highly controlled forms and languages of the law, the trial does not simply repeat the past. Rather, in stabilizing a linear succession of clear-cut distinctions between past, present, and future, the law performs a controlled repetition of the conflict to bring it to closure and to open up a negentropic and creative time in which the fractured past is regenerated as a condition of possibility for the return to social peace. In the form of either truth commissions or trials, or some other state-sponsored mechanisms, the fundamental presupposition upon which these post-conflict state interventions are based is that clear-cut distinctions between the past, present, and future can be made because time flows in one direction (see Grandin 2005; Rojas-Perez 2008; Wilson 2003).

Because of this normative element, the association of archaeology with the law in the context of forensic investigations of mass state atrocity brings about a series of transfigurations in how the discipline approaches its object and constitutes its authority. As a semiautonomous social field, the law has its own forms of knowing and reasoning, both individualizing and forensic (Bourdieu 1987; Luhmann 1989). In determining what counts as *a* legal fact, which in turn will ground *a* legal judgment with universal implications, the work of the law circumscribes particular events and thus requires the constitution of particular legal subjects and objects in the form of *a* victim, *a* perpetrator, *a* crime, *a* witness—all of which are then related to preexisting universal rules. In the legal arena, the site of excavation becomes *a* crime scene (i.e., a space defining—almost literally—an inside and outside of the law), where only those legally authorized can participate in the game of establishing the legal truth, and the archaeologist becomes an expert witness (i.e., a legal subject endowed with the symbolic capital necessary to assist the law in gaining certainty). More tellingly, as Tuller shows in chapter 5 in this volume, the archaeologist must submit to strict regulation in respect to the production and circulation of legal evidence.

More important for my purposes in this chapter, the law establishes a particular relation with the lay voice. As Bourdieu (1987) argues, the abstract claims of equality and the universality of the law hide the fact that, by definition, one of the first operations of the legal field is to either exclude or subordinate the ordinary voice to the expert voice. The legal world is a semiautonomous social field in which questions of who speaks, who is listened to, and how to speak are mediated by forms of symbolic power that determine who has the competence to speak and the authority to be heard. Thus, if a controlled recovery of the past implies by definition the political need for a circumscribed social field in which experts endowed with symbolic capital participate in the games of truth out of which knowledge is produced, the formalization of the law imposes additional power determinations. In the post-conflict legal and political assemblages that deal with past atrocity, the ordinary voice is always already *doubly* excluded or subordinated to the voice of the expert.

Archaeologists appointed as legal experts thus embody two determinations of power: the power that comes from their being expert in their discipline and that which comes from their being the legal authority in the site of excavation. In this condition, bearing the double authority of the one who knows how to know and the one authorized by the law to produce a particular knowledge about the past, the voice of the forensic expert cannot relate to the lay voice except in terms of either exclusion or subordination of the latter. In this sense, the irruption of the "drunken dude" in the site of exhumation in Los Cabitos could not be explained except as a stroke of luck and fortune accompanying the legal and technological undertaking. At any rate, it is the presence of contingency disguised as luck.

OBJECTING VOICES

If the past is the "object" of the law and forensic sciences, then we can say, following Latour (2000), that with the irruption of the "drunken dude," the past "objects" to how it is produced and spoken of in the scriptures of law and forensic sciences. This objection is voiced from outside the legal universe not only because the "drunken dude" is not a (formal) part of the legal investigation, but also because he voices an experience that has been excluded from the particularizing work of the law. Moreover, he enters into a scene that is highly charged with symbolic power to challenge the forensic gaze trained to read traces and clues and gain access to the invisible past. The Quechua-speaking intruder "objects" to the authority of the Spanish-speaking expert witness on the basis of the authority of his own experience of being a survivor. The "drunken dude" may be external to the legal universe, but he is internal to the painful experience of violence and state terror of which Los Cabitos is a gruesome trace.

As the area most heavily affected by the internal war, Ayacucho is a place of stories in which each person has a story to tell. Following Cavell (1994:12), we can say that the worst has come to be known here and, for that reason, one's pain, small or large, "need not go unsaid and unaccompanied." Whether in one's own experience, such as the unnamed intoxicated man's, or a relative's, a neighbor's, a friend's, or an acquaintance's, everyone has witnessed how terror and violence devastate individuals, families, and communities and how, because of their mechanical repetition, violence and terror became ordinary. One's personal biography and specific places are thus intimately associated in the experience of pain and suffering derived from violence. That these stories of pain, small or large, do not go unsaid or unaccompanied or, say, unauthored depends not only on the conditions of possibility for saying and acknowledging (Das et al. 2001), but also on the question of the arrogation of voice.

Elsewhere (Rojas-Perez 2010) I elaborate on the specific conditions of possibility for the "drunken dude's" arrogation of voice in the context of the legal and forensic investigation of practices of state atrocity in Los Cabitos. For the argument in this chapter suffice it to say that his arrogation of voice clearly appears not to be tied to the question of rights. Since he is external to the legal universe of the criminal investigation (and, perhaps, precisely because of this very externality), he could have remained silent out of indifference, complicity, fear, or denial. And yet, he decides to speak because the "object" under investigation is a crucial, perhaps defining, experience in his biography. He speaks his experience from the inside of that experience—an experience that, by definition, cannot be subsumed by the law and hence is excluded. Truth, then, arrives not as a result of the legal and disciplinary technologies that aim to achieve a controlled recovery of the past, but almost literally from their outside. Truth in Los Cabitos arrives as an event. It takes place as a result of the survivor's objection, which forces its way through the controlled past of the forensic experts.

By arrogating voice for himself, the (drunken) survivor speaks for all in this land who have their pain, small or large, that "need not go unsaid and unaccompanied" (Cavell 1994:12). It is a singular voice; and because it is singular, it is universal. Thus, the past lingers all over this place of stories, perhaps awaiting the disruptive moment in which somebody else arrogates voice for herself, and speaks for everybody else while speaking for her biography, singular but universal.

DESÁNIMO, OR THE LEGAL EXPERT'S SOUL

As "native" archaeologists, the legal experts themselves experience in the site the tension between ordinary and expert voices as articulated in the Spanish notion of *desánimo.* "Desánimo" as a noun can be translated as disheartenment, discouragement, sadness, or disappointment. It is the opposite of *ánimo* (enlivening, encouragement). During my fieldwork I repeatedly heard the archaeologists uttering "desánimo" to express their disappointment with the outcomes of their work. And yet, in strictly forensic terms, there were no reasons for such disappointment. The excavation slowly but steadily succeeded in proving that a killing field functioned at the headquarters of the counterinsurgency campaign in the Peruvian south-central Andes, and the work provided crucial evidence to prosecute the atrocities. If the work of these experts was making a decisive contribution to the criminal investigation of one of the major cases of state atrocity in modern Peruvian history, why were they still disappointed? Clearly, their reaction came from the fact that, in almost two years of work, they had not been able to find a single complete body besides those found in early 2005. All they had recovered were heaps of ashes and uncountable fragments of charred human bones. Not being able to find more complete bodies was a source of desánimo for them; and this strikes us as a paradox because, if we were to speak in purely formal terms, they already had "bodies of evidence" for prosecution.

It could be argued that this anxiety about not finding complete bodies responds to the fact that the "humanitarian aspect" of the excavation (Fondebrider 2002) was missing—the expectation that the archaeological work would facilitate the return of individual bodies to their relatives for proper burial. Elsewhere (Rojas-Perez 2010, 2013), I have shown how important the recovery of the individual missing body has become for post-conflict state projects of bringing legal and cultural closure to past state atrocities because it serves to complete a story of suffering and redemption by which both law and culture reconstitute the broken social order. But it seems to me that desánimo comes not only from the legal-forensic or humanitarian regions, but also from the fact that the forensic experts in Los Cabitos are themselves witnesses of the experience of violence and suffering they study now as an object in their condition as experts.

In search of certainty, both the law and forensic sciences demand that archaeologists objectify and distance themselves not only from the investigated object but also from their own personal experience of it. However, the forensic archaeology team in Los Cabitos engages in what Buchli and Lucas (2001) call an "archaeology of the contemporary past"—namely, an archaeology that deals not with the "recent past" but with the present and, as such, with contexts that are textually and discursively rich. For these authors, the "recent past" implies events close in time, whereas "contemporary" refers to the "now." The difference is between proximity and identity. In the former, the "object of study" remains at some distance; there is still some gap, no matter how small, between the archaeologist and what is studied; in the latter, any gap is constantly contested and collapsed because the archaeologist is implicated more immediately than in any other kind of archaeology (Buchli and Lucas 2001:10).

The most immediate way in which the archaeologists are implicated by their "object" in Los Cabitos is that, as "natives," that "object" is a central part of their own biographies. Like most Peruvians and Ayacuchanos of their age, they are familiar with experiences of violence and massive suffering, the material remains of which they are studying now. The internal war in Peru marked their biographies and, like the "drunken dude," they inhabit a place of stories. The archaeologists are also in possession of personal stories of suffering and devastation—whether pertaining to a friend, a colleague, a classmate, an acquaintance, a relative, or even themselves. In this sense, the contemporary past in which they are digging is an ongoing past—that is, their now. We may ask here to what extent these and other associated experiences of suffering returned to them in the site, particularly in the very moment in which they recovered ashes or fragments of human bones. We may ask what it means for them to return to the site of devastation as "experts."

Joyce (chapter 10, this volume) powerfully argues that human remains are not simply inanimate matter. They are more than just evidence (see also Crossland 2009a). During my fieldwork I observed how, while following scrupulously archaeology's disciplinary rules and assumptions, at certain moments the forensic experts turned the procedure into a kind of ritual in which they treated the shattered human remains as anything but mere "objects" or "artifacts." They related to the remains with a certain reverence and referred to them as belonging to a present person. "It is his knee," "it is his femur," "it is her rib," they said whenever they found fragments of bones and recovered them for analysis. This use of language reveals a tension between two modes of relating to the remains: the body as evidence and the body as person (Crossland 2000, 2002, 2009a; Joyce, this volume). As persons, the dead have agency, and one specific way in which this agency is expressed is providing the information they have to experts who can hear them (e.g., see Fredy Peccerelli in Carrescia 2008).

But to speak of the body as a person is to speak of the body as a set of relations. The unnatural destruction of a specific human body expresses the utter destruction of the human relations it formerly embodied. The inability to recover these bodies gets translated not only into the inability to remake our relation to them (a relation, say, in the form of their proper burial) but also into the inability to remake our relation to ourselves (a relation, say, in the form of mourners). Something very personal thus continues to be missing with the missing body, and desánimo speaks of that loss of our relation to others and of being lost to ourselves in this site of devastation, a point that Crossland and Joyce explore in the introduction to this volume.

There is yet another way in which the archaeologists in Los Cabitos are implicated by their "object." They are dealing with the material remains of processes of violence and state terror that are not entirely situated in the past and that continue to haunt the present in the logic of what I have called the "finished/unfinished past" (Rojas-Perez 2013). Unsurprisingly, given its highly sensitive political and historical significance, the forensic excavation was constantly subjected to institutional and political pressures and constraints that sought to undermine it. The threat of physical violence does not disappear with the official inauguration of the "post-conflict" era (Rojas-Perez 2008) and looms over the investigation in several disguises. The question for these archaeologists seems to be, what is the position of the expert witness in this context? (Fondebrider in chapter 2, this volume notes that this is not unusual in investigations of mass killings; see also Sanford 2003b.) Is the forensic text they are producing enough to unmake state terror—which is to say, to master it? Is the rationalization of the past by means of the controlled language of the law enough to unmake state terror?

Desánimo, I suggest, seems to articulate a certain skepticism regarding the work of the law in contexts of the investigation of state atrocity. It voices an intuition that the rational procedures and controlled language of the law and disciplinary power, while crucial in unmaking denial, are not enough to bring about justice and unmake state terror as a condition of possibility for recovery in the aftermath of atrocity. Desánimo also articulates a certain distancing of archaeology from forensic sciences. As a discipline interested by definition in the social, archaeology looks at the broader contexts of power relations that shape specific forms of the social and the cultural. In desánimo, there is the intuition that the possibility of justice and the impulse to remake a world in the aftermath of devastation, while grounded in the work of the law, cannot be confined to the narrow and controlled realm of the law or, more precisely, as I show in the next section, of the trial. This intuition also highlights that an irreducible dimension of justice in the face of state atrocity, its substance, needs to be found and founded elsewhere.

POST-CONFLICT SILENCING OF ATROCITY

On May 26, 2011, a Lima-based special court of the Peruvian judiciary started a trial in the Los Cabitos case. The prosecutor charged seven former high-ranking officers of the Peruvian army with the torture and forced disappearance of dozens of terrorism suspects in 1983—the year the Peruvian military seized control of the Ayacucho region to wage a counterinsurgency war against the Maoist Shining Path.[4] It was one of a dozen trials concerning human rights that began after the advent of the democratic transition in late 2000, all of which have aimed at coming to terms with the atrocities of the past and establishing the grounds for a post-conflict democratic social and political order based on a culture of human rights. Because some perpetrators were effectively prosecuted, including former president Alberto Fujimori, who was sentenced in April 2009 on charges of gross human rights violations during his tenure (Burt 2009; Youngers and Burt 2009), some observers rushed to comment that Peru had become an exemplary case of how democratic transitions can turn wartime politics of denial, forgetting, and impunity into post-conflict politics of truth, memory, accountability, and justice for survivors.

And yet, this optimism, which emerges from the fact that trials concerning human rights are being conducted in the country, does not account for the fact that despite the post-conflict incitation to truth, memory, and accountability, a dense wall of public silence usually encircles them. The Los Cabitos trial is a striking case in point. Given that it is perhaps the most important legal case in contemporary Peruvian history, from a purely liberal perspective one would have expected that the case would attract widespread public attention. Such a perspective presupposes both the existence of a national audience and the willingness to deliberate openly about atrocities the public supposedly did not know about. Trials are endowed with both cognitive and affective powers through which the law ends conflict and finishes the past by means of sanctioning truth, producing a *consensual* understanding about such a past (Ost 2005; Savelsberg and King 2007).

However, in chilling contrast with the trial of Fujimori, the Los Cabitos case hearings have gone unnoticed by a wide national audience. The former had live national TV coverage from the beginning to the end and provoked intense public debate; the latter have had almost no press coverage since the beginning and have provoked no public conversation whatsoever. In the former case many people, including members of the political elite, often packed the hearings; in the latter, besides the defendants and the legal practitioners, there have rarely been other attendees—except perhaps some bystanders from time to time. In the former case, the plaintiffs and the defendant's relatives actively engaged the Spanish-speaking public arena in order to advance their case; in the latter, the Quechua-speaking plaintiffs from Ayacucho could not even attend the hearings because they could not afford to travel 20 hours round trip by bus to Lima every week. (I attended the hearings during the early stages of the trial, from late May to August 2011, and then from June to August 2012, during the stage in which the survivors of torture and the relatives of victims of forced disappearance were cross-examined.)[5]

It might be possible to attribute this public silence *only* to the historical problem of who speaks and who is listened to—and hence whose memory enters into the public arena—which is determined by conventions and structures of symbolic power in ethnic, class, and gender-based hierarchies (see Trouillot 1995). However, at stake here is also the particular object named "state terror" and the temporality of a finished/unfinished past in which the assemblage of post-conflict state rule dwells. On one hand, as mentioned above, moving within the assemblage of liberal rule, the post-conflict state claims legitimacy on the basis of its ability to break with the arbitrary and violent past by (re)establishing the rule of law as a means of constituting the social order. In this sense, finishing the past is a condition of possibility of the post-conflict state. On the other hand, in the continuous work of refounding its order the post-conflict state leaves the past unfinished. By invoking the object "terrorism" as a permanent threat, the post-conflict state not only repeats forms of violence associated with the past, bringing back technologies of control that proved to be "effective" during the internal war, but also seeks to forget its own violence. This temporality of the unfinished past is internal to the work of state power in that it produces both the sorts of new threats against which the post-conflict state can legitimize its violence *and* the grid of affects, such as fear and shame, necessary to establish its control over suspect populations (Green 1999; Rojas-Perez 2010).

It is in this temporality of the finished/unfinished past that we need to situate the public silence surrounding the Los Cabitos trial. This silence certainly suggests that there is not a homogeneous public willing to deliberate about past atrocity in order to reach a consensual understanding of the past. Rather, as Trouillot asserts, the production of historical narratives, or the "truth" about the past, "involves the uneven contribution of competing groups and individuals who have unequal access to the means for such production" (1995:xix). But it also suggests that the specificity of the object "state terror" always already establishes a particular kind of conversation (among experts) in which the idea of the "state" as a principal of intelligibility of the social order needs to be rescued. Thus, while initially authorizing speech about the object "atrocity," trials of the perpetrators of state atrocity are not necessarily about addressing the truth, memory, and suffering of the victims, but about modulating what is to be socially said, or not said, and remembered, or forgotten, about such atrocity and such suffering. The survivor's suffering is thus institutionally appropriated for the sake of more transcendent tasks—instituting the social order, avoiding future conflict, and legitimizing the post-conflict state (on the question of institutional appropriation of suffering, see Das 1995).

JUSTICE IN THE MARGINS OF STATE LAW

In addition to public silence, perhaps the most striking manifestation of the institutional appropriation of suffering in post-conflict Peru is the fact that, because of the impossibility of their identification, the human remains recovered during the forensic exhumations in Los Cabitos have not been recognized as "the body of the victim" within the existing categories of human rights crimes established in the Peruvian penal code. In the category of extrajudicial execution and aggravated murder, victims must be identified. In the category of forced disappearance, the body of the victim is by definition missing. Because these remains cannot be individualized and identified, they have been considered just "contextual evidence" for the purposes of the prosecution. In short, the disappeared continue to be disappeared while the unidentified human remains stay packed in cardboard boxes piled up in IML storage rooms in Ayacucho.

And yet, the reappearance of their missing relatives, either dead or alive, has been the central demand of justice that the (excluded) relatives of the disappeared have formulated throughout the years. Elsewhere (Rojas-Perez 2013) I contend that the forensic excavations in Los Cabitos open up, for the first time in more than 30 years of vain search, the possibility for a *where* in which the bodies of their missing relatives *might be* dwelling. The ashes and charred fragments of human bones recovered in the excavations *might be* their missing relatives' remains; however, since the identification and individualization of these remains appear for now impossible, the relatives cannot be certain. Yet a fissure has already cracked the unending temporality of the disappearance. As I (2013) have written elsewhere, the possibility of assigning their missing relatives' remains a *whereness*, or, at least, an imperfect locality, affects the indefinitely prolonged uncertainty that engulfed these mothers' lives all these years. It punctuates the duration of the disappearance (2013:161). The subjunctive mood (Good 1994) of the "might be" serves to imagine that death is the most probable mode of being of their missing relatives.

Paradoxically, the fact that the disappeared have not been brought back into being as legal subjects, cultural subjects, or historical subjects within the institutionalized structures of legal and disciplinary power allows for the possibility of a line of flight through which the idea of justice in the face of state atrocity escapes the edifice of the trial. And this possibility is clearly associated with the emergence of the Quechua-speaking survivors' (ordinary) voice, which claims their experience of suffering and appropriates collectively the remains recovered during the forensic excavation to constitute forms of mourning and justice—without the body—as a response to ongoing state terror. In this sense, the "failure" of forensic archaeology is the condition of possibility for the recovery of (ordinary) voice as a manifestation of a form of justice that takes place in the realm of the law, but outside the purview of the trial (see also Sanford 2003b). It is an invitation to have a more nuanced and complex understanding of the problem of post-atrocity justice, one that is related to but goes beyond the work of the law.

CONCLUDING COMMENTS

Some chapters in this volume discuss compellingly the forensic aspect of forensic anthropology by interrogating either its normative characteristics (Tuller, chapter 5, Thompson, chapter 4), its epistemological assumptions (Walsh-Haney and Boys, chapter 7), or its social and political contexts (Fondebrider, chapter 2). Others approach in fascinating ways the anthropological aspect of forensic anthropology by interrogating its position and relations with broader debates within the discipline of archaeology (Geller, chapter 8, Martin, chapter 9), by asking how forensic anthropologists voice their experience outside the constraints of disciplinary grammars (Crossland, chapter 6), or by examining how they talk about their "objects"—the dead (Joyce, chapter 10). My chapter has approached the anthropological aspect of forensic anthropology by attempting to situate the work of forensic anthropology (in the site) within broad political and cultural contexts of power and by looking at how, as a truth-making discipline, forensic archaeology moves tensely between the shores of state making and justice making. Given that manufacturing state legitimacy and opening up possibilities for justice are not the same, it seems perfectly clear that in contexts of forensic investigation of mass atrocity, particularly where recent experiences of state terror are at stake, this tension between state making and justice making is unavoidable.

As the Los Cabitos case illustrates, there is no doubt that the intervention of forensic anthropology in contexts of criminal investigation of state atrocity is decisive in providing hard evidence to constitute a legally authorized truth about atrocity. However, as a field of expertise, forensic archaeology might get trapped in the assemblage of post-conflict state rule by authorizing a truth that is institutionally appropriated and adapted to the needs of legitimacy of post-conflict state institutions. Conversely, the field might become an intercessor of forms of justice that, while related to the work of the law, go beyond the pronouncement of legal institutions. It is an unavoidable tension that does not have an easy solution—and perhaps should not have one—if one avoids either denying it or plainly embracing thoroughly one aspect of the equation.

The complexity of post-atrocity situations, as described by Fondebrider in this volume, invites forensic anthropologists to embrace this tension and live critically with it. This, it seems to me, would be the beginning of what Thompson (this volume) asks forensic anthropologists to do: to embrace more fully the anthropological aspect of forensic anthropology. Then, perhaps, the idea that the object "state terror" is in several respects an ongoing past that not only continues to shape the post-conflict society, but also always already implicates the forensic anthropologist personally, can gain some purchase and persuade practitioners about how the intrinsic political nature of their "object" is not just a theoretical problem but one that bears upon the fundamental question of what it means to have justice served in these contexts. This question implicates us all and invites us to listen to how the ordinary voice emerges in the highly politically and symbolically charged sites of intervention of the law and disciplinary power.

Acknowledgments

Grants for my dissertation research came from the National Science Foundation (project no. 0518950) and the United States Institute of Peace. I am grateful to the legal and forensic personnel of the Ministerio Publico and the Instituto de Medicina Legal of Ayacucho, Peru, for allowing me to participate and observe their work in a difficult political context. I salute and admire their work, and pieces like this chapter are meant to foster conversation on common preoccupations about the crucial question of the *desaparecidos* in Peru. I am also grateful to Zoë Crossland and Rosemary Joyce for their invitation to participate in the SAR advanced seminar of which this edited volume is a compelling product. Finally, my thanks to all the participants at the seminar and to the two reviewers who provided valuable feedback on an earlier draft of this chapter. Any errors and weaknesses in this piece are, certainly, mine alone.

Notes

1. All the names of the legal and forensic personnel are pseudonyms except for the prosecutor, who is a public figure. The term "hoyada" is an idiosyncratic derivation of the Spanish noun *hoyo* (hole). It may be translated as "the hollow."

2. Since the first task group disbanded in mid-2002 due to a series of political and technical disagreements that ended up with the experts of the EPAF stepping down from representing the CVR, reorganized teams including international experts conducted these procedures. For accounts of these beginnings, see EPAF n.d.; and Equipo Forense Especializado, http://www.mpfn.gob.pe/iml/efe.php (accessed December 12, 2012).

3. Alarcon is the legal advisor for the Ayacucho-based National Association of Relatives of People Kidnapped, Detained, and Disappeared in Peru.

4. As a matter of expediency, the Peruvian judiciary decided to split the case into three separate cases, according to the year in which the crimes were committed. These legal cases are thus referenced as Los Cabitos 1983, Los Cabitos 1984, and Los Cabitos 1985.

5. At the time of writing of this chapter, the Los Cabitos trial had not yet concluded.

4

Deconstructing the Ideal of Standardization in Forensic Anthropology

Tim Thompson

In an article reviewing the pedagogical efforts under way in forensic anthropology, Galloway and Simmons (1997:801) state that "the future of the discipline is dependent upon establishing further standards and guidelines for training and status beyond those that are currently in place." Arguably, almost 20 years later, we are no further forward. However, one of the key changes since their work is the growth of the discipline into new areas, notably the development of forensic archaeology. "Forensic anthropology goes far beyond osteological analysis," write Dirkmaat and colleagues (2008:48), and acceptance of this brings with it a number of issues. These include standardizing a broad discipline that involves the examination of bodies both living and dead, both fleshed and skeletalized, and both at home and abroad—and also the difficulties of identifying which aspects of forensic anthropological practice are to be standardized—all the while balancing the requirements of all interested parties, including the practitioners (Thompson 2003). What standardization offers is the opportunity to reduce variability and external influence (through the unification of definitions, methods, and practices), thereby providing confidence in the discipline from those who seek to utilize its strengths and an increased sense of professionalism on the part of practitioners. Thus, perceptions of credibility, as described by Galloway and Simmons (1997), lie at the heart of this issue.

Tim Thompson

The issue of standardization in forensic anthropology is not as straightforward as some would lead us to believe. The field is multifaceted, and the issue is compounded by the fact that "anthropology is a holistic discipline with fuzzy intellectual boundaries" (Skinner et al. 2003:82). Of course forensic anthropology is not the only forensic discipline to engage with the issues of standardization. Forensic pathology, toxicology, and genetics are already undergoing this process (Ferrara et al. 2010). Yet what is often neglected is a discussion of the other actors involved, or how the culturally embedded scientific paradigm that is codified into the discipline fits elsewhere in the world. Is standardization beneficial for all? Being mindful that "the archaeologist exposes temporal and spatial relationships that help explain how the bodies came to be in the observed state" (Skinner et al. 2003:84), it is clear that "bodies are evaluated; they certify and attest" (Petrović-Šteger 2009:67). This activity is inherently culturally specific and cannot be atheoretical. Too often we think of all this from a restricted viewpoint of "objective" forensic science and fail to appreciate the myriad other factors that complicate the notion of objectivity in this field (see Thompson 2008 for a dismantling of the notion of the objective forensic photograph and the implications of this for the discipline). Standardization is often seen as a neutral route to objectivity, and rarely do we question how it fits into an overall appreciation of the holistic consequentiality of our work. Yet it has implications beyond the practitioners that are often overlooked.

In this chapter I discuss the notion of standardization in forensic anthropology by describing the contexts in which forensic anthropology is applied, by examining some of the factors that affect this application in the field, and by discussing the concept and implications of standardization. The specific duties associated with the forensic archaeologist and anthropologist vary around the world (examples of different national perspectives can be found in Blau and Ubelaker 2009; Brickley and Ferllini 2007; and other chapters in this volume). Where I work in the United Kingdom the two are closely related but separate disciplines (one with a focus on search and recovery and the other with a focus on the examination of the body), and practitioners tend to do either one or the other. In this chapter when I focus on the examination and investigation of the body I use the term "forensic anthropology" and when discussing work around the grave itself I use "forensic archaeology."

Cattaneo (2007) argues that the first problem that the discipline needs to address is to actually define "forensic anthropology." She notes that the association with osteometry is too restrictive. An alternative is the term "bioarchaeology," which some prefer since they feel it unites the role of the anthropologist and the archaeologist and includes other biological sciences (Skinner et al. 2003). The broadening of the definition and scope of forensic anthropology has led some to refer to it as the "new forensic anthropology." This expansion is entirely legitimate and is not born from commercial interests but rather reflects a natural evolution of the field (Dirkmaat et al. 2008).

Regardless of the nomenclature, there is no doubt that forensic archaeology and anthropology have significant roles to play in international medico-legal contexts. There are numerous examples in the published literature of the contributions that both have made toward the resolution of cases ranging from single bodies to mass graves to devastating mass fatality incidents. Their potential importance is therefore beyond doubt. However, two points should be considered. The first is that despite their proven success, forensic archaeology and anthropology are very small components in the overall forensic investigative process, utilized in only a tiny percentage of cases. In the United Kingdom this point is sometimes lost in the noisy push to establish and validate these subjects in academic, educational, and legal contexts. The second consideration is that, despite the successes, there is an acknowledgment among practitioners that ours is a "fuzzy" science that relies heavily on practitioners' interpretation and experience. This has led some to argue that forensic anthropologists should "develop professional standards to which they hold themselves accountable and by which forensic scientists in other fields, who may call upon their services, can verify their competence" (Galloway and Simmons 1997:796). Despite this explicit acknowledgment of the nature of forensic anthropology, and considering the fact that it does involve a significant amount of practitioner interpretation, it is interesting that there is little discussion regarding the various factors that can influence interpretation and bar detailed analysis of observer error, as well as other dry methodological issues.

What is needed is discussion of the factors that influence how and when forensic anthropology is applied in the field. In this context, the implementation of standardization has been argued to be one of the most important goals of the forensic sciences in recent times, yet despite this, there has been little discussion of what this shift to standardization actually suggests for the wider context of forensic anthropology—for the political and social spheres in which it operates. Thus there are two key areas of concern for the standardization agenda: methods and personnel. But even this is a simplification. Regarding methods, there are issues to address in terms of both the formation of our techniques and their application to human remains; regarding personnel, the issues include appropriate expertise and individual interpretation. Complications arise when debates around the need for standardization conflate all of these, when in fact the end goals are significantly different. Therefore the question that I am interested in asking here is, in this complicated context is it enough to say that standardization simply makes things better without asking for whom and in what way? This chapter addresses these issues and discusses some of the tensions that can influence the application of forensic anthropology.

TENSIONS ASSOCIATED WITH THE SCENE

There are likely to be different goals and expectations at a crime scene. This can lead to tensions or awkwardness between those working together to resolve the incident, particularly if it involves a grave. These pressures speak to broader tensions that emerge from differences in the disciplinary orientation, training, and experience of those involved in the scene. Forensic anthropologists, with their relatively young discipline and strong connection to the deceased's body, are susceptible to these tensions. This situation is compounded by the fact that the number of forensic anthropologists working in the field, especially in human rights, genocide, and war crime investigation contexts, has increased dramatically since the late twentieth century (Komar 2003). Work by Steadman and Haglund (2005) demonstrates that between 1990 and 1999 the Argentine Forensic Anthropology Team (EAAF), the Guatemalan Forensic Anthropology Team, Physicians for Human Rights, and the International Criminal Tribunal for the former Yugoslavia utilized 134 anthropologists from 22 countries at nearly 1,300 sites in 33 different countries. Here I examine two tensions that derive from the application of forensic anthropology at the grave site: the first results from the physical work of the discipline, and the second from the expectations of the other interested parties (see too, Tuller, chapter 5, this volume).

The Application of Forensic Anthropology at the Grave Site

The different methods and techniques that can be used to create an osteo profile are often derived from the study and analysis of skeletal material from different contexts (see Walsh-Haney and Boys, chapter 7, this volume). However, due to the nature of human variation, methods generated from one set of remains may not be appropriate for another. Thus, population-specific techniques lose accuracy when applied to a different population (Garvin and Passalacqua 2012; Kemkes-Grottenthaler 2001; Komar 2003), and methodological differences make it hard to directly compare studies based on different populations (Wärmländer and Sholts

2011). Since this loss of accuracy may result in incorrect osteo profiles, this is an area that anthropologists are diligently addressing. The creation of effective standards for modern populations relies on the comparison of osteological methods against known antemortem information. Despite the number of bodies examined in the forensic context, this often may not be possible, thus resulting in small sample sizes for such work (Steadman and Haglund 2005).

Notwithstanding the specific circumstances required for it to reach its full investigative potential, forensic anthropology is a crucial tool when human remains are present at the scene of a crime (Cattaneo 2007). This is especially true when the scene contains fragmented remains, when there is a question regarding provenance (that is, are they modern or archaeological remains?), and when an assessment of taphonomic factors is required (Dirkmaat et al. 2008; Ferllini 2007; Mundorf 2011; Rogers 2005). Anthropology's strengths over other identification sciences (such as DNA analysis and fingerprinting) are that it can function well even after prolonged decomposition or degradation of the body and that it still works well on fragmented remains. Forensic anthropological analysis does not necessarily link human remains to an individual identity—that is, an osteo profile is not dependent upon an external database of individual identifiers (such as AFIS, for fingerprints) to produce useful results. This can be helpful if the investigators are uncertain that the individual identifiers of the deceased are present in such an external database.

Yet this last feature is also one of forensic anthropology's perceived key weaknesses, in that it rarely provides proof of positive identification. With this in mind, Kemkes-Grottenthaler (2001) highlights the tensions at the scene between anthropologists and DNA experts (who can provide such). Mundorf (2011) argues that in the mass fatality victim identification setting, the use of anthropology is lessening since practitioners can struggle to provide enough individualizing information about a person. However, this is not true in all contexts. That DNA analysis is of greater use in the forensic setting is only a reality under certain circumstances—in cases, for example, where there are funds available to undertake DNA sampling and analysis. However, one can see how DNA can be used to "verify" the work of the anthropologist and by doing so generate the sense of hierarchy among practitioners that led Dirkmaat and colleagues to go so far as to say that "DNA analysis techniques served to undermine the classic role of forensic anthropology" (2008:33).

Historically there have been tensions between anthropologists working in a forensic context and osteoarchaeologists (see Martin, chapter 9, this volume). The work undertaken by a forensic anthropologist might be viewed as easily undertaken by an osteologist. This fails to appreciate or acknowledge the extra responsibilities, interpretational challenges, and consequentiality of the forensic context (Galloway and Simmons 1997), and is an effect of a misperception of what the subject involves through focusing on methods while ignoring context. The purpose of the forensic sciences is to assist the courts, yet it may be that those in the legal profession do not fully understand the scientific methods or processes of application and interpretation of forensic anthropology, and thus may not be able to effectively evaluate the scientific evidence. Likewise, the scientists may lack an understanding of legal and judicial processes (Girdwoyn and Tomaszewski 2009; Grivas and Komar 2008). Both of these issues are due to perceptions and to how workers are exposed to the other's discipline and in what manner.

There is also the possibility of tensions at the scene between anthropologists who originate from different countries and cultures with differing work practices. Related to this are tensions between forensic anthropologists with different levels of education and different assessments of the importance of academic achievement versus time spent in the field. Congram and Steadman (2008) raise this point when they question the motives of some forensic anthropologists who travel to work in other countries, especially when those countries may be well equipped to do the work themselves. These difficulties are further explored by Fondebrider, Tuller, and Rojas-Perez (chapters 2, 5, 3 respectively) in this volume. In the United Kingdom, there is also the possibility of tensions between forensic anthropologists as a result of the market-driven nature of forensic science and anthropology services (Cox 2009). Commercial competition may impact personal and professional relationships, especially if there is the chance of further work in the future. Indeed, one of the concerns facing some freelance forensic anthropologists at the moment is whether they can effectively compete for work against the larger forensic providers. This is part of a wider issue, and Welsh and Hannis note, "In the UK, the forensic science sector is complex...because in each of the jurisdictions within the UK there are different models and particularly because of the split between state provision of some aspects of forensic process and the commercialization of others in England and Wales" (2011:140; see also Cox 2009). Thus it could be argued that standardization in the United Kingdom would be of real benefit, but there may well still be problems if this starts to cross national, cultural, and jurisdictional borders.

The Influence of Other Actors in the Narrative of the Site

In an earlier paper (Thompson 2003), I highlighted the key interest groups in the application of forensic anthropology in the field: the public, the police, the legal system, students, and the media. All five of these have an influence, to a greater or lesser degree, on the narrative of a given grave site. I argued there that the police expect further contributions from forensic anthropology to aid their investigation; that the legal system expects the provision of evidence that it can use in the courts; that students expect interesting and relevant courses; and that the media expect to use the subject in their reporting and program making. All of these are still relevant, and they impact how forensic anthropology is applied and how its practices and conclusions are represented and disseminated, which in turn affects the application of the subject in future work. Zoë Crossland's discussion in chapter 6 in this volume of the representation of forensic anthropology in fiction is a case in point. Where my 2003 discussion fell short was in the consideration of the public. I tended to consider "the public" as people separate from the investigation itself, but still with a loose vested interest. Of course, victims, survivors, and family members of those associated with the scene should also be included in this group. The human rights context provides a powerful illustration of the tensions created by differing claims, and I use two groups in particular to illustrate the implications of a potential standardization in forensic anthropology.

The first group includes those in the legal system. In human rights abuses cases, it is these individuals who will orchestrate the investigation and take it to a conclusion. These may be military, civilian, and law enforcement agencies (Komar 2003) and, potentially, members of families (Steadman and Haglund 2005). The legal system may provide a single prosecutor or may develop wider truth commissions. These are the organizations for which the forensic anthropologist will be working, and their aims and goals will vary over time, with changes in personnel, and from region to region and country to country. They are likely to also insist on the presence of a monitor, whose role it is to supervise the excavation and examination of the remains. These are strict roles with well-defined boundaries (Skinner et al. 2003), but tensions can exist when the boundaries are not clearly articulated or are ignored. Petrović-Šteger uses the phrase "the political deployment of mourning" (2009:48), and the legal system, and consequently the forensic anthropologist, becomes deeply involved in this. This leads to the second group and to one of the most discussed tensions created by the forensic anthropological investigation of human rights abuses: that created by the interaction of forensic anthropologists and archaeologists with grieving members of the public. I will illustrate my point with a few examples.

During 2003–2004, Maja Petrović-Šteger spent time in the field in Serbia and Bosnia-Herzegovina undertaking an ethnographic study of those involved in the forensic investigation of the mass graves there. She notes (2009) that despite the acknowledgment that good cooperation between international forensic experts and local volunteers is a prerequisite for the International Commission on Missing Persons (ICMP) to work effectively, it was decided to exclude local workers from the professional processes of recovery of the bodies. She explains the rationale: since it was often difficult to tell the ethnicity of those in a given mass grave, the ICMP did not want any particular group to be seen as being favored or allied with the forensic team. This clearly makes some sense in the complicated environment that is the former Yugoslavia (see Tuller, chapter 5, this volume). However, this course of action "provoked dissatisfaction among the people personally involved in searching for their loved ones' 'remains'" (Petrović-Šteger 2009:54). In addition, advice was often given to the forensic experts not to mingle with the local population. Certainly in my time in the region, I was strongly advised against speaking any language other than English for fear of being viewed unfavorably by one group or another.

By contrast, Victoria Sanford (2009), in her work following the forensic investigations of the mass graves in Guatemala, notes the important role that family members have in directing the attention of the forensic scientists to sites and locations of interest. Like Flavel and Barker (2009:430), who note that the "exhumation of clandestine graves is usually a community event in Guatemala," Sanford describes the closeness of the survivors and their relatives to the grave site and their immediate need to interact with the personal effects recovered. This is very different from the experiences in the former Yugoslavia and raises interesting questions about how the discipline might be reimagined as a more community-based practice in line with the model developed by the EAAF and others in Latin America and also, to a lesser extent, the Joint POW/MIA Accounting Command. This would pose a real challenge for forensic anthropology since this runs contrary to how it is currently taught and practiced by people working in the United Kingdom and in much of the United States.

There are times when the involvement of the families of the disappeared with the forensic anthropologists is deeper than just attendance at the grave site. Through their work with the Special Unit of Human Rights of the Forensic Service of Chile, Claudia Garrido Varas and Marisol Intriago Leiva have investigated a large number of high-profile human rights cases deriving from the period of the military government of 1973–1990. In one example involving the recovery, analysis, and identification of 15 disappeared individuals (Garrido Varas and Intriago Leiva 2012), they describe how the investigation began with a discussion between the prosecutor and the families of the victims that incorporated aspects of the proposed methodology. They describe the importance of communication and relations between the forensic investigators and the families of the victims. It may be that the differential treatment of the public in these examples reflects the different political histories of the conflicts and attempted resolutions. The authors state:

> Human rights cases in Chile are particularly delicate in this respect, as during the dictatorship, these cases were analyzed by the same [forensic] institution that is doing the analysis today, although things have changed considerably since democracy was established in 1990. For the families, this experience makes them victims again; they had to go through this process twice, under the same institution, even in the same building. It is not guaranteed that the families will believe or trust the new analysis, regardless of the results. (Garrido Varas and Intriago Leiva 2012:e23)

The public and families of victims do not always support the work of the forensic anthropologists. Opposition to forensic excavation has been seen in Spain, where investigation of the civil war graves is viewed by some as opening old wounds (Congram and Fernández 2010; Ferrándiz 2013). Congram and Fernández (2010:23) note that the "subject of mixed support for mass grave exhumations by primary stakeholders…has been largely, shamefully, avoided in forensic anthropology literature." In her paper on the investigations surrounding the disappeared in Argentina during the junta government of the 1970s, Crossland describes how certain family groups and associations vocally opposed the exhumations since they placed too much emphasis on identifying the dead and not enough on eliciting admissions of guilt: "They insist on public judicial accountability by those responsible; until then, they insist on remembering their disappeared relatives as they were in life rather than in death" (Crossland 2002:121).

One of the particularly difficult aspects of the resolution of crimes against humanity is that both parties involved (that is, the victims and the perpetrators) may be living in the same town or region. Hinton (2002) describes the difficulties of Cambodian victims and family members seeing the perpetrators of the violence in the normal, everyday course of their lives. This may be more likely in situations where the violence is meted out on civilians by civilians, such as in Rwanda, rather than in more militaristic campaigns of violence and terror. The proximity of victims and possible perpetrators can also provide challenges to the forensic investigation in terms of judging the authenticity of information provided by members of the public, since the investigators often do not know in what capacity they were involved in the conflict. Related to this, Ta'ala and colleagues (2006) note the difficult situation of utilizing the assistance of those who perpetrated the crimes to fully understand the methods of execution and context of death, in order to help interpret the forensic evidence. The example they refer to is the brutal four-year rule (1975–1979) of the Khmer Rouge in Cambodia, which resulted in the death of approximately 1.5 million Cambodians due to starvation, disease, or execution—around 20 percent of the population (Hinton 2002).

From the examples I have highlighted here, it can be seen that key forces acting on the application of forensic anthropology at the scene involve the relationships between forensic anthropology and other forensic and crime scene sciences, the (mis)perception of the task and scope of the subject, and the claiming of the application of forensic anthropology by non-anthropologists. With so many tensions at work, it is of interest to question how standardization (which seeks to reduce variability and external influences on the subject) will affect this milieu.

STANDARDIZATION IN FORENSIC ANTHROPOLOGY

Forensic case studies are often concerned with establishing a "standard biological profile" (Kemkes-Grottenthaler 2001:71); this avoids the question of what the "standard" is referring to. Instinctively one would assume a profile that included components such as estimations of sex, age at death, stature, and so on (Blau and Ubelaker 2009). But the issue of standardization in forensic anthropology concerns much more than this; it focuses on the selection and application of anthropological techniques in addition to determining who should or should not be practicing—the appropriate application of appropriate methods in appropriate contexts by appropriate workers. Thus, the question of standardization is not a straightforward one to answer, and again forces us to ask what exactly we mean when we ask for standardization.

The recovery of human remains from a grave site without following appropriate archaeological methodology will invariably result in a loss of vital information (such as body parts, stratigraphical information, or an understanding of anatomical associations). It could also result in damage to the body, which will lead to a loss of forensic intelligence (Cattaneo 2007). It is therefore imperative that those undertaking such work are competent to do so. Few would argue with this. But how do we address the issue of standardization if, as Cattaneo (2007) has argued, there is still an issue of definition? Not only do we have difficulty in stating what forensic anthropology in the twenty-first century is, but it is becoming an increasingly multidisciplinary field that functions in an increasingly wide range of contexts (Black 2003; Dirkmaat et al. 2008). Further, as Steadman and Haglund's (2005) and Mundorf's (2011) research shows, forensic anthropologists are also being used in a wider variety of roles, which can include the collection of antemortem data, the development of databases, and involvement in management and logistics. It is worth noting that some workers (such as Skinner et al. 2003) suggest that this expansion of roles may not be appropriate, and some indicate that naïveté about the roles and functions of the other forensic sciences and related areas may be problematic. This broadening of the purview of forensic anthropology generally, much of it supported and encouraged by anthropologists themselves, makes it difficult to devise all-encompassing standards that fit neatly in all situations and roles.

Standardization of Field Methods

It is not possible to talk about standardization in any form in forensic anthropology, and particularly with regard to methodology, without reference to the highly significant *Daubert* rulings. In the United States, the case of *Daubert v. Merrell Dow Pharmaceuticals* focused on a claim that birth defects were the result of prenatal ingestion of the drug Bendectin, which is designed to aid with morning sickness. In 1993 the Supreme Court issued its guidance on the admittance of scientific evidence, following debate surrounding crucial evidence in this trial. Related to this is a later case, *Kumho Tire Company v. Carmichael* (1999), which focused on a claim that a tire that burst and resulted in a car accident was faulty and the accident did not result from abuse by the car's owner. The admissibility issue here concerned whether the evidence on the condition of the tire was scientific, and thus subject to *Daubert*, or was more technical in nature.

The *Daubert* tests for forensic science are reproduced in a number of publications (such as Christensen and Crowder 2009; Grivas and Komar 2008; Holobinko 2012; Sommer 2010), but can be summarized as the following:

1. The theory or technique must be falsifiable, refutable, and testable, that is, subject to empirical testing.

2. The theory or technique has been subjected to peer review and publication.
3. Error rates are known or can be calculated.
4. The theory or technique is generally accepted by the relevant scientific community.
5. Standards and controls concerning the application of a given technique exist and are maintained.

It is difficult to overstate the significance of this ruling in the forensic sciences in the United States and also farther afield. Somewhat slowly, forensic anthropology has awoken to the implications of Daubert and is beginning to actively address them through discussion and critical reevaluation of the techniques and methods it uses (Christensen and Crowder 2009). Unfortunately forensic anthropologists may face difficulties in trying to mold the discipline to fit the *Daubert* standards, since the field uses a combination of quantitative and qualitative methods (Christensen and Crowder 2009) while also coping with the range of variation in the human skeleton.

The *Kumho* case was able to clarify some of the issues initially raised by the *Daubert* ruling, and these also impact forensic anthropology: experts can develop theories based on their observations and experience, all forms of expert witness will be held to the *Daubert* standards, and the *Daubert* guidelines are flexible and may not be applicable in all cases. Although it is still argued that observational methods are too subjective (Christensen and Crowder 2009; Garvin and Passalacqua 2012), the key point from the *Kumho* case is that the *Daubert* standards are not necessarily applied in all cases (Grivas and Komar 2008). This may include forensic anthropology. It should also be noted that not all states apply the *Daubert* standards (Holobinko 2012). Interestingly, in Page and colleagues' (2011) study of 548 US cases where the admissibility of forensic evidence was challenged under *Daubert,* only 6 cases where the forensic identification evidence was excluded focused on a failure to use accepted or approved methodology. The *Daubert* ruling thus illustrates the tension between the desire to standardize scientific practice for legal purposes, and the need to retain a definition of science that can encompass the range and continually developing nature of scientific practices.

One means of addressing the above has been through standard operating practices (SOPs), which are common throughout the forensic sciences and are adopted by all forensic providers. Fundamentally they confirm that any given technique is being undertaken in the most appropriate manner for the legal questions being asked, and they ensure that the results from any one lab are directly comparable to another. Such SOPs have appeared in forensic archaeology (Hunter and Simpson 2007; Skinner et al. 2003) and are now beginning to materialize in forensic anthropology. In this context, the key significance of SOPs is that, as Hunter and Simpson (2007) point out, a failure to adhere to what has been defined as best practices in the field may jeopardize any subsequent legal proceedings.

Standardization of Expert Knowledge

Throughout all discussions of standardization in anthropological methods, credibility is a key issue. In forensic science generally, the concern about "standardization" tends to focus on the analysis of the evidence itself. How do we argue with any confidence that the measurements and calibrations our equipment provides or the results that derive from our forensic laboratories are scientifically and technically valid (Malkoc and Neuteboom 2007)? Likewise, "evidence tendered should be based on validated scientific knowledge; all tools and procedures deployed should have been subject to independent testing to demonstrate compliance with their stated claims" (Sommer 2010:12). But we also need to consider workers too, and not just methodology. Alan Kershaw, the former chief executive of the United Kingdom's Council for the Registration of Forensic Practitioners (CRFP) states that we need to ensure that "the courts and the public can reasonably trust [forensic scientists'] professionalism, their ethicality, their integrity" (2001:226). Black (2003:187) notes the "court's insistence on greater precision, detail and commitment from its experts." This is absolutely valid in forensic anthropology, too, but we also have additional standards to consider: those that underlie the very techniques upon which our discipline is based.

With regard to the standardization of personnel, considerable debate focuses on education and training. In 2003 Black bemoaned the growing number of academic institutions offering degrees with forensic titles in the United Kingdom; in 2009 Presley and colleagues noted the continued expansion of this area. When Welsh and Hannis (2011) reported the findings of their research into forensic science degrees in the United Kingdom, there had been an increase in students studying forensic science from 2,191 in 2002–2003 to 5,664 in 2007–2008. Cattaneo (2007) notes, however, that the issue has actually less to do with academic qualifications than with experience and training. This is also mentioned by Galloway and Simmons (1997). Cattaneo clarifies that the problem is that across Europe, training is not homogeneous and quality cannot be ascertained. Brickley and Ferllini (2007) also note the lack of appropriate teaching in forensic anthropology. A key issue is that there is evidence to show that students who have completed their degree courses view themselves as competent to practice—yet theoretical knowledge alone is clearly not enough (Galloway and Simmons 1997; Girdwoyn and Tomaszewski 2009). This is a problem since many of the UK forensic providers have little confidence in the knowledge and skills of many UK forensic science graduates (Welsh and Hannis 2011), although Cox (2009) argues strongly that UK universities do not purport to offer competency in the forensic context. In order to address these issues, the Chartered Society of Forensic Sciences has developed component standards by which the educational content of both forensic archaeology and anthropology degrees can be assessed (see Thompson 2013a, 2013b).

Related to this is the need to ensure that any results produced by a worker in one country are just as valid if transferred to another country (Malkoc and Neuteboom 2007). Kershaw (2001) raises the issue of the internationalization of standardization, while Komar (2003) notes potential problems associated with different levels of education and training in international contexts involving anthropologists from different countries. Nonetheless Cox (2009:32) argues for us to "celebrate the diversity of backgrounds" rather than viewing differences per se as a problem to be resolved. One of the interesting aspects here is whether we view the Western scientific and forensic paradigm (around which standardization is based) as being more valid than those developed in other parts of the world (where we may be plying our trade). Indeed, this is an issue that I (Thompson 2013b) discuss in relation to forensic education, and Fondebrider's discussion (chapter 2, this volume) shows that by adopting a less overtly Western paradigm, forensic anthropology functions effectively in these situations.

We can also see that there is an issue with the standardization of language in forensic anthropology. Rogers (2005) provides a helpful example: the use of the term "historic" with regard to human skeletal remains varies in different countries. The importance of standardized terminology in the forensic setting has also been highlighted by Girdwoyn and Tomaszewski (2009). Duhig and Martinsen (2007) argue for clarity in terminology, for example, between the definitions of anthropology and pathology and even of osteology and anthropology. But they also add new and highly nonstandard terms, such as "paramortem," so unfortunately in the end, despite their good intentions, they just add to the confusion.

IMPLICATIONS OF STANDARDIZATION

We can see that the issue of standardization has strands that focus on methods (the formation of and application of) and strands that focus on the anthropologists themselves (in terms of expertise and interpretation).

For the standardization agenda to progress, these all need to be addressed. But we cannot fully explore the impact and implications of this in the field without again referring to the actors described above. Otherwise, what would be the point of standardization, if not to impact these people?

It has been argued that better investigative work is only possible with greater practitioner and institutional collaboration and harmonization. International standards may be the way to achieve this (Malkoc and Neuteboom 2007), and SOPs may be a means of achieving international standards. Yet Hunter and Simpson (2007:268) suggest that SOPs are "idealized" and processes for "fair weather" conditions. Thus it seems that the reality of a situation can impact the ability of a practitioner to follow a given SOP. This may also help to explain why SOPs are so common in forensic laboratories, where conditions are controlled and do not vary, and less common for field-based subjects (such as forensic archaeology), where every grave site differs, and political and environmental influences can fluctuate not just throughout a single deployment, but throughout a single day of a single deployment.

With the "myth of the supremacy and infallibility of science, long trusted by juridical science and jurisprudence" (Ferrara and Pfeiffer 2010:343) now gone, one can see why SOPs are attractive since the *Daubert* rulings, where the issue of the admissibility of evidence shifted from the conclusions of a given technique to the method itself (Christensen and Crowder 2009; Dirkmaat et al. 2008; Grivas and Komar 2008). This has significant implications for a science that attempts to measure human variation. It also makes one wonder whether forensic anthropologists should "alter established approaches in response to a legal precedent or in response to furthering scientific investigation" (Grivas and Komar 2008:773). Thus we ask whether it is appropriate for legislators to state the standards required of forensic anthropology, a subject with which they have little experience, or for the judge to determine whether the scientific method used has been developed in the normal course of scientific investigation (Grivas and Komar 2008). Even the more "robust" methods tend to demand at least some observer interpretation and opinion, and by "trying needlessly to force powerful qualitative techniques into quantifiable categories, anthropologists may inadvertently be lessening the effectiveness of their methodologies and testimony" (Grivas and Komar 2008:774).

Ideally, the methods chosen by the practitioner should be based on scientific reasoning and merit, not preference or familiarity (Christensen and Crowder 2009). Yet how does this fit with situations such as the one in Chile mentioned above, where family members and other interested groups are involved in the process of exhumation? Indeed, in their survey of practitioners, Garvin and Passalacqua (2012) note a diversity of aging techniques used and a lack of standardization in the age estimation process. We can also see that an obsession with quantitative methods and the creation of error rates has occurred as a result of *Daubert*, and although Christensen and Crowder (2009) argue that all qualitative data can be analyzed numerically, this is somewhat simplistic and as a process vastly devalues the richness of this form of data. In terms of error rates, *Daubert* does not necessarily state that we need low error rates, just that we need to be able to state what they are (Christensen and Crowder 2009). But since there is a general lack of suitable reference samples, these may essentially be unknown.

Some other questions also arise when we consider the implications of applying standardization in the field. There is the issue of the speed of development of our techniques. What can one do if the raw materials or the techniques are developing faster than the rate of testing, publication, and general peer acceptance (Sommer 2010)? Further, with this requirement for peer review and publication becoming so important, as Sommer (2010) notes, journal articles effectively are compulsory. On the one hand, this is quite acceptable and fits with our current model of practice; however, it does mean that members of the public have to pay to gain access to these publications if they want to further their own knowledge of the subject. Also, how do the local workers helping in developing countries gain access to such materials?

All of this leads to the question, would standardization in forensic anthropology help in all situations? Perhaps it would mean that we could have more confidence in the results and conclusions of our anthropological methods; certainly, Garvin and Passalacqua (2012) imply this with regard to age estimation. But some contexts would still remain problematic. For example, in some human rights contexts, the skeletalized remains in a given mass grave may derive from individuals with very similar osteological profiles. Thus the work involving the thousands of mostly young adult male victims at Srebrenica (Komar 2003) would be little affected. Mundorf (2011) makes a similar point by drawing attention to the disaster victim's identification context. Likewise, if the aim is to compare an osteo profile to antemortem records, the quality of the profile will make little impact if the antemortem records are inaccurate, incomplete, or nonexistent (Congram and Steadman 2008; Komar 2003). Grivas and Komar (2008:771) suggest that there is even "an acknowledgement by the court that science is too complex to evaluate with a single set of standards." Further, would forensic practice really benefit from a rigorously applied set of standards that is not flexible enough to take account of the needs of families? Perhaps this is less of an issue of standardization and more one of flexibility or enforcement. But even if we accept that standards can be adapted to nonstandard situations, this still does not answer the question of who sets the standards and how "ideal" conditions are defined and by whom. This brings us back to the discussion of Euro-American assumptions of how a crime scene operates, how practitioners are trained, and so on.

IMPLEMENTATION OF STANDARDIZATION

If it is decided that standardization in the field is a desirable aim, then a key question becomes to determine how this is to be achieved. Three possible avenues are available: via practitioners, via professional and academic associations, and via education and training centers.

Practitioner Competency

Until fairly recently, the United Kingdom had a model for the implementation of standardization in the forensic sciences. The short-lived Council for the Registration of Forensic Practitioners was devised to be used by the courts to ascertain the level of competence of a given forensic specialist. The register was opened in 2000 (Black 2003), and forensic anthropology and archaeology were two of the disciplines that it covered. Note that despite the discussions above about the different types of standardization, this scheme's sole purpose was the application of knowledge, rather than what comprised said knowledge. Arguably this was one of its major weaknesses—that it was merely assessing how practitioners presented information, not whether that information was correct or appropriate.

During the establishment of the CRFP it was decided to adopt a universal assessment approach, where every practitioner would be assessed in exactly the same way (Kershaw 2001). Since the credibility of any practitioner is dependent on the credibility of the scheme determining their credibility, it is no surprise that CRFP chose this comprehensive option. Black (2003) provides significant details and the rationale for the scheme in forensic anthropology in her paper in a forensic anthropology special edition of *Science and Justice*. The whole process was confidential (Kershaw 2001), as it would need to be to ensure independence. However, Kershaw (2001) notes that it would also need transparency and accountability in a number of areas, including the selection of assessors. Skinner and colleagues (2003) add an interesting point about the difficulties of assessing the professional conduct of a forensic anthropologist if that anthropologist is a friend. This is a fairly small discipline after all.

It is not just the practitioners who can be assessed; their place of work can also be vetted. For example, international standards can be achieved through the ISO scheme, and indeed this is currently being implemented. The ISO 17025 (2005) standard is being increasingly adopted as a yardstick against which forensic science laboratories are measured to determine their competency to perform tests and calibrations, including sampling, the use of standard and nonstandard methods, laboratory-developed methods, and validation (Lentini 2009; Sommer 2010; Warren et al. 2011). For some forensic anthropologists in the United Kingdom this may cause a problem, since they may be self-employed practitioners or work out of a university and therefore not have the use of a laboratory that will fulfill the ISO 17025 criteria. There are also cost and resource implications for the ISO standards, so again it is uncertain whether all countries can achieve such levels.

Professional Associations

Associations and professional bodies have a significant role to play in this drive for standardization because of their ability to cross state boundaries and avoid political dealings. For example, in their work investigating medico-legal protocols across Europe, Ferrara and colleagues (2010) found that 84 percent of the 32 countries investigated have a national society of legal medicine. Engagement of the professional bodies could lead to the more effective harmonization that Malkoc and Neuteboom (2007) argue for, since those groups could facilitate the successful internationalization of standardization. Other (nonprofessional) groups are also working in this area, and a good example is the Scientific Working Group for Forensic Anthropology (http://www.swganth.org), which was co-founded by the Federal Bureau of Investigation and the US Department of Defense's Central Identification Laboratory in 2008 and has since produced a number of important advisory documents. Elsewhere (such as in Europe), there are a number of anthropology associations and other organizations working on standardization. Coordination between these bodies would seem to be a priority in order to avoid the development of competing sets of standards for the same practice in any one country.

Education and Training

The situation with regard to the teaching of forensic anthropology led Skinner and colleagues (2003:91) to recommend a "revolution in our training philosophy." Galloway and Simmons (1997) suggest that we consider explicitly addressing the number and nature of degrees provided (their implication is to reduce the number offered), and we must simultaneously consider how well education systems are set up for forensic education. (This is something that Girdwoyn and Tomaszewski [2009] argue has been identified and actively addressed in Poland.) It is also true that "the accountability for the knowledge component of forensic professionals falls largely on colleges and universities" (Presley et al. 2009:74), even though Cox (2009) argues that colleges and universities state clearly that they offer education in the subject and not training. Thus the priority of the forensic community is knowledgeable and competent practitioners, the origins of which start in higher education, yet the priority of universities is to ensure a successful, vibrant, and stable institution. Popular classes in forensic sciences can be a lucrative element of university course offerings, but are not necessarily designed to produce forensic professionals. Rankin and colleagues (2012) suggest involving practitioners in degree development, assessment, and research, but generally it falls to the professional bodies or government regulators to mediate the different priorities of the forensic community and the universities. This intervention will invariably involve the creation of guidelines in terms of what topics should be included in forensic courses if they are to be viewed as providing learners with a suitable education and training for a career in forensic anthropology. As noted above, this has been expressly addressed by the Chartered Society of Forensic Sciences in the United Kingdom (Thompson 2013b). Lentini (2009) notes that the content taught in degree courses can become a form of implicit methodological and practice-based standardization.

Associated with this is the need for ongoing training throughout a career. This is important since it ensures that the forensic scientist is kept up to date with current techniques, and mitigates the risk of practitioners repeating the same errors every time they perform a technique, perhaps through a lack of experience with the method or being improperly taught in the first place (Christensen and Crowder 2009). There is often a requirement to undertake such ongoing training in order to maintain one's accreditation, which is entirely appropriate in some contexts, but again disadvantages those working in parts of the world where these resources are not readily available.

One of the key problems with training forensic anthropologists is providing them with a realistic setting in which to work. Mock graves are a popular choice, but these tend to focus on the methods and not on the interactions with other agents, and in this they exemplify the European and American orientation toward forensic practice. A different approach may be to employ virtual worlds where not only can a mock grave be created, but training can be given in working with other experts, interacting with other interested agents, and nonmethodological components of the process, such as reporting and legislative paperwork. Further, because the whole experience is virtual, the trainees and those doing the training can be from all over the world, thus ensuring that the most appropriate expert is on hand. This form of training is already being used successfully in the mass fatalities context (Cohen et al. 2012).

CONCLUSIONS

I have noted the significance of the individual interpretation of skeletal remains (an issue expanded on by Geller, chapter 8 and by Walsh-Haney and Boys, chapter 7, this volume). This is influenced by many things, from the quantity and quality of our education to our experiences in the field. The general assumption is that the application of standards in the subject will limit problems of variability in approaches and the perhaps inappropriate conclusions that this can bring. But is this an appropriate thing to do, and will it work? Of course we do not want inexperienced practitioners making mistakes in the field, but even those workers fully au fait with our methods will draw on their own individual experience to interpret the results of these methods. Forensic anthropology is really the application of both "technical and experiential knowledge" (Congram and Steadman 2008:162). This is the nature of a discipline that attempts to read human development and variation from the skeleton, and indeed the results of Garvin and Passalacqua's (2012) practitioner survey show this to be the case. Perhaps we just need to accept that forensic anthropology is not wholly a quantitative science; perhaps we need to acknowledge and embrace more explicitly the "anthropology" in forensic anthropology. Indeed, I would argue for this approach following the vivid demonstration of confirmation (and other cognitive) biases in anthropological methods (Nakhaeizadeh et al. 2013; Nakhaeizadeh et al. 2014), the effects of which can be disguised by the sheen of scientific authenticity provided by quantitative methods.

Malkoc and Neuteboom refer to the European Union and the motto of "unity in diversity" (2007:125), and conceivably of greater importance than just standardization are the continued collaborations between workers and interested parties, and the acceptance that these can lead to divergent methods that are appropriate to different contexts. Highly specialized sophistication on its own is limiting, and the greatest improvements in the forensic sciences have come through interdisciplinary developments (Ferrara and Pfeiffer 2010) and international collaborations (Girdwoyn and Tomaszewski 2009). Generally, we presume that these international collaborations focus on improving methods, but a transfer of working philosophies should also occur. In the field, Steadman and Haglund (2005) argue, a more multidisciplinary approach makes the investigation of human rights abuses more successful, and Mundorf (2011) argues for the same in the mass fatalities context.

In all this discussion of improving forensic anthropology, we must not lose sight of whom we are actually improving things for. Of the five groups of agents I discussed in my 2003 paper, perhaps the most significant are the legal and public groups. In terms of the legal group, we should remember whose job it is to actually establish identity. It is not the anthropologist, but rather the military, civilian, and law enforcement agencies, and each has its own criteria for determining and concluding identity (Komar 2003). Forensic anthropology is just one part of a chain of events that leads to the courtroom, to an identification committee, and so on. We must not forget that in terms of helping the courts or commissions reach their goal, science provides assistance and is not a determinant (Sommer 2010; Tuller, chapter 5, this volume). In terms of the public group, as Steadman and Haglund (2005:7) state, "it is essential that forensic anthropologists strive to maintain focus on the people they serve—the victims and their families." But how to marry the demands and desires of these different groups? Congram and Sterenberg (2009) provide a suggestion based on their time investigating the mass graves in Iraq. They note that some mass graves were designated as "forensic" or "evidentiary" excavations and some as "humanitarian." The former were presided over by the forensic investigators while the latter were supervised by mainly Iraqi groups. At first glance, this seems like a useful solution, but it still implies some form of hierarchy of importance, which may not align to a local population's view. Clearly, this is a complicated issue that requires greater discussion, as Fondebrider outlines in chapter 2 in this volume.

There is no doubt that the issue of standardization is one of the most pressing in forensic anthropology at the moment, yet as I have shown, there are difficulties in applying this concept to our subject. These difficulties arise from a number of issues, some because of the qualitative nature of the subject's methods, some because of variations in training, and some that are context-specific and derive from cultural and historical assumptions of what constitutes appropriate practice. None of my discussion here should be interpreted as suggesting that we should not use standards in forensic archaeology and anthropology. Rather, we should recognize that this tool comes with its own problems and entailments, and that perhaps it sometimes seems to hold out a false promise of security and neutrality in a situation that is by definition unstable and shifting and in which many different stakeholders are involved. Further, as is discussed in other chapters in this volume, our work can be objective but is not neutral; it is inevitably goal-oriented. Unless all of these issues are addressed, the standards produced and advocated will not be satisfactory from all perspectives and will lead to challenges in the application of forensic anthropology around the world in the future.

5

Identification Versus Prosecution

Is It That Simple, and Where Should the Archaeologist Stand?

Hugh Tuller

Increasingly, archaeologists and biological anthropologists are assisting in investigations of large-scale contexts of gross violations of international law (Blau and Skinner 2005; Cox 2003; Haglund 2001; Steadman and Haglund 2005). While these experts have played a significant role since the 1980s (Doretti and Snow 2003; Fondebrider 2004), there has been a substantial increase in their involvement since the mid-1990s, when international tribunals investigating the atrocities in the former Yugoslavia and Rwanda began. The training that archaeologists and biological anthropologists receive is compatible with the techniques that crime scene investigators employ when collecting physical evidence. Their participation at these kinds of crime scenes is usually not only welcomed, but sought after. However, as the opportunity to become involved in this international work increases and more archaeologists and biological anthropologists begin working in these contexts, they must be cognizant of their roles and responsibilities as *forensic* experts. In this chapter I focus specifically on forensic excavation and the problems and perspectives of those involved. For simplicity, I will use the term "forensic archaeology" to describe the work of both archaeologists and biological anthropologists who employ archaeological methods and techniques in the search for and excavation of human remains. (See Crossland and Joyce, chapter 1, this volume, for discussion of the relationship between forensic archaeology and anthropology.)

The sensitive nature of forensic work, with its potentially grave consequences, is very different from a research or academic environment. Practitioners must understand their roles as forensic investigators, their responsibilities (to family members, the courts, their employer, and other stakeholders), and the restrictions that they must operate under. Even forensic practitioners experienced in domestic police work need to be aware when working internationally of who is employing them and what that organization's goals are. They may find the transition from domestic forensic work to international work a surprising one.

In this chapter I explore the relationships that forensic archaeologists have with stakeholders, primarily the institutions and states that employ or contract with them to assist with large-scale international investigations. In particular, I address the practitioner's role in the often-cited dichotomy between the identification of victims and the prosecution of perpetrators, asking what the responsibility of archaeologists is, regardless of their employer's objective. While my main focus is on the different auspices under which forensic archaeologists may find themselves working internationally, I also use domestic investigations for contrast.

GOALS, STANDARDS, AND RESTRICTIONS

Some authors have suggested that there are three goals of the investigation of mass killings: the identification and repatriation of victims' remains (humanitarian goal), the collection of evidence for the criminal or civil prosecution of perpetrators (legal goal), and the creation of an accurate historical record of events to counter politically skewed or revisionist histories and to provide family members with an understanding of what happened to their loved ones (historical goal) (Ballbé and Steadman 2008; Haglund 2001; Juhl and Olsen 2006). These goals appear straightforward and logical; however, they are less neatly defined in practice. While investigations into political violence hold the *potential* to realize these goals, in practice all three are not regularly attempted at the same time.

Forensic investigations of mass graves are ultimately a manifestation of a political solution designed to deal with past violence that has upset social norms and institutions. Exemplifying the tensions inherent in forensic investigation are accounts by other authors who describe these investigations as a dichotomy between *identification* and *prosecution* activities (Baraybar et al. 2007; Blau and Skinner 2005; Cordner 2005; Komar and Buikstra 2008). These activities encompass humanitarian and legal goals, respectively, but one goal may be the focus of an investigation at the expense of the other. Either the investigation will focus on the identification of victims, or it will attempt to gather incriminating evidence to prosecute perpetrators. Political, temporal, and resource constraints will usually not allow both to happen concurrently with equal emphasis.

Creating a historical account of events should not be envisioned as a separate task, but rather should be seen as one of the potential outcomes of mass grave excavation. The creation of historical narratives is part of the archaeological process. Mass graves are often designed to hide past events and foster uncertainty as to what happened to the missing people. Perpetrators can promote their own versions of events in the absence of other evidence. A proper excavation, regardless of whether the investigation is designed to locate and identify victims or to collect courtroom evidence, can help reveal what occurred at a mass grave site. By uncovering features and artifacts, including the dead themselves, archaeology can help connect past events to tangible evidence and thus transform historical narratives.

The context of a forensic excavation is very different from that of conventional archaeology in that the work is conducted at a scene of crime, and this affects how findings are presented. In conventional archaeology, when a site is excavated there is a professional obligation, and in many cases a legal one, to report the findings in a format that is available to other archaeologists and interested parties. Usually this entails the creation of an archaeological report that details the background of the site, the excavation methods employed, and ultimately the findings, interpretations, and conclusions. When published, the report becomes available to a wide audience. For example, other archaeologists may use the report to help support a regional theory; social or cultural anthropologists could use it to contrast prehistoric, historic, and contemporary cultural associations; governmental organizations may find it useful to promote local heritage; or indigenous groups may find it helpful to support their oral histories. The pursuit of conventional archaeology and the publication of findings generate public awareness of history, foster cooperation between different fields of study, and help us understand who we are by extending our knowledge of the past beyond the limits of written history.

Conversely, the work that a forensic archaeologist performs is usually for the specific and perhaps limited purpose of identifying victims or prosecuting perpetrators. With these goals, certain types of restrictions, not usually placed on conventional archaeologists, are regularly assigned to the forensic archaeologist. These restrictions set guidelines not only for how the work is conducted, but also on how and where findings can be presented. Regardless of whether the excavation is part of a large-scale international human rights violation investigation or assisting a local domestic police force in a missing persons case, it must be remembered that the work is being conducted at a scene of crime, with all the sensitivity such situations demand. Just as police crime scene investigators cannot speak freely about or release their reports to the general public, neither can a forensic archaeologist. Even if temporarily contracted, the forensic archaeologist is a member of the crime scene investigation team and is thus held by the same legal and ethical restraints as police investigators when dealing with sensitive information. Only on rare occasions will a forensic excavation report be made public, and this is usually to demonstrate to stakeholders a level of transparency in the investigative process. When it does happen, such a release of information is usually in the form of a carefully edited or redacted summary issued by the government or organization conducting the investigation.

A good example of an organization releasing such information is when the International Commission on Missing Persons (ICMP), an intergovernmental organization that strives to find and identify missing persons, provided a summary report on the excavation of a series of mass graves and related features at a police training camp near Belgrade, Serbia. I was employed as a forensic archaeologist by the ICMP at the time and took part in both the excavations and the eventual writing of the summary report. The victims in the graves were ethnic Albanians who were reportedly killed in Kosovo, their bodies collected and placed in covered trucks, and then driven approximately 350 kilometers north out of Kosovo and into Serbia proper, where they were eventually deposited into these graves. Through the course of the excavation we identified five mass graves and three additional features associated with the creation of the graves and the cremation of bodies, which were first dumped on the surface of the ground prior to burial. The burning of the bodies and moving them with heavy machinery caused much postmortem trauma and disarticulation of body parts. Consequently, a large number of body parts were recovered separately that could not be reassociated to a specific individual victim. Although a minimum number of individuals found in each grave was established, the actual number of victims could not be calculated at the time of excavation due to this disarticulation. (DNA analysis would later assist in providing the final number of victims.)

The excavation and the autopsies, which were conducted on site, were monitored by observers, and at times news agencies were granted permission to visit the ongoing activities. Although these observers were briefed on the number of graves, associated features, the types and number of remains recovered (complete bodies and unassociated body parts), they would sometimes report these incorrectly, most likely out of misunderstanding the terms used and the context of the burials. Discrepancies in the reported numbers caused confusion and concern among stakeholders and the general public. For anyone following the case in the media, the numbers seemed to move. The changing numbers fed into conspiracy theories of those who denied that the killings took place (or at least not to the extent that was reported), who charged that the investigation was a politically motivated fraud. The result was repeated misinformation and outright untruths being disseminated by standard media agencies, independent bloggers, and conspiracy publications. As can be imagined, this misinformation caused great anguish among the family members of the missing people.

The ICMP, which has a strong relationship with the various victim groups in the region, was particularly sensitive to family inquiries regarding the excavation and identification processes. In an effort to make clear the results of the excavations that took place at the police training center and to help explain why a final number of victims could not be given at that time, the ICMP asked us, the archaeologists involved, to produce a summary report of the activities. A separate detailed excavation report had been written for each of the seven graves and features, but these contained evidentiary information that the Belgrade authorities and the International Criminal Tribunal for the former Yugoslavia (ICTY) in The Hague could use in their court systems. To produce the summary, all seven reports were combined into a single narrative and carefully edited so as not to release any sensitive personal information regarding particular victims or evidence not yet publicly released. The finalized summary was given to the Kosovo Albanian family groups, the Belgrade and Kosovo authorities, and interested NGOs, and it was eventually posted on the ICMP website (http://ic-mp.org/wp-content/uploads/2008/02/icmp-fsd-16-04-2-doc.pdf) for the general public. While the summary report could not quiet the conspiracy theorists and deniers, it did serve as a talking point for the ICMP to explain to more rational minds the steps that were taken in order to locate, recover, and identify these particular victims from Kosovo and, by extension, ICMP's process in resolving missing persons cases throughout the Balkans.

The seven detailed excavation reports, associated field notebooks, photographs, digital and sketched maps and section drawings, evidence logs, and chain of custody documents are all still considered restricted information. We, the archaeologists, also remain under restrictions as to what we can present and publish. Anyone involved with the excavations and all the supporting documentation are potentially subject to subpoena, and if called upon we must appear in court. It is in the court system that this sensitive information (called "evidence") is presented for review and critique.

Similar systems of documentation control are present at domestic organizations as well. The Joint POW/MIA Accounting Command (JPAC), where I currently work, is tasked with the search, recovery, and identification of US military and civilian employees who went missing during past wars. The scientific arm of JPAC is the Central Identification Laboratory (CIL), where the forensic archaeologists, anthropologists, and odontologists work. The CIL is accredited as a forensic laboratory through the American Society of Crime Laboratory Directors/Laboratory Accreditation Board and adheres to the International Organization for Standardization (ISO) 17025 requirements for standard operating procedures for excavation and for laboratory analysis. In addition to the work conducted on past wars and as part of its accreditation requirements, the CIL also assists the Honolulu Medical Examiner's Office and various Hawaiian police departments with their current cases. When contracting with these organizations, the CIL offers them the option of receiving a full report on the work done or a consultation, which can be a verbal opinion or a summarized written opinion. What the medical examiner or police department does with the reports or opinions is up to them. The CIL will not release any information on the case to other outside sources. All notes, photographs, maps, and other documentation that the forensic practitioners create during the course of their work is maintained in the CIL files. This ensures that all the results and the documentation of how those conclusions were derived can be presented to the medical examiner, police, or a court of law any time in the future, even in the absence of the individual who did the analysis or conducted the excavation.

Many forensic anthropologists are professors working out of universities, but like the CIL, they work closely with local medical examiners and police agencies (see Walsh-Haney and Boys, chapter 7, this volume). Others may work directly in a medical examiner's office or with a police agency. All these organizations have (or should have) protocols and ethical guidelines that protect the sensitive work, including written reports, documentation of the casework, and limitations on what can and cannot be made public—including in journal articles and books.

IDENTIFICATION VERSUS PROSECUTION: AN EXAMPLE

Although differences exist between conventional and forensic archaeology in how professional standards and codes are created, applied, and enforced, they share many of the same principles, methods, and techniques.

Simply put, forensic archaeology is defined as the application of archaeological field and laboratory techniques in a legal context (Blau and Skinner 2005); it is not the application of "forensic" techniques to archaeology (e.g., taking the fingerprints of an Egyptian mummy is not forensic archaeology). There is nothing too different or special in the manner in which a forensic site is processed compared to a conventional archaeological site; the difference is just in the purpose of the excavation and the manner in which findings are presented. Forensic archaeologists should be as concerned as their counterparts with the site history, the formation processes, and understanding the patterns of human behavior that took place before, during, and after the creation of a grave feature. Just like conventional archaeologists, forensic archaeologists need to document this behavior in as clear a manner as possible. In an international post-conflict context, the resulting reports and evidence can help meet two of the possible goals of investigation: identifying the victims and collecting evidence of criminal activity. However, it may turn out that an employer does not necessarily want a full archaeological recovery with all the data, and could insist that only a portion of the evidence be collected. In such cases the employer is actually ignoring or at least limiting the third goal of mass grave excavation: the creation of an accurate historical record. Strictly following an employer's limited objective could preclude such history from being recorded.

A large-scale investigation that is focused on the prosecution of criminals accused of genocide, for example, may not choose to dedicate time and energy toward recovering information that could lead to the individual identification of victims. As I explain in more detail below, the ICTY, which was dealing with thousands of bodies excavated from mass graves, focused on evidence collection for war crimes and crimes against humanity prosecutions and left the process of identification to woefully underfunded and understaffed local forensic institutes. A second international effort focused on the humanitarian identification of these victims had to be created to deal with this in the aftermath. Unfortunately, the manner in which the criminal investigation processed the remains sometimes created difficulties for the identification process.

The opposite could be true in an investigation focusing on the identification of victims, which might see the collection of criminal evidence not only as a misuse of limited resources, but even as a threat to the mission of the agency. An organization that touts itself as a humanitarian operation seeking to heal the wounds of war through the recovery and identification of the dead may feel that the collection of criminal evidence could jeopardize its neutrality and sabotage its goals of reconciliation. The ICMP based in Sarajevo, while working side by side with police investigators, did not initially want its forensic practitioners to record observations of criminal behavior for these very reasons. While not all investigations are as polarized as this, certainly the contrast in investigative goals can place the forensic archaeologist in an awkward situation. On one hand, forensic archaeologists should process sites in a conventional archaeological manner, which would help to capture data for a historic narrative. On the other hand, their employers may want to restrict their activities and the information derived from them, depending on their particular objectives. These are all problems that archaeologists working outside the academy in contract situations face on a daily basis. However, in the context of human rights investigations the stakes are greater, the emotional investments more profound, and the ramifications more serious.

Perhaps the quintessential example of the division between large-scale investigations focused on the prosecution of perpetrators and those aimed toward humanitarian efforts to identify victims is the coexistence in Bosnia-Herzegovina (BiH) of the International Criminal Tribunal for the former Yugoslavia and the International Commission on Missing Persons. The ICTY is an ad hoc legal body of the United Nations, established in 1993 by Security Council Resolution 827 to prosecute serious crimes committed during the series of wars in the former Yugoslavia. While ICTY investigations of mass graves have taken place in the nations of the former Yugoslavia, including BiH, the tribunal itself is located in The Hague, Netherlands. The Sarajevo-based ICMP is an intergovernmental organization that was established in 1996 at the G7 summit in Lyon, France. Its original goal was to locate and identify people who had gone missing during the 1991–1995 Balkan conflicts, but it has since expanded its role outside of the Balkans. The creation of the ICMP was motivated in great part by the fact that The Hague's prosecution mandate did *not* include the identification of the individual victims who were being recovered and autopsied. Both the ICTY and the ICMP employed forensic archaeologists (the ICMP still does) to assist with mass grave excavations. However, cooperation between the organizations was never fully realized. (I first worked for the ICTY and, later, for the ICMP.)

The ICTY processed thousands of sets of remains during the years it conducted criminal investigations. Whereas group identification was sought to examine accusations of ethnic cleansing, war crimes, and genocide, the organization had no directive to identify individual victims. For trials, the manner and cause of the death of individual victims were important findings because that evidence could be used to demonstrate criminal activity. While identifying individuals may help "humanize" a statistic for the court and its audience, the individual identification process does not prove wrongdoing and ultimately takes resources that could otherwise be used for further forensic evidence collection. As a result, most of the ICTY-recovered remains were never identified, although in a number of cases a presumptive identification was made. This occurred when identifying materials or documents were found in association with the remains, or when family members visually identified a body prior to its initial burial. This kind of identification is open to error and cannot stand up as evidence in court (see Crossland 2013). The ICTY's unidentified remains were subsequently either reburied or placed in storage as unknown individuals. Sometimes these remains were still commingled when buried or stored, which created problems when identifications were later attempted. Rainio and colleagues (2001) have asserted that the focus on the collection of evidence for prosecution alone was appropriate given that a forensic team's role in international interventions is to support a prosecutor's investigations. They suggest that "local agencies" should be the ones to identify individual victims.

Although the ICMP is not really a "local agency" in the context put forth by Rainio and colleagues (2001), the organization has taken on the task of identifying the remains left by the ICTY and also supports the efforts of other agencies. Indeed, the ICMP is a well-regarded international organization whose mandate includes fostering cooperation between governments, empowering civil society initiatives, and supporting the creation of laws and institutions that help to identify victims of political violence and natural disasters. Without the efforts of the ICMP, which have been hugely successful given its DNA-led identification process, "local agencies" in the Balkans would have been utterly overwhelmed. They had neither the expertise to perform identifications on such a scale nor the resources to attempt such an undertaking, particularly considering they had just endured several years of war.

Since the ICTY and the ICMP had different mandates and were created at different times by different international bodies, a significant lack of coordination developed between the two. This discordance has resulted in added complexity for the identification process. While the ICTY provided the ICMP with the locations of the remains and background information concerning them, the autopsy reports and related documentation (i.e., the prosecutor's autopsy evidence) were taken to The Hague for the tribunals. In addition, the ICTY employed multiple teams over the course of the years of its investigations, which led to record-keeping inconsistencies

(Baraybar et al. 2007). This situation caused confusion for the ICMP as its forensic practitioners tried to follow up on the autopsies. Because of the lack of information and the inconsistencies in records, all the ICTY-recovered remains had to be reexamined, and those who had been reburied were exhumed. Not only did this activity place a greater burden on the ICMP than was necessary, but it further traumatized family members, who did not necessarily understand the difference between these "IC" organizations and their different aims nor, perhaps more important, why the identification process was taking so long (Wagner 2008). Much of the ICMP's time and effort has been dedicated to public outreach just to educate and inform family members.

The situation in BiH between the ICTY and the ICMP—two organizations working in the same country, each pursuing different investigative goals—is not the norm. However, it does serve as a good example of how one investigative goal can have a negative effect on another unless there is careful planning and coordination. Is the separation of investigative mandates, which is at the heart of this issue, even necessary? More specifically, should an employer's specific mandate determine how individual forensic archaeologists conduct their work? And what role do archaeologists have in resolving the potential impasse between their professional obligations as archaeologists and the goals of an investigation?

IN DEFENSE OF THE DISCIPLINE

Archaeology is similar to crime scene investigation in that the purpose of both is to figure out what has occurred in the past at a particular location. To do so, archaeologists and crime scene investigators use many of the same tools and processes to tease out and record relevant information from a site. Both also adhere to the same mantra: you only get one chance to get it right. Archaeological excavation and crime scene processing are inherently destructive to the site, so a failure to record an observation or collect a piece of evidence may mean that data are lost forever. Care must be taken when a site is processed so this information is maintained for further analysis.

Of course, not *everything* can be collected. There is a limit to what should be sampled and recorded, and decisions on how a site is processed will influence what can be collected. Archaeologists and crime scene investigators hedge their bets when collecting evidence, gathering what they feel is enough information to understand and explain what has happened at a site. One could, for example, sample every sediment anomaly at an excavation, but will the effort to process each sample add to the understanding of a site? Understanding which artifacts, features, and observations to record comes from proper training and experience in knowing how to frame research questions in respect to the particular investigation being conducted.

Forensic archaeologists hired to conduct a large-scale post-conflict investigation should carry out the work in a careful manner utilizing their training and experience. Yet, we can see how an organization's narrow investigative objective may conflict with the forensic archaeologists' professional obligations, possibly creating an impasse between them. This situation could put the forensic archaeologists in a difficult position where they have to confront the employer regarding accepted archaeological practice. In this case, at question is the employer's potential rejection of standard expectations for archaeological excavation and recording. Consequently, I believe that forensic archaeologists should stand up for the profession and make the case for as full as possible documentation of the crime scene, given that they will have only one chance to do it right. Relevant artifacts, features, and observations must be recorded so they do not disappear, and this is what forensic archaeologists should emphasize when confronted by an organization claiming that its mandate should dictate how a site is processed. One may have to convince the employing organization that the collection of additional data is not a waste of resources or harmful to its image. There are good arguments that can be used for organizations that focus on prosecution and for those that are interested in identification.

I have personal experience in arguing with employers about professional archaeological obligations. Although it was never enjoyable, I do believe my efforts paid out. I began working at the ICMP soon after my contract with the ICTY ended in 2002. The ICTY of course was in the prosecution business, and my employment with the tribunal involved recording and collecting criminal evidence at mass grave sites, such as shell casings, soil samples, and mechanical excavation markings in the soil. When I transferred over to the ICMP I was told by my fellow practitioners, who had been there for a while, not to record such evidence, that my job at a mass grave was only to recover the bodies. Local police agencies and prosecuting judges were on scene to handle the collection of criminal evidence. However, these local authorities were not trained in archaeology and relied on the ICMP forensic experts to guide the excavation. The ICMP experts were the ones who were digging and who recognized when they uncovered something of potential significance for the prosecution, but we were being told not to include such information because it could harm the ICMP's mandate of neutrality.

The situation we found ourselves in led to a minor split in the Exhumation and Examination Section of the ICMP, and culminated in several heated discussions in the organization. Ed Hoffine, the head of the forensic unit in the ICMP at the time, was in charge of all forensic activities in the organization, including the Exhumation and Examination and the DNA Sections. While Hoffine was instrumental in establishing the ICMP's DNA laboratories and much of the organization's success is due to his vision of a fast, low-cost, DNA-led identification system, and although I have the utmost respect for his work and consider him a friend, he is a DNA scientist and was not familiar with forensic archaeology. In one discussion I had with him, I argued that sending archaeologists to a crime scene and not allowing them to record their observations could have bad consequences for both the individual archaeologist and the ICMP as an organization should any of the archaeologists be summoned to court to testify. Digging around a crime scene without recording observations could be viewed as improper (and possible criminal) conduct. At the very least, the defense would be able to show that the experts conducting the excavation were incompetent, and thus that any evidence recovered by the local police is questionable. The backlash would be against not only the archaeologists, but also the organization that sent them. What would family members think of the identification process if the ICMP's experts were shown to be incompetent? Trust was on the line.

I informed Hoffine that if the ICMP sent me to excavate a grave, I was professionally obligated to fully record all my observations. Moreover, family groups had been voicing concerns over justice, and they wanted to know *what happened* to their missing members—not just that they had died, but how and where, what were the causes, and when it occurred. Other archaeologists voiced similar opinions. Subsequently there was no further discussion between us about what to record and what not to record at the graves where the ICMP worked. If there was any confusion among the ICMP management before, it had now become clear that archaeologists would record all observations and include their findings in their reports.

Blau and Skinner (2005) contend that the forensic archaeologist has a professional obligation to undertake the full and detailed recording of excavations so that prosecution can always be a future choice. While criminal trials may not be under way at the time excavations are taking place, they could be conducted in the future. In Argentina, for example, after the toppling of the military dictatorship, the new government granted amnesty from prosecution to the perpetrators of the Dirty War (1976–1983) in which approximately 50,000 people were disappeared. This amnesty was codified in two laws, the Full Stop Law and the Law of Due Obedience, which were enacted in 1986 and 1987, respectively. Since 1984, the Argentine Forensic Anthropology Team (EAAF) has been using archaeological techniques and methods to excavate suspected clandestine graves of the missing. In 2001, the two amnesty laws were annulled based on their incompatibility with international law and the obligations of the state. It may have taken 18 years since the end of the military dictatorship, but investigations and trials could now be conducted. Even though the EAAF had no authority or mandate to record criminal evidence during the years of amnesty, because its members had conducted proper archaeological excavations of clandestine burial sites, those reports can now be used as evidence in a court of law (Luis Fondebrider, pers. comm., 2010).

An agreement not to report potential criminal activity may be made out of necessity to avoid tension and possibly the breakdown of cooperation between former combating sides. Such is the case in the current search, recovery, and identification process happening in Cyprus under the auspices of the Committee on Missing Persons, which includes members from both the Greek and Turkish communities and the United Nations (Committee on Missing Persons in Cyprus 1981). None of the parties involved, including the forensic archaeologists, can ignore the fact that they may end up excavating crime scenes. Indeed, if the political climate in the region where they are working changes and criminal trials begin, individual archaeologists could be summoned to testify as to what they did and observed at a site. Recording what took place needs to be a requirement, or one risks not being able to justify one's actions in court and possibly having a criminal case dismissed because of a lack of due diligence on the part of the expert.

An additional consideration that may not be clear to an employer is that the full recording of possible criminal activity may contribute to the organization's goals of identifying remains and providing a history of events for surviving family members. Families have the right to know the fate of their missing members. This means that they have the right to receive not only their loved ones' identified remains, but also the knowledge of what happened to them from the last time they were seen alive to when their remains were found. Forensic archaeologists will often find themselves in the unique position to answer these questions (Dirkmaat et al. 2005; Skinner 1987). Excavation should be able to determine what happened before, during, and after an event. Limiting what the forensic expert is "authorized" to record will inhibit this understanding. Documentation of perimortem trauma to the bodies may be a difficult concept for a humanitarian employer to support since it is clearly within the context of criminal investigations. Nevertheless, such documentation can help develop a history of what happened at a site (e.g., close-range gunshot wound to the back of the head versus explosion trauma) and may also help with the identification of victims (Tuller 2012). The ICMP again provides a good example. While its goal is the identification of missing people, the ICMP has come to understand that family members often want to know as much as they can about what happened, and the organization supports the collection of all information. The ICMP now believes that telling the story of a mass grave is just as important as telling the story of the bones excavated from it.

The converse also holds true. A prosecutor's office is interested in recovering evidence that can be used in trial proceedings. If a certain part of the archaeological documentation of a site is perceived as contributing to the identification of victims, the prosecutor's office may consider this to be outside its purview and seek to stop that activity. To counter this attitude Tidball-Binz (2006) makes a compelling argument that the identification of remains should be just as important to a prosecutor (and every forensic practitioner) as the collection of criminal evidence. He reminds us that international humanitarian law, as contained in the four Geneva Conventions and their two additional protocols, recognizes and protects the right of families to know the fate of their missing loved ones. In addition, in 1992 the UN General Assembly passed the Declaration on the Protection of All Persons from Enforced Disappearances, which defines such disappearances as a government's refusal to acknowledge the detention or the detained individual's whereabouts (which would include clandestine grave sites). If an employing organization is perhaps too focused on the prosecution of criminals at the expense of the identification of individual victims, it may need to be reminded of these international laws and declarations. The employer and its forensic expert employees are liable if those laws are ignored.

Equally, if archaeologists working for a prosecutor uncover evidence that is contradictory to the prosecutor's case, they are still obliged to record and present it. The same holds true for police crime scene investigators. To do otherwise would be withholding evidence, and all parties, including the prosecutor's office, understand this concept. A prosecutor may not be pleased with such contradictory evidence, but recording it supports the objective of the criminal investigation to establish an accurate account of what took place. Archaeologists who are tasked to search for and excavate graves should recognize that they are working in a context that is usually much larger than their employer (politically, socially, and legally) and that their employer may lose sight of the future consequences of the work. In such cases, it may be up to the archaeologist to educate the employer about an archaeologist's professional obligations and the fact that international humanitarian law supports the families' right to know about their missing members. This is not to argue that a prosecutor of atrocity crimes should get into the business of individual victim identification, but to make clear that by conducting the work in accordance with professional standards, archaeologists are supporting the prosecutor's goals while still guaranteeing that information will be available for any future identification efforts.

As professionals, regardless of national differences in training and expectations (see Thompson, chapter 4, this volume), forensic archaeologists should strive to excavate to the highest standards, record relevant information to help understand the site's formation processes, and make the argument that doing less would hurt the goals of the organization they are working for and could put themselves in legal jeopardy. While one investigative goal may be presently pursued, that does not mean that the other will not be pursued in the future. By recording all relevant evidence in a conventional archaeological manner, the data will still be useful in years to come if an alternative investigative goal is pursued. An organization or ad hoc commission may not need all the information in an archaeologist's field notes or final site report to achieve its particular goal; however, this information should not be perceived negatively. Archaeologists are obligated to conduct excavations as their profession demands, and the organization that has hired them should understand this, use what it needs from the information that is generated, and then make arrangements for the safekeeping of all records for possible future review.

CONCLUSIONS

Just as archaeology is not simply the search for and recovery of artifacts, neither is forensic archaeology only the search for and recovery of missing people. Practitioners of both fields are interested in broader questions than what the artifact or piece of evidence can provide on its own. In particular, site formation processes and past patterns of human activity are keys to providing context for the artifact/evidence. This helps investigators to understand the history of a site and creates a narrative of events beyond simple assumptions. Without understanding how something got to a particular place, we cannot know what it means in the big picture, and so both fields strive to discover what took place at a site in the past and why it occurred in such a manner. However, this is where conventional and forensic archaeology diverge.

Whereas conventional archaeology operates mainly in the academic realm or as contract work, forensic archaeology—by definition—is primarily part of the criminal justice system. Because of this, the manner in which site interpretations are presented can be very different between the two. For the forensic archaeologist, a conservative approach to site interpretation is imperative since speculative assessments, if false, can have devastating consequences for all stakeholders (e.g., the victim's family, the accused, the archaeologist, the justice system). One may view the forensic practitioner's insistence on just "showing the facts" as perhaps failing to engage with recent critiques of the production of archaeological knowledge and the role of interpretation in the practice of archaeology (see discussions by Crossland and Joyce, this volume). However, the narrow focus by forensic practitioners on the documentation of empirical facts is chosen consciously and out of necessity. While forensic archaeologists explore all the avenues of possibilities, they report only on the evidence they know they can support. Speculation in a court of law is like chum to sharks (and lawyers) and will end poorly for the forensic archaeologist who dabbles in it.

In addition to cautious interpretations, forensic archaeologists regularly work under restrictions not seen by conventional archaeologists. Some of these—for example, restrictions on publishing case work—should not be viewed as negative (contra Steele 2008) but as necessary to protect the neutrality of the justice system (which in turn aims to protect all the stakeholders involved). While forensic archaeologists should be familiar with the medical-legal systems of their home nations and should understand the reasons for certain restrictions given their particular domestic justice system, when it comes to large-scale international investigations, the reasons and restrictions may be completely different from the domestic ones they are used to operating under. Thus, forensic archaeologists should examine the restrictions that will be placed upon them before blindly accepting them.

International organizations or institutions may attempt to regulate what is permissible to record and publicize based on their particular investigative goals. Some international investigations will aim to find and identify the missing people, while others will seek evidence to prosecute perpetrators. Deviation from the investigation's goal could be viewed as a waste of resources or as a danger to the organization's agenda. Restricting what can or should be recorded when conducting an investigation is likely to conflict with archaeology as a profession. An employer may view the archaeologist's skill set as a toolbox from which it can pick and choose which methods and techniques to use for any particular investigation. In contrast, archaeologists should view their contribution in a broader sense: the purpose of an excavation is to understand what has occurred at a site regardless of the purpose of a particular investigation.

It is in archaeologists' interest to understand the context in which they work, their employer's goals, the reasons for various restrictions on collecting and presenting site data, and the potential conflicts that may develop between these goals and their professional obligations. Considering all of this, archaeologists must be ready to educate the organizations they work for as to what it is we actually do as a profession and how fully documenting all relevant site information, instead of being viewed as a liability or waste of resources, can contribute to the end goals of the organization and beyond.

6

Writing Forensic Anthropology

Transgressive Representations

Zoë Crossland

In Thomas Holland's novel *One Drop of Blood* the forensic anthropologist Dr. "Kel" McKelvey contrasts the world of academic archaeology—"a house of cards" characterized by "speculation and extrapolation that could never be proven"—with forensics, which "was proved daily." In forensic work "the identities matched or they didn't. You were right or you were wrong—little room for debate" (Holland 2006:200). Certainly, the scope of forensic archaeology seems to be narrower than that of the rest of the discipline. Whereas most archaeological narratives tell about former ways of life, reconstructing the shared practices and beliefs of past communities, forensic archaeology deals with biographical questions centered on specific people: who are they, and how did they die? The restricted scope of this inquiry seems to make for work that is less conjectural than mainstream archaeology (see Tuller, chapter 5, this volume). But despite the appeal of the "pragmatic, fact-filled world of forensics," Kel has more to add. He recounts that he has started "feeling doubts where there had been none before." Kel does not doubt the quality of his work, but rather wonders about the ethics of intruding upon people's lives. He has no relish for "playing God": "Who gave him the right, who gave the U.S. government the right, to wade waist-deep into people's grief.... The majority of the families affected by the identification of war dead were grateful.... But not everyone" (Holland 2006:200).

This brief interlude two-thirds of the way through the novel points to some of the ambiguities of forensic anthropological work, ambiguities that rarely surface in the wider North American academic literature. The professional literature deals mostly with questions of method, although it has expanded since the late 1990s to encompass legal and ethical concerns as well as the logistics of working abroad (e.g., Burns 1999; Ferllini, ed. 2007; Steadman 2003). In contrast, the self-presentation of the field in mass-market literature is less restrained. Anthropologists describe the sensory experiences of forensic practice and tackle issues that are often left out of academic discussions. These popular texts reveal something of how the discipline is imagined and how the work of forensic intervention is authorized. They share an emphasis on the distinct status of the anthropologist as a specialist who speaks for the dead, and in doing so they show how the figure of the forensic expert negotiates the tricky and morally charged work of dealing with the dead.

In the United States, forensic anthropological practice is located in a tradition of criminal investigation, with close links to the police and local medical examiners (see Walsh-Haney and Boys, chapter 7, this volume). Forensic archaeology is considered to be a dimension of this practice, and accordingly in this chapter I discuss forensic anthropology broadly conceived. The term "forensic" is tightly tied to science and the law in the present-day imaginary, but the word's origins in the Roman place of assembly point to another important dimension. The rhetorical sites of deliberation where forensic anthropologists construct their arguments include the present-day public forum of the law court, but they also range more widely. In this chapter I look at the popular sites where forensic anthropology is disseminated to nonacademic audiences and consider how this work of public communication is also drawn into the constitution of the forensic anthropology field. As in the rest of anthropology, forensic practitioners write for specialized journals aimed at an audience of peers and develop textbooks that are directed at a student readership. But they also reach out to a range of publics in ways that diverge from the usual modes of anthropological textuality. In addition to writing unpublished case reports for legal and police purposes, forensic anthropologists are commonly asked to provide quotations and interviews for newspapers, magazines, and television. Perhaps growing out of this experience the field is also defined by mass media accounts composed by anthropologists themselves.

In exploring the forums where forensic anthropology is defined and communicated I focus on two genres of popular writing by forensic anthropologists. The first is fiction, usually composed as thrillers or detective stories (J. Bass 2006; Holland 2006; Koff 2011; Manhein 2012; Reichs 1998). The second is broadly autobiographical (e.g., Brkic 2004; Koff 2004; Manhein 1999; Morris 2011; Rhine 1998), including books co-authored with journalists or trade writers (Bass and Jefferson 2003; Mann and Williamson 2006; Maples and Browning 1994; Ubelaker and Scammell 1992). This flourishing fictional and autobiographical literature composed by practitioners themselves seems to be an English-language phenomenon, concentrated primarily in the United States. Such popular portrayals also seem to be specific to forensic anthropology, in contrast to other parts of the anthropological field. Considering the comparatively small number of active forensic anthropologists, the efflorescence of autobiographical and fictional accounts is striking. Perhaps the closest parallel may be found not in anthropology, but in the diverse texts composed around humanitarian work across the world. James Dawes (2007) has explored some of this wider art and literature, arguing that it can constitute a form of testimony, a working-through of disturbing experiences as well as an attempt to deal with the fraught nature of representing others' trauma. The popular forensic anthropological literature does not at first glance seem to be engaged in such a project, with the exception of a couple of more literary memoirs (Brkic 2004; Koff 2004), but it does use certain imagery recurrently. Some of that imagery comes from the long history of detective fiction, which underwrites much of the literature, but some of it also is deeply embedded in the epistemic categories through which evidence and inference are understood. This reveals some of the ways in which forensic knowledge is imagined and communicated in North American contexts, as well as the conceptual role of the scientist-investigator in its production (cf. Joyce 2002b; Pluciennik 1999). Most strikingly, these texts demonstrate how the corpse acts as an imaginative resource for thinking through the charged relationships between fact and value in the work of forensic interpretation.

Studies of the public dissemination and reception of scientific work show the unbounded, interdisciplinary, and multisited nature of the discourse around science (Clemens 1986; Lewenstein 1995; Turney 1998), demonstrating that, given the public nature of the scientific enterprise (Callon and Rabeharisoa 2003; Gregory and Miller 1998; Rabinow 1999), it is important to consider all textual modes through which knowledge circulates. Most research into the textual forms through which science finds its way into the public domain has focused on popular science writing, looking, for example, at the ways in which expert speech is reported by journalists (e.g., Calsamiglia and Lopez Ferrero 2003) or considering how the boundary between the public and the scientific expert is articulated and maintained (Bensaude-Vincent 2001; Fahnestock 1986; Gieryn 1983). In this respect, a number of studies have shown the complex paths that scientific facts trace in their circulation through technical and popular literatures and other venues (Latour 1987; Lewenstein 1995; Myers 2003). These studies suggest that there can be no clean demarcation between popular knowledge and scientific research. In an influential article published in 1990, Stephen Hilgartner warns against characterizing the translation of science into popular accounts as a movement of distortion and simplification. Instead, he observes that the movement between scientific research and the popular consumption of science is more fluid and interactive than this model suggests. This may be seen in the degrees of expertise between scientists working in different disciplines; most researchers will rely on popular accounts to some extent to keep up on developments outside their field.

Danette Paul (2004:34) suggests that mass media accounts can be important for the spread of knowledge in and across fields, and comments that scientists often use such texts for teaching purposes and in their research. One example is the online accounts of the identification by University of Leicester archaeologists of Richard III's remains in 2012. These circulated rapidly between colleagues via email and Facebook and surely found their way into a number of lectures and academic sources in advance of full publication. Popular accounts are also important for attracting research funding and students; in the field of forensic science they are also influential in the translation of scientific findings for court proceedings. In the context of North American forensic practice, such popular texts also entail a pedagogical objective, educating law enforcement agencies and others about the benefits of forensic anthropological and archaeological recovery and analysis. Douglas Ubelaker observes that knowledge also moves between police and forensic anthropologists. Not only do forensic anthropologists communicate their findings to a broader public, but "police work [is] a source for invaluable data about present populations that [are] unavailable from ancient sources" (Ubelaker and Scammell 1992:18). Given this wide-ranging impact, the popular literature may be seen as part of scientific discourse in its own right (Myers 2003:269).

This flow of knowledge can provoke anxieties about the correct transmission of ideas between different cultural domains, as foregrounded in debates around the "*CSI* effect" (Morris 2011:15–18). Named after the police drama *CSI: Crime Scene Investigation* and its spin-offs, the term has been used to articulate worries about the potential ill effects of fictional portrayals of forensic science on real-life courtroom situations (Cole and Dioso-Villa 2007; Mopas 2007). Anthropologist Alan Morris explains that these depictions create problems "by creating the misconception that forensic science can solve crime as quickly and definitively as it is done in television crime shows" (2011:16). The *CSI* effect has prompted discussion by attorneys (A. Thomas 2006) and forensic practitioners (Hanby and Bennell 2008; Patry and Smith 2008; Smith et al. 2008) as well as studies to assess how it might influence juries' assessments of forensic data (Cole and Dioso-Villa 2009; Schweitzer and Saks 2007). Morris describes how he was drawn into precisely this issue when he acted as an advisor for an episode of the British television program *Primeval*, which was set in South Africa. The script suggested that lead-210 isotope analysis could be used to date skeletal remains although "the technique is still being refined and very few forensic laboratories use it" (Morris 2011:17).

These crossings between fictional imaginings of forensic work and the professional use of forensic science are not a new phenomenon, however. The public space of forensic detection as articulated in an English-language, North Atlantic context has a history of interwoven fictional and factual strands that stretches back to the nineteenth century. Edgar Allan Poe's Dupin stories, published in the 1840s, and Arthur Conan Doyle's (1986[1893]) later Sherlock Holmes fiction are perhaps the most well-known fictional sites where forensic detection has been defined and explored. Ronald R. Thomas (1999:5) has shown how these and other popular contemporary narratives both anticipated forensic methods and commented on them. Indeed, he notes that Edmond Locard—one of the pioneers of forensic science—recommended Poe and Conan Doyle as reading material for his students. This great interest in forensic techniques meant that—just as with the lead isotope analysis—they appeared in fiction before they had been developed for police use.

The use of fingerprinting techniques to trap criminals was anticipated in Mark Twain's *Life on the Mississippi* (1883:239–240), and in *The Tragedy of Pudd'nhead Wilson* (1894) Twain described the use of fingerprint evidence in court well before it was used by police in the United States (Cole 2001; R. Thomas 1999:201–219). Fictional accounts of forensic practice in the United States can therefore be placed in a long tradition of narrative experimentation with the possibilities for forensic science. In the texts of the nineteenth century, it was not simply technology that was imagined, but also another way of knowing, a detached "ratiocination" (as Poe termed it) that allowed detectives to make inferences from evidence. In the careful delineation of how inferences are made from human remains, this strand persists. Below, I outline the different genres of popular texts in more detail. I then turn to the themes that emerge in fictional and autobiographical accounts and consider how forensic anthropological practice is imagined in North America.

WRITING FICTION

Forensic anthropology seems to lend itself particularly well to the thriller genre. In addition to Holland's work, there are three other series of popular books that have been developed around and by forensic anthropologists, and others are in development. Aaron Elkins's novels about Gideon Oliver, the "Skeleton Detective," are an early example of thrillers written by an author with some training in forensic anthropology. The first Gideon Oliver book (Elkins 1982) deals with a university professor who gets caught up in Cold War espionage and who draws upon his four-field anthropological training to help solve the case. Elkins stands in contrast to other forensic anthropologists who write fiction in that he describes himself as a full-time writer and former anthropologist. However, perhaps because of the competition from the other writers, he notes that he remains active "in real-life forensics by serving as the forensic anthropologist on the Olympic Peninsula Cold Case Task Force" (http://www.aaronelkins.com).

Elkins's pioneering forensic anthropological thrillers were followed by those of Kathy Reichs, who published her first novel, *Déjà Dead*, in 1997. Unlike Elkins, Reichs's primary occupation is as a forensic anthropologist. Reichs is now professor emerita of anthropology at the University of North Carolina at Charlotte, and her author page at Simon and Schuster informs us that she continues to consult for the Laboratoire de Sciences Judiciaires et de Médecine Légale in Quebec. In addition to numerous publications in academic journals, Reichs has also edited a key textbook on forensic osteology (Reichs, ed. 1998). Her fictional alter ego, Temperance Brennan, the heroine of 17 forensic thrillers as of 2014, has a remarkably similar biography, closely shadowing Reichs's employment history. Further obscuring the boundary between herself and her fictional avatar, Reichs has developed her series for television. In a move that could come straight from the pages of Poe or Jorge Luis, in this portrayal Temperance Brennan writes forensic thrillers featuring an anthropologist named Kathy Reichs. Reichs is probably the most well known of all the forensic anthropologists who write for a lay audience, given the popularity of her books and the success of the television show (*Bones*) based on her characters. Michelle Stoerr (2011) places Reichs's novels in the wider genre of specialist thrillers, or *fiction à substrat professionnel* (FASP), a form of narrative in which the plot and characters are grounded in the details and workings of professional environments (Petit 1999, 2000). FASP thrillers are written by authors—such as Patricia

Cornwell and Michael Crichton—who have some experience of the professional situations described; their characters grow from the life experience and history of the author.

Like Reichs's work, the Body Farm series of thrillers is firmly embedded in this genre. The series features Bill Brockton, a forensic anthropologist loosely based on the personality and career of William Bass, the founder of the Anthropological Research Facility (ARF) at the University of Tennessee (known informally as the Body Farm). Bass co-writes his novels with Jon Jefferson, and the two authors take the combined nom de plume "Jefferson Bass." William Bass is a certified diplomate of the American Board of Forensic Anthropology (ABFA), as are Reichs and Holland, and as in Reichs's novels, the Body Farm series pays close attention to the institutional details of Brockton's work, carefully illustrating the professional networks to which forensic anthropologists belong. Similarly, Thomas Holland's two thrillers featuring Kel McKelvey delineate the bureaucratic expectations and institutional arrangements at the Central Identification Laboratory in Hawaii, where, like Holland, the character is the scientific director. The books draw on Holland's work for the Department of Defense's Joint POW/MIA Accounting Command (JPAC), but Holland (2006:337) is careful to note that although his novels are "inspired by cases and situations that I have been involved with over my career," they are fictional stories that do "not reflect reality."

The forensic thrillers of all these authors are strongly linked to a central character, a forensic anthropologist whose expertise draws upon and is authorized by that of the authors themselves. This is flagged in the author biographies of Reichs, Bass, and Holland. Holland's novels list the places where he has carried out "successful forensic investigations"; the blurb on Reichs's books gives a précis of her academic career, certification, and positions; and the dust jackets of Bass's books explain that he is "a world-renowned forensic anthropologist" who "founded the University of Tennessee's...Body Farm...a quarter-century ago." "The real deal," proclaims Reichs on the front cover of the Jefferson Bass novel *Carved in Bone*, while inside, Dr. Henry Lee, the "author of *Cracking Cases*," writes that this "isn't the typical murder mystery based on fantasies. It offers terrific forensic details and the science of solving cold cases." Holland's novels are plastered with rave reviews from other thriller writers extolling his credentials as a "leading expert in his field." Echoing Reichs's terms, author Linda Fairstein suggests that "forensic investigators don't get more real than Thomas Holland."

Another entry into the genre has been made by forensic anthropologist Mary Manhein, whose novel *Floating Souls* (2012) is set in Louisiana, where

Manhein is based, and revolves around an anthropologist named Maggie Andrepont. Finally, another title, *Freezing* (2011) by Clea Koff, varies the template a little by featuring a pair of forensic anthropologists, Jayne Hall and Steelie Lander, who work out of an office in Los Angeles, profiling missing persons. This book is positioned as a "Jayne and Steelie mystery," suggesting that a series of novels is planned. As with the other texts, Koff's training is important. She prepared the ground for the series by publishing a memoir about her work as a forensic anthropologist in Rwanda and the former Yugoslavia, and her website details this experience. It also notes that she founded the Missing Persons Identification Resource Center, a nonprofit organization based in Los Angeles. As in the case of Jayne and Steelie, this organization develops forensic profiles of missing people and attempts to match them with unidentified human remains held by coroners' offices across the United States.

Heather Walsh-Haney (2011) suggests that Reichs's novels (and, I would add, those of other forensic anthropologists) not only make the most of the public appetite for criminalist thrillers and police procedurals, but also act to offset the fantastical portrayal of forensic anthropological techniques in popular culture. Although the remarkably close shadowing of real-life anthropologists by their fictional avatars has a demonstrably pedagogical and public relations dimension, this doubling is also vital for the authority and resonance of the text. *Carved in Bone*, the first Body Farm novel, suggests in an endnote that "some novels are pure fiction; others are fiction that is built on a foundation of facts. This book is of the latter type" (J. Bass 2006:321). The experience and expertise of the authors are at the heart of these forensic thrillers. To use Michael Taussig's (1993:2) words, the representation of forensic anthropology in such texts "shares in or takes power from the represented," underwriting their popularity and giving them the sheen and aura of scientific authority.

This emphasis on the authentic nature of the authors' forensic knowledge is reiterated in the genre of autobiography. Like the novels, these memoirs revolve around central characters, documenting their careers, hopes and fears, successes and failures. Among other things, both the novels and the autobiographies provide a way to demonstrate the training, inferential abilities, and wealth of experience of forensic experts. In a courtroom context the evidence of an expert witness can be attacked on the basis of character, expertise, and experience, and the autobiographical elements of the popular literature work to deflect such suggestions. Here then is a double move from fact to fiction and then back, by which the anthropologist's expertise authorizes the claims of the fictional character, and the fictional account in turn demonstrates and confirms the expertise of the author. In this way, as Taussig has argued, the representation acts back upon the represented.

LIFE HISTORIES

The autobiographical narratives vary somewhat in format, but in contrast to the fictional accounts, most turn around a series of case studies. Douglas Ubelaker, a curator in physical anthropology at the Smithsonian Institution, made an early entry into the genre in 1992, when he co-authored *Bones* with Henry Scammell, a journalist and trade writer. Their book explored different elements of forensic anthropological research by describing a variety of cases in which Ubelaker had been involved. Of all the early popular accounts of forensic anthropological work, Ubelaker's text is probably the most theoretically engaged, presenting his reflections on questions of truth and objectivity. It was followed a couple of years later by *Dead Men Do Tell Tales* (1994), co-authored by William Maples and Michael Browning. A distinguished service professor at the University of Florida at Gainesville, Maples was a pioneer in the forensic anthropological field. He consulted for law enforcement agencies and the US Army's Central Identification Laboratory and established the C. A. Pound Human Identification Laboratory at the University of Florida. His autobiographical account was also composed around high-profile cases in which he had been involved, such as identifying the remains of the last Romanov czar, Nicholas II.

Two other autobiographical accounts tread a slightly different terrain and speak to the increasing international impact of forensic anthropological techniques, as well as to the growth of the field. *The Stone Fields* (2004) emerged from Courtney Angela Brkic's experiences working as a forensic archaeologist as part of a team in eastern Bosnia. In a textured narrative that is matted with emotion and the pain of the past, she entwines her experiences of forensic work with her family's history in the former Yugoslavia. Clea Koff's *The Bone Woman* (2004) deals with Koff's experiences as an anthropology graduate student volunteering in Rwanda, Bosnia, Croatia, and Kosovo. It is as much a reflection on the frustrations and dangers of forensic anthropological research in post-conflict situations as it is a description of the techniques and methods of forensic anthropology.

However, most memoirs published by American authors stick to the true crime genre and stay within the well-established tropes of detection. Accounts by Stanley Rhine, Mary Manhein, Robert Mann, and William Bass similarly present a series of case studies structured around narratives of investigation, for the most part concerning criminal cases in the United States. Stanley Rhine was a professor of anthropology at the University of New Mexico when he published *Bone Voyage* in 1998. He is now retired but remains listed as a diplomate on the website of the American Board of Forensic Anthropology. Manhein, a fellow of the American Academy of Forensic Sciences, has published three accounts of her investigations, *The Bone Lady* (1999), *Trail of Bones* (2005), and *Bone Remains* (2013), her titles emphasizing her osteological expertise. Robert Mann's book *Forensic Detective* (2006), written with Miryam Ehrlich Williamson, is explicit in claiming the ground of detection for its subject. Mann is another ABFA diplomate and, like Thomas Holland, works at JPAC in Hawaii, where he is the deputy director of the Central Identification Laboratory. William Bass has written two popular nonfiction books, *Death's Acre* (2003) and *Beyond the Body Farm* (2007), both co-authored with Jon Jefferson. Bass's books describe his experiences establishing the Body Farm; like the other nonfiction texts, each short chapter illustrates a particular case and shows how forensic anthropological research can contribute to knowledge about the manner of death and the identity of the dead. Finally, Alan G. Morris's *Missing and Murdered* (2011) is an account of his experiences working as a forensic anthropologist in South Africa. Like Brkic's and Koff's texts, this account considers some of the complexities of international forensic practice, and in this respect it is probably no coincidence that all three authors have roots in more than one country. Morris (a Canadian trained in the United States and South Africa) is more reflexive than the authors of some of the other texts in his assessment of the assumptions wrapped up in forensic anthropology. He deals, for example, with the charged question of the racial classification of human skeletal remains, an issue that is rarely considered in any depth by other popular writers.

Both novels and autobiographical "detective" narratives perform the accumulated experience of their authors and demonstrate their skill with inferential reason, giving additional weight to forensic expertise. Claims that mass media forensic narratives are grounded in a bedrock of fact are remade through the inclusion of illustrative figures that could be found in any undergraduate text. These are found both in autobiographical narratives, such as Ubelaker's *Bones* (which includes figures, a glossary of terms, and a list of ABFA diplomates), and in the novels. Jefferson Bass's first book includes diagrams of the human skeleton taken from William Bass's textbook, *Human Osteology: A Laboratory and Field Manual* (first published in 1971), gesturing toward a pedagogical motivation.

All these mass-market texts publicize the work undertaken by their authors and presumably help in raising awareness and funds for their research. They aim to reach far beyond an academic audience and target the huge market for crime fiction and true crime stories. This is helped by endorsements by other popular authors. Bass describes how Patricia Cornwell contacted him to help with research for her novel *The Body Farm* (1994) and observes that her book led to more public interest in his work. Cornwell, the author of numerous thrillers featuring medical examiner Kay Scarpetta, subsequently wrote a preface to Bass's memoir, *Death's Acre.* On the front cover of William Maples's autobiographical *Dead Men Do Tell Tales* (Maples and Browning 1994), Cornwell provides an enthusiastic review quotation: "an incredible story brilliantly told—a masterpiece." On the front cover of *Bones,* Douglas Ubelaker's memoir, she suggests that the author is "one of the finest forensic sleuths of our time." Given the anxieties about the real-life effects of fictional portrayals of forensic practice, the easy movement between fictional detective genres and the apparently factual description in popular forensic anthropological texts is striking. Crime novelists write introductions to nonfiction narratives by forensic anthropologists; fiction is composed by forensic practitioners and incorporates claims to scientific veracity. If the protagonists of forensic novels act as thinly disguised doubles of their authors, the bifurcation of the popular literature into autobiography and fiction reinscribes this doubling, setting up parallel forensic anthropological worlds, real and imaginary. Circulating through both are forensic facts, which seem curiously resilient in their deployment in fiction, as of course do forensic anthropologists.

In both popular autobiographical accounts and the FASP literature, it is remarkable how often technical terms for the skeleton are provided, untranslated into ordinary English. Stoerr suggests that in this way the reader learns "about both scientific method and the scientific indicators that the forensic anthropologist relies on during the skeletal autopsy" (2011:88). In her first novel, *Déjà Dead,* Reichs describes Temperance Brennan's analysis of skeletal elements from a young woman. Brennan calls over her colleague Claudel, and pointing through a magnifying glass to "the upper border of the hip," she shows him "an irregularity": "the iliac crest was in the process of attaching itself when death had occurred." Brennan does not explain this, instead moving to examine another bone.

> I returned to the body to examine the clavicle, certain of what I'd find. I withdrew the sternal end from the water and began to tease away the tissue. When I could see the joint surface I gestured for Claudel to join me. Wordlessly I pointed to the end

> of the bone. Its surface was billowy, like the pubic face. A small disk of bone clung to the center, its edges distinct and unfused.
>
> "…So?" Sweat beaded his forehead. He was hiding his nervousness with bravado.
>
> "She's young. Probably early twenties." (1998:28–29)

Although this dialogue offers some interpretive information (the billows on the bone tell something about age at death), it also withholds much. The use of terms such as "iliac crest," "pubic face," and "sternal end" seems to presuppose some knowledge of the skeletal system. The terms also serve a nonreferential performative function, designed to elicit a sense of knowledgeable expertise and confidence in the anthropologist's judgment. This is reiterated by Brennan's absorption in her task, her calm and neutral manner in contrast to her flustered co-worker, and her "certainty" of what she will find, even before examining the bone.

These accounts do complicated work. While demonstrating the parallel authority of both fictional and real-life anthropologists, they also allow a certain rhetorical and representational freedom that is not available to authors in other venues. In *Déjà Dead* Brennan reflects on the aftereffects of murder on the victim. "It plunders one's dignity as surely as it has taken one's life.… The victim becomes part of the evidence, an exhibit, on display" (Reichs 1998:21). She blames the indignity of autopsy and analysis on the violent cause of death, but is also uncomfortable about her part in it: "Number it. Photograph it. Take samples. Tag the toe. While I am an active participant, I can never accept the impersonality of the system. It is like looting on the most personal level. At least I would give this victim a name" (21). Similarly, in autobiographical accounts anthropologists explore elements of forensic work that rarely find their way into the professional literature. Bass, for example, finishes most chapters in *Death's Acre* with a reflection on the dead person and the tragedy of that person's death. The autobiographies and novels provide a space then to think about the dead as people and to consider the ambiguities of dealing with the dead, as well as the wider repercussions of forensic work.

TRANSGRESSION AND MEDIATION

The figure of the double that is created by these texts seems to be important in understanding the peculiar popularity of forensic anthropological narratives. The anthropologist is split into two related personas: the real-life individual represented in autobiographies and the fictional double, who mirrors the skills and life history of the author. This splitting has precedent in detective fiction. In Poe's short story "The Purloined Letter" (first published in 1845), Liahna Babener (1988) has observed, the guilty party, Minister D—, seems to act as a double and counterpart to Dupin. Sherlock Holmes has a degenerate double in his nemesis, Moriarty, who seems to mirror the detective's unusual abilities and proclivities (Greenslade 1994:103–106). Forensic anthropology texts do not split the detective along these lines, however. Rather, the double is constituted in a way that might seem at first sight to provide a means to split the subject matter of forensic anthropology into fact and fancy, restricting certain topics to fiction and leaving others solidly contained in the realm of empirical truth. Bass and Jefferson (Bass 2006:321) contradict any such easy reading, however, by explaining of their first novel that "although the story is fictional, the science is factual." Fact then can move between genres, underwriting both fictional claims and the weight of autobiography. This fluid transition seems to strengthen the claims of scientific fact: it is resilient even to its representation in fiction, retaining its truth in the midst of a fabricated tissue of story. What then is the relationship between fictional and factual anthropologists?

It is not only the underlying claims to fact that link fiction to autobiography. The sentiments and statements offered by fictional anthropologists are often shared by their real-life counterparts. Whether biographical or fictional, the popular literature positions the forensic anthropologist as someone who is in a special relationship to the dead. As William Maples explains, "Death to me is no terror of the night but a daylit companion, a familiar condition, a process obedient to scientific laws and answerable to scientific inquiry" (Maples and Browning 1994:2). The forensic anthropologist is someone who can translate the corpse, literally and metaphorically: dead bodies can be dug up, removed, and displaced, and their language can be interpreted and communicated to the living, but only if the anthropologist remains impartial and objective. This special status is restated through graphic descriptions of human remains and the demonstration of the forensic anthropologist's resilience and determination in dealing with them. Fictional accounts can be particularly gruesome in their descriptions, if not aiming to shock the reader, at least attempting to convey some of the sensuous experience of dealing with the dead anthropologically.

Jefferson Bass's first novel opens at the Body Farm with the protagonist, Dr. Brockton, experimenting on a corpse in front of a sheriff's deputy. Deputy Williams blanches, flinching at the sight, and Brockton explains: "'What you're seeing here is forensic science in action.' With that, I reached down and wrenched the knife from the back of my research subject with a flourish. The blade popped free with a wet, sucking sound. A blob of purplish goo arced toward the deputy and plopped onto his left shoe, where it quivered moistly.... This time, I caught him before he hit the ground" (J. Bass 2006:6). This description delights in the transgression of social norms, locating expertise not so much in the experimental protocol as in the ability to withstand such sights and sounds. Similarly, in *Dead Men Do Tell Tales*, Maples writes that he seldom had nightmares, but that when he did they were "usually flitting images of the everyday things I see on the job: crushed and perforated skulls, lopped-off limbs and severed heads, roasted and dissolving corpses, hanks of human hair and heaps of white bones" (Maples and Browning 1994:1). This recognizes what Julia Kristeva (1982) has termed the "abjection" of the corpse. Kristeva argues that the abject cadaver provokes horror because of the way in which its transgressive physicality seems to break down the boundary between bodily inside and outside and between subject and object. In both these examples attention is paid to that boundary's violation. Whether pierced by Brockton's knife or "perforated," "severed," or "dissolving," the abject corpse is something that is normally thrust aside and hidden from view. In these terms, exhumation and bodily dissection violate expectations around the dead and engage with something that should be kept aside and away from living communities (see Buchli and Lucas 2001; Graves Brown 2011). However, in a denial of the abject, forensic anthropologists are positioned as specialists who occupy a protected space that allows them to deal with things that are forbidden or repulsive to ordinary people. In mediating between the dead and the living, forensic practitioners are shown to inhabit a zone of transgression where normal practices can be subverted in the search for truth. In *Death's Acre* Bass acknowledges that the research carried on at the archaeological research facility "required us to sidestep society's customary treatment of the dead" (Bass and Jefferson 2003:206). This makes the forensic anthropologist a liminal figure, someone who inhabits the zones and spaces that others shun or are barred from. Emphasizing this betwixt-and-between status, Maples writes, "I have gazed on the face of death innumerable times.... For me, every day is Halloween" (Maples and Browning 1994:2).

THE PUZZLE OF THE DEAD

In introducing William Bass's co-authored memoir, *Death's Acre*, novelist Patricia Cornwell suggests that forensic experts such as Bass can "hear the dead speak." This is a task of interpretation of a "secret language" (Cornwell 2003:xi). The answer here is encrypted—hidden and disguised in the secret language of the corpse. Consistent with this perspective, forensic work is commonly explained as a form of intellectual puzzle; this metaphor demonstrates a concern with the logic of forensic evidence while also emphasizing the limits on interpretation. Courtney Angela Brkic's (2003:138–159) short story about an Argentine forensic anthropologist in Bosnia describes how "he thought of himself as a solver of puzzles. The bones were pieces that, together, made a picture" (143). Douglas Ubelaker observes that "scientists in general tend to be puzzle solvers, and there are times when it seems that the best metaphor for forensic anthropology would be the jigsaw puzzle" (Ubelaker and Scammell 1992:260). Such imagery suggests that only one solution is possible and that the body's clues invite its discovery. William Bass reiterates this: forensic anthropology cases are "intellectually irresistible...scientific puzzles demanding to be solved" (Bass and Jefferson 2003:5). The search for the clues that will solve a puzzle allows the violation of expectations about the treatment of the dead. As Bass explains, "Everything I see and smell is a source of data, a possible key to discovering the truth" (240).

In placing the intellectual challenge posed by the dead at the front and center of forensic work, even the most repugnant attributes of the decomposing body can be co-opted as evidence in the search for the truth. Metaphors of decryption remake the dead body into a problem to be solved. Bass explains: "When I'm studying a crime scene...I never regard it as a death; to me, it's strictly a case" (Bass and Jefferson 2003:240; cf. Brkic 2003:145). Affirming this view, Reichs's character Temperance Brennan reflects that "the murder scene was a clinical exercise. No problem. Dissect it, study it, solve the puzzle" (Reichs 1998:28). In emphasizing the ability to tolerate such work, these authors figure the murder scene both as a corpse to be dissected and as an intellectual riddle. Here the dead body is associated metonymically with the broader facts of a case, and both are positioned as puzzles to be deciphered. Making the same rhetorical move from dead body to evidence, Maples and Browning (1994:2) explain that the solution to the mystery of a violent death can be sought and discovered if one has "the stomach, the knowledge, the experience and the perseverance to reach with both hands into the rotting remnants of some dreadful crime, rummage through the bones and grasp the pure gleaming nugget of truth that lies at the center of it all."

Lying jewel-like in the very body of the corpse, the truth lies waiting to be found by those who are strong enough to search for it. Here the search for the truth and the violation of the body are closely linked to the courage and integrity of the expert. In this respect it is significant that in the FASP novels the process of autopsy often causes a negative reaction in morally suspect characters (e.g., J. Bass 2006:6) or in those with major character flaws (e.g., Reichs 1998:29). The fictional narratives may take a little more pleasure in the grisly details of the corpses that litter their texts, and they allow their protagonists more freedom to act inappropriately, but they present the same concerns as the autobiographical texts and use similar language to do so. Memoirs and case studies perhaps frame such questions more explicitly than the novels do, but in discussing the disturbing properties of the dead and the process of decrypting the clues of a crime scene they draw on the same rhetorical tropes to think about the work of forensic anthropology.

The doubling of the forensic anthropologist is not designed then to separate and corral certain prohibited topics into fiction. Instead it seems to be more epistemic. Poe's second Dupin story offers some insights. "The Mystery of Marie Rogêt," first published in 1842, was inspired by the real-life murder of Mary Rogers in the New York area the previous year. As Matthew Pearl observes in the introduction to a 2006 edition of the stories, in the 1845 version of this tale Poe played with the "boundary between fiction and history" (xi–xiv), counterposing a footnoted editorial narrative against the fictional account. Pearl notes that Poe the narrator and Poe the editor seem to disagree about the nature of the story, with Poe the narrator positioning the text as fiction and in a coincidental relationship to the original murder case, while Poe the editor's footnotes suggest that the story about Marie Rogêt could reveal the truth about what happened to Mary Rogers. Pearl quotes Poe the editor as observing that "under pretence of relating the fate of a Parisian *grisette,* the author has followed, in minute detail, the essential, while merely paralleling the inessential facts of the real murder of Mary Rogers." The story is founded on the "essential" facts—and because of this "all argument founded upon the fiction is applicable to the truth" (Pearl 2006:37). Here Poe suggests that facts can be stripped from their New York context and retain their ability to show the solution to the puzzle of Rogers's death. Yet at the same time he makes visible the representational strategies through which the murder of Mary Rogers was translated into New York newspaper accounts and through them into Paris-based fiction, acknowledging the ambiguity at the heart of any true crime story—that it is both a story and a truth claim. The story simultaneously puts into question the relationship between the facts of a case and their textual representation, and denies that it is an issue. This relationship is also at stake in mass media accounts of forensic anthropology, but it is rarely addressed head on. Instead, writers take an oblique approach in which metaphors of encryption and an emphasis on the special status of the forensic specialist stand in for more explicit analysis of how facts get spun into stories.

Just as the anthropologist is positioned in these texts as someone who is able to mediate between the dead and the living, able to transgress societal norms in the service of justice, he or she is also located as an intermediary between fact and its representation. To decipher the dead is to speak for them and to make representation to others on their behalf. This is to implicitly recognize the ambiguities of the evidence of the dead; facts may shape one's conclusions, but they also need to be interpreted and translated into language. In foregrounding metaphors of decryption, popular forensic texts tacitly acknowledge the mimetic work of representation, which transfers facts from the realm of the dead body to the realm of text and testimony. This acknowledgment is also made apparent in popular descriptions of the effort to represent the dead faithfully and without outside influence.

Forensic anthropologists mediate between the dead and the living both through the transgressive handling and analysis of human remains and through speaking for the dead and testifying on their behalf. The doubled figure that haunts popular anthropology texts is not a bifurcation that splits the anthropologist into two contrasting parts, but rather a doubling that draws upon this transgressive mediation between the dead and the living to conceptualize and explore the problematic relationship between fact and value. In this figuring, the dead inhabit the realm of truthful fact while the living dwell in the messy and complicated realm of representation. Forensic anthropologists are uniquely able to move between the two parallel fields faithfully and without betraying either that which makes them human or the truth of the dead. Just as facts remain uncontaminated by fiction in their perambulations through the mass-market novels, so forensic anthropologists can circulate freely between realms that are constituted as opposed and distinct in popular forensic texts. The work of expertise shields the forensic protagonists from pollution through contact with the dead, and from the claims and demands of the living. Yet, at the same time, in recognizing evidence as somehow like the abject corpse, there is an incipient realization of the ways that the evidence of the dead has the potential to decompose the boundary between object and subject, between fact and value.

The puzzle that is solved through forensic work is thus not simply the question of what happened to the dead. It is the puzzle of how to rearticulate the dead with the living. As Kathy Reichs puts it, "I could use my science to solve a puzzle. I could provide a family with closure" (preface to Owen 2000:8). William Bass, reflecting on the skull of one unclaimed woman's remains, muses that she "had been someone's daughter, someone's wife, someone's mother. Now she was reduced to a case" (Bass and Jefferson 2003:45). Unconnected with her family she remained in the liminal space of the university teaching collection and was not reburied. This was someone who would be given a funeral only if relatives are identified to claim her. The imagery of the anthropologist as cryptologist offers a great deal, but it comes with entailments that discourage close attention to the relationships that sustain and entangle forensic anthropological practice (as explored throughout this volume). Both fictional and popular accounts often express a sense of responsibility to the living and the dead, and acknowledge the ways in which the biographies of the living and the dead are entwined, but the attendant emphasis on the special status and expertise of the anthropologist seems to hinder attempts to engage with the wider entanglements of forensic work. The work of forensic anthropology tends to be imagined as a narrow methodological and inferential task, yet it has profound social repercussions. As Ubelaker remarks at the end of *Bones*, the work that forensic anthropologists carry out in the United States often involves the impoverished and indigent, people who die not only from violence but from neglect and hardship "in the midst of...the richest, most powerful nation in the history of the world" (Ubelaker and Scammell 1992:289). He suggests that for one poor, abandoned individual, the work of forensic analysis was "her last opportunity to be recognized, to express her plight, to have her identity documented and to leave some record of her life" (289). The issues and questions raised in the popular literature create opportunities to think about broader societal issues that are of relevance to the whole discipline. Opening up new rhetorical tropes for conceptualizing forensic practice and fully exploring the repercussions of those that are well established might also have the effect of allowing some of these questions to enter more easily into the field.

Acknowledgments

Thanks to Michelle Stoerr for sending me a copy of her 2011 article and to the members of the SAR seminar for wonderful feedback on this chapter.

7

Creating the Biological Profile

The Question of Race and Ancestry

Heather Walsh-Haney and Serrin Boys

Forensic anthropologists bear witness to the interplay of biology, culture, and public policy through the identification of skeletal markers of age, sex, height, and ancestry, which are used to help establish the positive identifications of decedents (Cattaneo et al. 2010; Holobinko 2012; Turner 2005). The number of unidentified decedents has increased dramatically over time, and so too has the number of missing individuals. According to the National Institute of Justice, the number of missing persons increased from 450,000 in 1980 to nearly 900,000 in 2010, thereby creating an immediate demand for techniques that can ascertain the identity of human remains stored in medical examiner's offices,[1] in indigent cemeteries,[2] and uncovered from mass graves (Fondebrider 2009; Hinton and O'Neill 2009; Sanford 2003a).

In most international jurisdictions and in the United States, the medical examiner or coroner works to establish a positive identification via what these medical practitioners often term scientific, definitive, or objective rather than presumptive, punitive, or circumstantial means (FAME 2010; Tidball-Binz 2006). The former mode of identification tends to be statutorily defined and uses methods such as the comparison of antemortem and postmortem medical or dental radiographs or records, fingerprints, DNA analysis, or the acknowledgment of the person's identity by family members who recognize and stipulate to the identity of an intact corpse (e.g., absent decomposition, extensive facial trauma, or fire damage) in the presence of medical examiner or coroner personnel. The presumptive-punitive-circumstantial method of identification may involve a situation where a neighbor finds in the house of the missing individual a decomposing corpse wearing clothes and jewelry known to family members; or one in which the presence of a hospital or nursing home tag on the wrist of the corpse is presumed by the medical examiner or coroner to be correct; or one in which photos of tattoos can be compared to tattoos on the corpse. The forensic anthropologist reads the skeletal remains to record idiosyncratic markers or individualizing characteristics, such as distinctive dentition, old injuries, and pathology, to help the medical examiner or coroner establish the identification. These unique dental and skeletal anomalies accompany the skeletal biological profile, which ascribes the remains to broad categories of age, height, sex, and race or ancestry.

Law enforcement has the statutory responsibility to locate medical or dental records and radiographs and DNA samples and to conduct interviews and fingerprint comparisons to establish a legal positive identification (Holobinko 2012; see Florida Statute 406.145 as an example of law enforcement's statutory obligations). In so doing, law enforcement distills the forensic anthropologist's findings into biological descriptors that help families and friends refer to their missing loved one and provides the attributive terminology necessary to solve criminal cases. Variables such as age at time of death and height tend to be decoded by the anthropologist, family members, and law enforcement agency with relative ease. For example, if a numerical age range is given by a forensic anthropologist (e.g., between 18 and 26 years old) or if height has been determined, this poses few problems for the kind of questions that law enforcement might ask: "What year was your son born? He was last seen alive on what date? Was he five foot six, or approximately one meter seventy in height?"

Sex is usually described by forensic anthropologists as an ordinal number on a scale, often from 1 to 5, moving from female through probable female, indeterminate, probable male, and male (Buikstra and Ubelaker 1994). This nomenclature tends to be translated by most stakeholders into the terms male, female, or unknown. Such a heteronormative description and investigation of biological sex does not begin to capture the range of phenotypic and genotypic variation that exists, but it does provide a starting point for identifying missing persons. If identifying biological sex poses problems, the terminology of race used by medical examiners, law enforcement, family members, and forensic anthropologists to describe human remains in order to establish a positive identification is even less clear-cut. In this chapter we explore the issues involved in the ascription of race or ancestry to human remains.

DECODING RACE

One disconnect involves the use and interpretation of the term "race" by the various stakeholders. In the course of our forensic anthropology casework we have found that medico-legal practitioners and family members typically use race as a classification method that ties together shared biological (phenotypic) traits and social interactions (religion, language, beliefs).

Scholars see race as a socially constructed term used to classify and stratify populations based upon segmenting the clinal distribution of phenotypes into discrete clusters (Brues 1993; Cartmill 1998; Fuentes 2012; Goodman and Armelagos 1996; Lieberman et al. 2003; Paule 2013). Anthropologists have largely dropped the term from their vernacular in favor of the term "ancestry" in part because of the impossibility of classifying dynamic clinal distributions into types (Ousley et al. 2009; Sauer and Wankmiller 2009). Anthropologists also avoid the term because oppressive ideas concerning biological determinism, systemic and patterned biases, and subjugation emerge when biological traits and behavior are woven together by using the race concept (Caspari 2009; Gravlee 2009; Ossorio and Duster 2005). To remove themselves from the controversy, forensic anthropologists conduct ancestry skeletal evaluations as part of their forensic investigations (Sauer and Wankmiller 2009).

Forensic anthropologists recognize ancestry as a continuous variable parsed into categories, which places an individual within a genetic lineage distinguished by the morphological variations observed in human skeletal remains (Byers 2005; Ousley et al. 2009). They also describe ancestry groups as populations composed of people sharing common features derived from a mutual ancestor (Brues 1993; Caspari 2003, 2009; Gill-King 2005; Sauer 1992). More simply, a combination of visual (nonmetric) and metric shape and size differences in bones and teeth provide the forensic anthropologist with data that are used to assign the unidentified decedent to one of a limited number of groups that tend to be defined by geographic proximity, gene flow and gene drift, or the lack thereof (Albanese and Saunders 2006). For example, the bones of the eye orbit create a shape that has been found to correlate reasonably well with an individual's geographical lineage. Decades of anthropological study have established that angled, rectangular, and round orbits represent European, African, and Asian/Native

American ancestry groups, respectively. However, this is a simple translation of earlier racial terminology (Caucasoid, Negroid, and Mongoloid) into more neutral ancestry terms and leaves the underlying typology unexamined. Clearly, there is great variation in all three geographical regions, and eye orbit alone provides only a crude measure of ancestry. To focus on ancestry is to link together allele frequencies, geographic distance, and selective forces (the latter arising from environment, behavior, or mutation) in order to capture the genetic variability in and between populations (Caspari 2009; Jorde and Wooding 2006; Relethford 2009; Sauer 1992, 1993). Forensic anthropologists must base biogeographic relatedness, or ancestry, on the skeletal similarities and differences evidenced by evaluating variation in the shape and size of skeletal elements (Hefner 2009; Hurst 2012; Kallenberger and Pilbrow 2012; Ross et al. 2004). This is a crude estimation of the complexities of ancestry, but one that can be effective for identifying individuals in populations where different racial or ethnic groups are reasonably discrete and there is little recent history of gene flow between the identified groups.

The accuracy of the forensic anthropologist's assessment of ancestry relies on aligning the etic ancestry group assignment with the decedent's (emic) identity in life (Duray et al. 1999; Paule 2013; Sauer 1992). Unquestionably, misalignments may arise (1) due to emic and etic ancestry disconnects; (2) because familial relatedness cannot guarantee physical similarities; or (3) when the individual may be a nonconforming phenotypic outlier in relation to recognized "types" (Ellison et al. 2007; Hughes et al. 2011): populations are neither biologically bounded nor immobile. In order to improve ancestry accuracy rates, the Scientific Working Group for Forensic Anthropology (SWGANTH) stresses the use of nonmetric and metric standards and statistical analyses. However, our review of SWGANTH's ancestry working draft revealed a lack of consensus with respect to the terms "race" and "ancestry." Specifically, we noted that the document uses the two terms interchangeably. This speaks to the frequent and ongoing confusion of race with ancestry.

RACE IN GOVERNMENTAL, MEDICAL, AND LEGAL CONTEXTS

Despite the debates in anthropology, race remains a categorical variable prolifically used in governmental, medical, and legal contexts as well as throughout the hard and social sciences. Since its inception, the US Census Bureau has traced and collected race data, while stipulating more recently that race typologies do not conform to anthropological, genetic, or biological criteria (US Census Bureau 2014). Similarly, medical researchers codify race to describe differences between populations that may prove to be biomedically relevant, to promote equitable access to life-saving medical studies, to describe inequalities in access to health care, and to facilitate the portability of important biomedical information between patients, researchers, and policy makers, such as the World Health Organization, US National Institutes of Health, and Project Hope. Medical clinicians often "eyeball" the patient's race but use sociopolitically acceptable terms put forth by the US Census Bureau (Ellison et al. 2007).

In legal contexts, death certificates include race as a biologic descriptor to add legitimacy to the decedent's positive identification. The death certificate provides information necessary to resolve estate issues and validate social security and private insurance benefits claims by family members (Bertolli et al. 2007; Caveney et al. 2006). In addition, researchers use race categories from death certificates to study disease patterns, population life expectancy, and mortality rates. Because medical examiners and coroners eyeball race, a linguistic disconnect can exist between the way a medical examiner "sees" race categories and the way a decedent might have "seen" herself. This undoubtedly biases epidemiologic and mortality studies and may bring the validity of a positive identification into question (Ellison et al. 2007).

The issue of eyeballing race and subsequent misidentification was investigated by Bertolli and colleagues (2007) when they explored the effect that race had on health status and access to medical care. As part of an American Indian/Alaskan Native ethnicity validation workshop, these researchers demonstrated that the misidentification of race by medical examiners and coroners resulted in inequitable access to HIV/AIDS medications (for the families and sex partners of the decedent) and slow mobilization of medical staff to American Indian/Alaskan Native families in particular (Bertolli et al. 2007). Bertolli and colleagues observed that American Indian and Alaskan Native deceased individuals were consistently misidentified as white in 70 percent of the evaluated cases, Hispanic at a rate of 16 percent, black at 11 percent, and Asian/Pacific Islander at 2 percent; in 0.9 percent of the cases, race was not noted. However, rather than removing the biological descriptor of race, the working group recommended bringing tribal representatives into the race identification process. These examples raise questions about the effectiveness of the forensic anthropologist's move to use ancestry as a descriptor when racial terminologies predominate in the sociopolitical agencies with the power to define, identify, categorize, record, distribute, and legislate populations. They also point to the reasons that ancestry is frequently conflated with race in the literature.

MATCHING UNIDENTIFIED DECEDENTS TO MISSING PERSONS

Our review of three unidentified person databases in the United States—the National Missing and Unidentified Persons System (NamUS), the National Crime Information Center (NCIC), and the Florida Unidentified Decedents Database (FLUIDDB)—highlighted differences in race and geographic origin nomenclature as part of public policy (see Table 7.1). Shockingly, only one category appears in all three databases—white. This finding probably indicates the way in which white acts as an unmarked and unquestioned category, against which all the other types are variably defined. Ignatiev follows the racial reclassification of Irish immigrants to the United States during the mid-1800s in his book *How the Irish Became White* (1995). He finds that Irish immigrants were categorized as "different" or "nonwhite" upon entry into the United States, yet as they became an important part of the American labor force their race became "white." However, the Irish categorized themselves based on geographic location (and, by extension, religious affiliation as Protestant or Catholic).

This fluidity and variability in identity remains an issue today. Just as the Irish assigned themselves to groups based on geographic and cultural markers, the missing persons databases parse some of the population by geographic location and language affiliation. This procedure certainly complicates the process of matching missing people with unidentified decedents. These databases also classify people from single geographical locations (e.g., Samoa, Guam, Haiti) in isolation and do not provide categories for self-identification. In addition, each database uses racial terms not replicated by the others, such as "biracial," "mixed," and "unsure." The lack of homogeneity between these databases may be why the number of unidentified people grew from 4,000 to nearly 8,500 individuals from 2008 to 2013—a trend that began in 1990 (Paule 2013).

The monumental task of winnowing missing persons lists in order to match an unidentified decedent begins with a law enforcement officer sorting the lists by the date the missing person was last seen. Then, she continues to shrink the number of possible matches by sorting the list by sex and further still by age at disappearance. Subsequently, the law enforcement officer compares the final list of missing persons to the lists of unidentified decedents. With this information in hand, she contacts the possible next of kin and interviews them to assess the accuracy of the missing persons

TABLE 7.1. US RACE AND ANCESTRY CATEGORIES BY DATABASE

Database	Classifier		Race Classifier in Database																						No Classifier
	Race	*Ancestry*	*W*	*B*	*BAA*	*AAN*	*A*	*NA*	*AIAN*	*API*	*AI*	*NH*	*GC*	*S*	*OPI*	*H*	*HA*	*G*	*J*	*V*	*C*	*UNK*	*ALL*	*OT*	*DNC*
FLUIDDB	X		X																				X		
NCIC	X		X						X	X												X			
NamUS	X		X		X		X	X														X		X	
NCMEC																									X
US Census	X		X			X			X	X	X	X	X	X	X									X	
Dist. 20 MEO	X		X				X	X									X								
SWGANTH	X	X																							X
SWGMDI																									X
FORDISC 3.0	X		X						X							X		X		X	X				

Notes: FLUIDDB = Florida Unidentified Decedents Database; NCIC = National Crime Information Center; NamUS = National Missing and Unidentified Persons System; NCMEC = National Center for Missing and Exploited Children; Dist. 20 MEO = District 20 Medical Examiner's Office (racial categories delineated on fingerprint cards and as determined by Access, the death registration system used by the medical examiner in Naples, Florida); SWGANTH = Scientific Working Group for Forensic Anthropology; SWGMDI = Scientific Working Group for Medicolegal Death Investigation; FORDISC 3.0 = multivariate statistical analysis program and linked forensic databank.

W = White; B = Black; BAA = Black/African American; AAN = African American/Negro; A = Asian; NA = Native American; AIAN = American Indian or Alaskan Native; API = Asian or Pacific Islander; AI = Asian Indian; NH = Native Hawaiian; GC = Guamanian or Chamorro; S = Samoan; OPI = Other Pacific Islander; H = Hispanic; HA = Haitian; G = Guatemalan; J = Japanese; V = Vietnamese; C = Chinese; UNK = Unknown; ALL (Hispanic, Mixed, Asian, Native American, and Unknown are grouped together in one search function); OT = Other; DNC = Does Not Classify race, ethnicity, or ancestry in the database.

data and gain additional information about the missing individual's medical history. Unfortunately, as mentioned above, law enforcement's work does not tend to culminate in positive identifications, and the number of unidentified decedents and missing persons increases each year.

In order to determine what part ancestry plays in matching missing persons with unidentified decedents, Paule (2013) assessed the cases that law enforcement could evaluate when the descriptors of sex, age, and height were used to weed through the databases. Essentially, she set out to retrospectively investigate whether law enforcement was more successful in resolving a case when "race" was used to describe the missing person or unidentified corpse. Paule targeted the most widely used and successful database, NamUS, whose search fields include sex, race, and idiosyncratic trait information (e.g., body size, tattoos, dental alterations or anomalies). Because forensic anthropologists tend to agree that the most accurate nonmetric and metric assessments of ancestry arise from analysis of the skull (Giles and Elliot 1963; Gill 1990; Hefner 2009; Krogman and İşcan 1986; Rhine 1990), Paule (2013) compared cases that listed a race designation to cases where race was not determined, and she also indicated whether "race" was based on skeletal attributes of the skull (e.g., the skull was not absent). This was her attempt to query the database the way a law enforcement officer would proceed if the ancestry of the decedent was not known. Paule evaluated 513 total case entries with 409 being individuals of "unsure" race. She queried the database by including sex and age criteria, which nearly halved the sample size. When Paule evaluated the remaining sample by including race, the sample size decreased by 86 percent and thus reduced the workload for the hypothetical law enforcement officer. Paule's results underscore SWGANTH's inclusion of ancestry estimation as one of the group's best practices.

THE PROBLEM OF ETIC AND EMIC ANCESTRY CONGRUENCY

For more than 30 years, most forensic anthropologists accepted the racial vernacular used by missing persons and unidentified decedents databases in their reports because of the presumption that the terms most closely represent how members of the public categorize ancestry groups in general and themselves in particular (Abu El-Haj 2007; Cox et al. 2006; Dirkmaat et al. 2008; Epstein 2008; Gill-King 2005; Jantz and Ousley 2010; Ousley et al. 2009; Sauer 1992, 1993; Warren et al. 2008). Furthermore, based on the current SWGANTH position and the popularity of forensic anthropological database programs like FORDISC (Jantz and Ousley

2010),[3] the use of race or ancestry will not fall from the forensic anthropological vernacular in the United States any time soon because forensic anthropologists tend to believe that when estimated correctly, ancestry improves the soundness of other components of the biological profile. For example, Stewart and Kerley's (1979) research involving the metric assessment of sexual dimorphism in the femoral and humeral heads demonstrated that greater accuracy was achieved when the researchers knew the ancestry of the individual. Their results most likely arose from that fact that sex, age, ancestry, and other environmental factors co-vary in ways that are complex and not yet fully understood. However, refinements of methods and the addition of new reference groups will help forensic anthropologists understand and accommodate population changes over time.

Since the beginning of the twenty-first century, forensic anthropologists have worked to fill a void in the research concerning Hispanic populations by helping to identify Hispanic individuals via skeletal morphology (Anderson 2008; Anderson et al. 2008; Ross et al. 2004; Spradley et al. 2008). Spradley and colleagues (2008) examined the accuracy of long bone skeletal sexing standards for Hispanic populations. These researchers found that the accuracy of sex estimation from long bone measurements dropped significantly when they applied white and black standards to Hispanic individuals. This result clearly demands an adjustment in osteological methods, while at the same time it is fraught with the issue of conflating the many different ancestry populations from all over the Americas into one category of "Hispanic." This issue remains pertinent as FORDISC moves to include skeletal estimations for Hispanic ancestry. At its best, forensic anthropology appears self-regulating, like all good science. However, in order to understand the implications and effects of the social and morphological categories we use, it is important to remember the wider context for this science, as Fondebrider argues in chapter 2 in this volume.

Acting as a counterweight to those who support the precision of ancestry estimation via skeletal analyses, scholars point out that (1) in any particular trait, greater variability exists within a population than between populations (Goodman 1997; Lewontin 1972), and (2) social identity cannot be inferred from biological ancestry because the emic and etic viewpoints do not always align (Goodman 1997; Goodman and Armelagos 1996). Goodman (1997) discusses an example involving the misidentification of an isolated, partially fleshed leg found at ground zero of the Alfred P. Murrah Federal Building during the mass fatality response to the terrorist bombing in Oklahoma City. Reportedly, the forensic anthropologist identified the leg via nonmetric and metric means as a darkly fleshed white male. The leg actually belonged to Airman First Class Lakesha R. Levy, a 21-year-old black woman.[4]

The cautionary example of Airman Levy's misidentification has not remained unnoticed by forensic anthropologists. Ancestry advocates Hefner and colleagues (2012) empirically demonstrated that nonmetric traits do not consistently fall within the predicted ancestry groups. Hefner (2009:994) adds that there is presently a poor understanding of the variation within geographical groups and that individuals often display evidence of traits that would normally be ascribed to different ancestry or racial groups, showing the fallacy of the typological approach to ancestry prediction. Therefore, the discipline of forensic anthropology must challenge itself to explore the assumptions built into these and future methodologies (Hughes et al. 2011).

FINE-TUNING THE LANGUAGE OF ANCESTRY WITH IDIOSYNCRATIC FORENSIC ANTHROPOLOGY CASES

Having been involved in forensic anthropology casework for a combined 17 years, as student, laboratory technician, and forensic anthropology consultant, we have experienced the interplay between ancestry and positive identification for unidentified decedents. Walsh-Haney has watched with worry as medical examiners and law enforcement investigators translated 15-page forensic anthropology reports into one- and two-word racial or geographical ancestry adjectives for the NCIC, NamUS, and FLUIDDB databases (see Table 7.1). With concern, we have waited for weeks and months for DNA results to confirm our ability to use forensic anthropologic nonmetric and metric methods to align our etic ancestry findings with the decedent's emic ancestry identification. As of this date, thanks to our understanding of lineage as a factor in the morphology of traits used to identify individuals, we are unaware of any misclassified decedents. We also compliment the training provided by William R. Maples to Walsh-Haney regarding the understanding that as part of the legal system, we uphold the integrity of forensic anthropology by presenting the findings as accurately as possible rather than with a narrow or precise focus. For example, a contemporary, adult female skull that presented with traits from all four ancestry groups would be described as a female of undetermined ancestry, which increases the accuracy of the report. This is in contrast to increasing precision (narrowing our findings to the exclusion of ancestry groups) and thus assessing the adult female as most likely of Asian, Hispanic, or Native American ancestry based on the presence of flared zygomatics (cheekbones).[5] In the latter scenario law enforcement would most likely fail to consider other ancestry groups in missing persons database searches.

Clearly, ancestry/racial estimation has some utility in many situations and can provide positive identifications (e.g., Sauer 1992), but this is not straightforward. Below, we provide some examples from our casework involving ancient Native American remains and modern decedents of other ancestry groups. We highlight the process of ancestry estimation with case examples that both support and problematize the use of ancestry as a biological descriptor.

In the state of Florida and pursuant to Florida Statute 872.05, human skeletal remains belonging to individuals who died more than 75 years before their discovery lack forensic significance. Therefore, the case jurisdiction falls to the state archaeologist. Because Florida tribal representatives and NAGPRA (Native American Graves Protection and Repatriation Act, PL 101-601, 25 USC 3001) rules do not support destructive analyses, carbon-14 dating and DNA testing are last resorts. Thus, nondestructive methods and multiple lines of evidence are used (e.g., nonmetric and metric assessment; analysis of dental wear and attrition; taphonomic changes; provenience; associated pieces of physical evidence, such as stone points, antler tine points, pottery shards).

In 2012, we evaluated fragmentary and incomplete human skeletal remains found in the home of a deceased archaeologist. Suspecting that the remains may have been evidence of a modern forensic case masked as archaeological material, law enforcement transferred custody of the remains to the medical examiner. In turn, the medical examiner notified the state archaeologist, who recommended that we evaluate the remains to ensure proper disposition. The remains, contained in a cardboard box labeled with archaeological site information, consisted of multiple individuals. Following methods outlined in *Standards for Data Collection from Human Skeletal Remains* (Buikstra and Ubelaker 1994), *Skeletal Attribution of Race* (Gill and Rhine 2004), and others (Brothwell 1981; Deter 2009; Hinkes 1990; Rhine 1990), we estimated that these remains represented two adult Native Americans between 40 and 50 years of age. Specifically, we noted nonmetric traits, such as an elliptical maxillary arcade, complex cranial vault sutures, straight transverse palatine sutures, the absence of caries, and marked dental wear and attrition.[6] We did not conduct metric assessment using FORDISC 3.1 (Jantz and Ousley 2010) because the cranial remains were incomplete and fragmentary. Our macroscopic (using a 300x dissecting scope) and radiographic analyses revealed one antemortem dental abscess (Ortner 2003). Our skeletal findings, the taphonomic changes, and the congruency between the artifacts and the site information pointed to Native American ancestry. Upon receipt of our report, the state archaeologist accepted custody of the remains and associated artifacts in accordance with federal and state laws governing the disposition of archaeological Native American remains, artifacts, and burial sites.

Also in 2012, we evaluated human skeletal remains at the request of the medical examiner and in accordance with Florida Statute 472.08. Law enforcement investigators and human remains detector dogs had discovered the fragmentary and skeletonized human remains in a wooded area during a search-and-recovery effort. This had been undertaken to follow up a lead from a confidential informant regarding a missing white adult female. Crime scene investigators mapped and collected the remains. The medical examiner accepted custody of the human remains while law enforcement personnel kept and analyzed other types of physical evidence (e.g., cigarette butts, clothing, bullets). The medical examiner transferred custody of the remains to Walsh-Haney and requested that we conduct a full forensic osteologic examination.

We followed methods outlined in *Standards for Data Collection from Human Skeletal Remains* (Buikstra and Ubelaker 1994), *The Human Skeleton in Forensic Medicine* (Krogman and İşcan 1986), and others (Brooks and Suchey 1990; Gill and Rhine 2004; Hefner 2009; Lovejoy et al. 1985; Meindl and Lovejoy 1985; Moore-Jansen et al. 1994; Reichs, ed. 1998). Our bench work included the creation of a biological profile (age, ancestry, sex, stature, and evidence of antemortem pathology or trauma),[7] estimation of time since death, and analysis of perimortem pathology or trauma (i.e., injuries that occurred at or around the time of death). We also noted evidence of postmortem taphonomic changes (e.g., parallel marks in the bone created by rodents; warping and bleaching related to exposure to the elements; root etching). Our analysis revealed that the remains were consistent with one female between 37 and 60 years of age. However, we observed nonmetric traits from three ancestry groups on the cranial remains, demonstrating that many skeletal remains do not conform to any neat typological patterns. In particular, we noted European "white" (angled nasals, narrow nasal aperture, long nasal spine, receding zygomatics, S-shaped zygomaticomaxillary suture, parabolic dental arcade, and spatulate incisors), Asian or Native American (complex cranial sutures, including an Inca bone and straight transverse palatine suture), and sub-Saharan "black" (post-bregmatic depression)[8] traits.

Our metric assessment using FORDISC (Jantz and Ousley 2010) was inconclusive.[9] Due to the incongruence of the nonmetric and metric findings, we completed our report by indicating that ancestry could not be reliably estimated via skeletal analysis; therefore, we recommended that law enforcement and medical examiner personnel include all ancestry groups in their searches of missing persons databases. Furthermore, we noted that our age estimate, though accurate, would be more precise had ancestry been estimated. Several months after completion of the report and during Walsh-Haney's follow-up discussions with law enforcement and the medical examiner investigators regarding the case's resolution, we learned that DNA analysis had positively identified the decedent as a white woman in her fifth decade of life. According to law enforcement interviews, the decedent's family members (the legal next of kin) did not know of racial admixing in their family.

The question of how ancestry is involved in racial identity is fraught and complicated. Kaplan (2003) recounts the case of Wayne Joseph, an African American individual from Louisiana who migrated to Los Angeles and voluntarily submitted his buccal swabs to a genetic testing lab. He did this in order to assess the claim made by his friends and family that all individuals who self-identify as black are actually racially mixed. Kaplan reports that Mr. Joseph's DNA results indicated that he was 57 percent Indo-European, 39 percent Native American, 4 percent East Asian, and 0 percent "black" African. The DNA findings did not persuade Mr. Joseph (or his family) to change their racial identity, however. In this instance, the claim to a black lineage was an important element of the family's identity and worked to deny association with white oppressors in Louisiana (Kaplan 2003).

CONCLUSIONS

Despite prolific use by the US Census Bureau, various missing and unidentified persons databases, biomedical clinicians and researchers, and forensic anthropologists, the terms "race" and "ancestry" are not interchangeable. Rather, to scholars in the fields of anthropology, genetics, and medicine, "race" is a problematic concept that is used to prop up racist ideologies with false biological categories, while the term "ancestry" is not. However, in many cases, "ancestry" is used as a simple substitute for racial categories, and the underlying typological theory through which identifications are made is not examined or adjusted.

To address these valid concerns, we have made efforts to remove the term "race" from our scientific vernacular, not only supplanting it with "ancestry," but also trying to be aware of the limitations of conceiving of ancestry in terms of type groups. We base this choice on the knowledge that human skeletal phenotypes (1) are heritable and polygenic; (2) are affected by environmental and behavioral factors; (3) may result from mutation; (4) have temporal significance; and (5) may track population relatedness via clinal distribution. We understand that biological and social ancestry identification may not align when etic and emic viewpoints are incongruent or when scientific methods are misapplied, misinterpreted, or not revised with reference to population changes through time. We document these ancestry identification shortcomings by writing forensic anthropology reports that do not use unequivocal ancestry terms, and those reports are widely accepted and appreciated by the medico-legal community with which we interact. The challenges going forward will be to continue to interrogate how ancestry evaluations are embedded in unexamined typological thinking about race and to find new ways to talk about the skeleton that are not tied to the identification of unproblematized ancestry groups.

Notes

1. Walsh-Haney consulted with the Broward County Medical Examiner's Office (BCMEO) to analyze unidentified skeletal remains stored in that office. The BCMEO provides its human remains storage policy online (https://www.broward.org/MedicalExaminer/AboutUs/Pages/FAQs.aspx).

2. Walsh-Haney works with the Monroe County Medical Examiner to identify skeletal remains from one county mausoleum as part of the indigent burial program outlined on the county website (http://www.monroecounty-fl.gov/index.aspx?nid=281).

3. The software program FORDISC contains skeletal metric data compiled by researchers from the University of Tennessee Anthropological Research Facility for use by human skeletal analysts. The program generates discriminant functions related to sex, ancestry, and stature with the most current version of the program using up to 27 cranial, 9 mandibular, and 44 postcranial measurements that sort an unknown individual into one of 12 race/sex groups for crania or 4 race/sex groups for postcrania.

4. AFC Levy was buried with full military honors in Louisiana's Mount Olivet Cemetery.

5. Flared zygomatics tend to be observed with greater frequency among Asian, Hispanic, and Native American skeletal samples.

6. The central and lateral incisors were lost postmortem (as evidenced by the empty tooth sockets that lacked remodeling) and were not available for analysis.

7. These are diseases or injuries that occur in life, which are evidenced by a cellular response that tends to alter the bone's conformation, such as the pitting on a joint surface related to osteoarthritis.

8. Post-bregmatic depressions occur in European and Asian ancestry groups but occur in greater frequency in Africans (Blumenfeld 2011).

9. Posterior typicality probability = 0.530; *F* typicality probability = 0.828; R typicality probability = 0.811; chi typicality probability = 0.711. By following protocols outlined by the FORDISC 3.1 user's manual (Jantz and Ousley 2010), we ruled out size and measurement errors as contributing factors.

8

Hybrid Lives, Violent Deaths

"Seminoles" in the Samuel G. Morton Cranial Collection

Pamela L. Geller

In this chapter, I consider decedents in the Samuel G. Morton cranial collection whom the natural historian labeled "Seminole." These 16 individuals, who are represented only by their cranium or cranial fragments, died during the first half of the nineteenth century. I review the circumstances surrounding Morton's possession of these skulls and assess the decedents' marks of violence, both real and symbolic. I then offer a more extended discussion of two individuals who display morphological features that may indicate African ancestry. I recognize that such evidence of ancestry is fairly tenuous and controversial. With this in mind, these data are examined in light of additional information culled from historical and archival sources. There is great imperial arrogance at work in Euro-Americans' copious documentation. Read with a critical eye, however, these materials shed much light on past sociopolitical contexts. Accordingly, an examination of embodied differences can move beyond racialization to more nuanced understandings of ethnic identities and their genesis. Individuals of African ancestry labeled Seminole, for instance, may have something to tell us about Seminole maroons—runaway slaves, free blacks, and black people enslaved by Seminole Indians.

The relevance of Morton's (I use the possessive case ironically) Seminoles to forensic anthropology may not be readily apparent. Shared taphonomic constraints, techniques, and analytical standards aside, this historic case highlights conceptual concerns held in common by bioarchaeologists and forensic anthropologists. Specifically, the investigation of human remains can testify to the conjoining of state formation processes, systematic violence, and racialization of the other. In certain sociopolitical contexts—for instance, when mass killings or other human rights violations occur in modern nation-states—this intertwining is obvious. Researchers' practices then function to remedy social injustice, alleviate suffering, or facilitate repatriation (e.g., Sanford 2003a ; see also contributions in this volume by Fondebrider and Rojas-Perez, chapters 2 and 3, respectively). In the Seminole case, thinking about the past violent acts that engendered Morton's cranial collection is a necessary precursor for legislative redress in the present. To do so, however, may prove unsettling for some practitioners.

Just as problematic as the physical violence that yielded a scientific opportunity for Morton is the symbolic violence produced by his study of cranial capacity. Morton is certainly an unhandsome ancestor for anthropologists. Despite some scholars' reflections on the sins of our father (e.g., Gould 1978, 1981), however, notions born from his scientific racism continue to inform other practitioners' theory and practice. In this regard, forensic anthropology has been the most resistant to race's de-biologization, as evidenced by the ongoing assignment of race (or, more euphemistically, ancestry) into discrete, bounded categories. In defense of this "common-sense" method, some assert that the determination of race is feasible and necessary (e.g., Gill 1998; Sauer 1992, 1993; but see Smay and Armelagos 2000 for a critique of this position). Yet, queer scholar Annamarie Jagose (1996:102) reminds us of common sense's dangers: "It does not follow that those formations of knowledge which coincide with the discourses of common sense manifest some truth beyond analysis."

Racial typologization by forensic anthropologists may oversimplify identity, its (re-, trans-)formation, and contextual shape-shifting. As Walsh-Haney and Boys recognize in the previous chapter of this volume, the forensic identification of unidentified decedents' race or, in their preferred term, ancestry is not straightforward. Hence, distinguishing between etic and emic categorizations, especially in legal contexts, acknowledges that biology can be connected to ancestry, but identification is also often informed by personal conceptions, familial beliefs, and political definitions. The possible presence of Seminole maroons in the Morton collection, while a historical example, underscores this tension between etic and emic categorizations. Depending on the individual and circumstances, a Seminole maroon may have been kin, commodity, or ally in the nineteenth century. Etic imposition then has little to convey about self-identification, discordance between genotype and phenotype, and biological and social hybridization. It does, however, impart subtle messages about the ongoing maintenance of racial or ethnic purity and, accordingly, conjures the specter of white supremacy.

SAMUEL G. MORTON AND ME

The Morton collection has changed hands several times since the natural historian's death on May 15, 1851. In total, Morton acquired 967 skulls during his lifetime; he recorded 867 in *Catalogue of Skulls of Man and the Inferior Animals* (Morton 1849) and received an additional 100 skulls just prior to his death. James Aitken Meigs, an intellectual ally, continued to augment the collection in the years that followed. According to Meigs (1857:3), after Morton's death the collection increased by 67 skulls. In 1853, 42 of Morton's colleagues, who by all written accounts held him in high regard (e.g., C. Meigs 1851; Patterson 1854; Wood 1853), purchased the 1,034 skulls from his widow, Rebecca (née Grellet Pearsall), for the sum of $4,000. They then formally transferred ownership of the crania to the Academy of Natural Sciences of Philadelphia (ANSP).[1] In 1966, the ANSP loaned the collection to the University of Pennsylvania Museum of Archaeology and Anthropology (UPMAA). Over the decades, the collection's meaning has shifted in the anthropological imagination. My experiences with it are perhaps illustrative since Morton's skulls have long held a place in my scholarly pursuits.

As an undergraduate at Penn in the 1990s, my gaze, which should have been focused on the scratching that passed for my lecture notes, would instead meet the empty eye sockets of the crania. Stephen Jay Gould's *The Mismeasure of Man* (1981), published several years earlier, had besmirched the skulls' scientific value. Nevertheless, the collection has continued to arouse scholars' interest (e.g., Fabian 2003, 2010; Lewis et al. 2011; Michael 1988; Renschler 2007; Renschler and Monge 2008; Weisberg 2014). For instance, Lewis and colleagues' (2011) reanalysis of crania in the Morton collection suggests that Morton's data were reliable. Hence, they argue, personal biases held by Gould—not Morton—may have misinformed the former's conclusions.

Occasionally, my professors would pull Morton's specimens from the glass-enclosed cabinets that ran along the perimeter of my classroom. Curios would transform briefly into objects with pedagogical import. In subsequent years, my academic inquiry grew into ambivalence. Early in my graduate studies at Penn, I was hired to inventory Morton's skulls. Congress had passed the Native American Graves Protection and Repatriation Act

(NAGPRA) in 1990, and the university's compliance was necessary. The passage of NAGPRA perhaps hastened ANSP's decision to officially give UPMAA the collection in 1997. The challenges of complying with federal legislation were made readily apparent, as was the conditionality of ownership. Based on a preponderance of the evidence at the time, remains were culturally affiliated when possible. Next, notifications were dutifully sent to federally recognized tribes. Such was the case for the 16 skulls labeled "Seminole," whose contemporary descendants include the Seminole Tribe of Florida, the Miccosukee Tribe of Indians of Florida, and the Seminole Nation of Oklahoma.

In the various courses I teach, discussion of Morton's acquisition of skulls from Indian burial mounds highlights the connection between archaeology's formalization, scientific racism, and colonialism. Accordingly, students learn about shifting professional ethics and the passage of protective legislation like NAGPRA. To extend these lessons, my bioarchaeological study of the Morton collection has sought to verify the presence of individuals whose lives were contoured by interpersonal and structural violence. I see such positive identification as paralleling forensic anthropologists' work in contemporary legal contexts (in this volume, see Fondebrider, Thompson, Tuller, and Walsh-Haney and Boys). NAGPRA, after all, is human rights legislation enacted to address the effects of abuses perpetrated historically against Native Americans. Yet my work—which involves study of the collection's cranial remains, pertinent historical sources, and archival documents—has also revealed past misidentifications, specifically with regard to racial categorizations. Black Indians in the Morton collection, as I discuss below, require us to deliberate about scientific representation, racism, and race relations between all Americans, whether Native, colonizing, or forcibly relocated to the continent. My historical perspective sketches out the construction, not the inevitability or timelessness, of forensic anthropology's scientific methods and politico-legal frames.

SKULL COLLECTORS

Crania collecting in eighteenth- and nineteenth-century America was not undertaken in secret nor regarded as shameful, though it seems to have bordered on the gruesome (Fabian 2003, 2010). Morton was one of the more voracious and esteemed seekers of skulls. The gaps in his teaching collection catalyzed his efforts (Renschler and Monge 2008). His *Catalogue of Skulls of Man and the Inferior Animals* begins: "I commenced the study of Ethnology in 1830; in which year, having occasion to deliver an introductory lecture on Anatomy, it occurred to me to illustrate the difference in the form of the skull as seen in the five great races of men" (1849:iii). To this end, Morton made many solicitations from the comforts of his writing desk, which were answered by the slave-owning planter, amateur paleontologist, US Army surgeon, and others.

Political events would prove serendipitous for Morton and his associates. On May 28, 1830, President Andrew Jackson signed the Indian Removal Act. Though it did not have strong support, as evidenced by the small margin of 102 yeas to 97 nays with which it passed in the House of Representatives (Perdue and Green 2001:89–90), the act had dramatic repercussions. The law legitimized land seizure by the US government, admittedly at a steep cost in life and fiscal stability. Under the guise of paternalism, Jackson's "solution" set in motion violent clashes between US troops, frontier settlers, and American Indians. Nation building during colonial expansion involved the appropriation of land, resources, and the physical remains of the vanquished. Postcolonial reflections expose the often glossed-over and insidious nature of procurement.

On April 4, 1867, the federal government officially sanctioned the collecting of crania. As noted in Circular No. 2, US surgeon general Joseph K. Barnes "called on military medical officers to collect crania together with specimens of Indian weapons, dress, implements, diet, and medicines" (1867–1868:167). The fruits of these labors were originally housed at what was then called the US Army Medical Museum,[2] and Natives' body parts were not the only ones sampled. From May 1862 onward, US Army surgeons had been charged with collecting "specimens of morbid anatomy, both medical and surgical" from white soldiers and citizens. Investigation of these remains was intended to improve "the health and well being of the nation's military, and ultimately its civilian population" (Stone 2011:3). Yet, even prior to these formalized efforts, collecting occurred with frequency. Wherever the US Army roamed from the early 1800s onward, graves of both the ancient and the newly deceased were reopened and plundered. Peters (1997), for instance, describes Zina Pitcher and Henry Schoolcraft's activities in Michigan. The former was a US Army surgeon, while the latter was the US Indian agent appointed to the Lake Superior Chippewas (Ojibwes); Pitcher collected skulls, which he later sent to Morton, as early as 1825.

The Native bodies strewn across battlefields were routinely relieved of their heads by US soldiers. Decedents' fragmented parts were then transported far from their ancestral lands and final resting places, a marked contrast to the care afforded many slain US soldiers. Morton's scientific study of "racial" differences facilitated the identification and constitution of the nation's internal enemies and legitimized their violent conquest.

Unequivocally, he found opportunity in American Indians' epidemiological catastrophes, military defeats, and forced migrations. The Natives of Florida, particularly those who lived and died during the time of the Second Seminole War (1835–1842), provide a particularly tragic example.

An abbreviated history of Seminoles residing in colonial Florida follows. I have drawn from other scholars' accounts, which offer far greater detail about the events preceding the Second Seminole War (e.g., Baptist 2002; Covington 1993; Garbarino 1989; Lancaster 1994; Missall and Missall 2004; Mulroy 2007; Perdue and Green 2001; K. Porter 1996; Sturtevant and Cattelino 2004; Weisman 1989, 1999); additional information beyond the narratives of Euro-American writers can be found on the Seminole Tribe of Florida's website (http://www.semtribe.com/History).

According to Sturtevant and Cattelino (2004:429), Seminole ethnogenesis occurred at the start of the eighteenth century when a distinct identity crystallized for Creek bands that had moved into northern Florida. These peoples were collectively referred to as *simaló·ni* and later *simanó·li*, the Creek (or Muskogee) word for "wild, non-domesticated (plants and animals)" (Sturtevant and Cattelino 2004:431). Other scholars identify the term "Seminole" as a corruption of the Spanish word *cimarrón*, meaning "wild one" or "runaway" (Missall and Missall 2004:7; Perdue and Green 2001:92). Coexisting under the designator's larger umbrella were diverse groups with varied political agendas. In common though, Seminoles took issue with the increasing US presence in the Florida frontier. Destructive and deadly clashes occurred from 1812 onward, as did Seminole migration to Florida's eastern and southern regions. The 1823 Treaty of Moultrie Creek, which created a land-bound reservation roughly 4 million acres in size, offered a temporary solution for its 32 begrudging signatories. But, if anything, the treaty highlighted growing divisions among the Seminoles. Rather than being viewed as a collective, the members were identified in official verbiage as the "Florida tribes of Indians" (Missall and Missall 2004:66). The expansionist policies of the United States soon resulted in broken promises and intimations of westward migration. Subsequent treaties negotiated with some Seminole leaders, especially the 1832 Treaty of Payne's Landing, which voided all Seminole land claims, worked to realize the aims of the Indian Removal Act. Those Seminole groups that relocated prior to 1836 did so to avoid further violent confrontation with the US Army. For the remaining groups, fierce resistance to removal was the only option. These events preceded and provided the backdrop for Morton's acquisition of "Seminole" skulls.

Of the 16 Seminole skulls in Morton's collection, 7 have been identified as warriors. Such identities, coupled with the physical marks of interpersonal violence, indicate that many met their ends during the Second Seminole War's numerous conflicts. The circumstances surrounding Morton's possession of the cranium labeled 97-606-604 are detailed in *Crania Americana* (1839:166–167):

> This remarkably characteristic Indian head was presented to me by my friend Dr. G. Emerson of this city, who at the same time favored me with the following historical memorandum. "Seminole warrior, slain at the battle of St. Joseph's, thirty miles below St. Augustine, in June 1836, by Captain Justin Dimmick [*sic*], of the First Regiment United States Artillery. At the commencement of the action Captain Dimmick rode forward, and received the fire of the Indians at a distance of about thirty yards. The Captain's horse being struck on the neck and flank, he dismounted; and the Indians, supposing him to be badly wounded rushed towards him to scalp him. At that moment Captain D. raised his gun, (a double-barrel fowling piece,) and shot both of the Indians in succession: he then seized the musket of a soldier who stood near him, and sprang upon his enemies, one of whom (the subject of the annexed drawing) he found already dead, by a ball through the head."

Forensic analysis of the skull confirms the violence described in Dimick's report. The shot's entry is clearly visible on the individual's left parietal and its larger exit hole appears on the right one. In a different account of the event, secondhand though it may be, US Army assistant surgeon Jacob Rhett Motte confirmed Dimick's use of a double-barreled fowling piece (1953:115). The size and shape of the entry and exit points are consistent with the spherical lead shots of fowling pieces. It is also possible, however, that Captain Dimick used a musket to kill the man numbered as 97-606-604; this weapon was ubiquitous during the time of the Second Seminole War.

The type of weapon used is not simply a matter of trivia, but rather conveys important sociohistorical information. During the first half of the nineteenth century, fowling pieces were deployed to quell insurgents. In the 1831 revolt led by Nat Turner, for instance, both blacks resisting enslavement and slave-owning whites used fowling pieces (Aptheker 2003:56). Double-barreled weapons like fowling pieces were also, of course, frequently used to hunt small game (Needham 1817:163–178). As a consequence, they were generally regarded as weapons of sport rather than military armament. Congressman William Montgomery of North Carolina said as much to the House of Representatives in January 1839. He was particularly critical of the escalating costs associated with the Second Seminole War, given the US Army's repeated failures to secure Florida. Officers, he railed, had grown accustomed to life's luxuries and civilities, which robbed them of their ability to fight and command. A request from Major General Thomas S. Jesup, commander of the US Army, dated December 12, 1836, for "double barrelled guns" was regarded as evidence of such weakness and was met with indignation. These guns, in the estimation of Montgomery, would allow the capture of bloodthirsty Seminoles, but certainly not their eradication. "Are these the kind of officers that we are to send a large army of men under...to defend our frontier inhabitants against the Seminole warrior, with his unerring rifle and his bloody scalping knife and tomahawk" (Montgomery 1839:269). Montgomery's demonization and dehumanization of Seminoles, while not a unanimous view, was representative of many in powerful positions who enacted legislative policies. Morton's skull collecting, with its corporeal fragmentation and purported scientific neutrality, helped hasten the transformation of Seminoles from immediate threat to historic footnote.

THE SURGEON: EUGENE HILARIAN ABADIE

Emerson's procurement of the skull numbered 97-606-604, by way of Captain Dimick, draws attention to the varied individuals Morton called on for assistance. The most proficient supplier of Seminole skulls was Eugene Hilarian Abadie. Abadie was born in Millau, France, on August 16, 1810. On September 1, 1818, he and his father, Hilarian, arrived in the United States aboard the *Eagle* (Tepper 1986:1). His two older brothers and two sisters would later disembark from the same ship on June 18, 1819 (Tepper 1986:1). The circumstances for the family's relocation are unknown. It may have been that Napoleon's nation building made for politically turbulent times in France, especially for those families with aristocratic roots, like the Abadies (Pittman 1903:xiii). Regardless, his immigrant's tale reads like a success story in contrast to the tragedy that unfolded for those migrating along the Trail of Tears. Philadelphia became the Abadie family's new home. Eugene enrolled in the University of Pennsylvania's Medical School and graduated with an MD in March 1833 (Lippincott 1919:500). Penn most likely was the setting for his introduction to Morton, a fellow alumnus (Class of 1820) and an active member of the Philadelphia scientific community.

In the summer of 1836, Abadie was appointed as an assistant surgeon in the US Army. So began his long active military service, which, according to his obituary in the *New York Tribune,* "was exceeded only by that of two other officers in the Medical Department" (Anonymous 1874). As his first military appointment, Abadie served as "Surgeon to Emigrating Indians" during the Creek Confederacy's forced migration westward. Abadie's colleague Jacob Motte placed him in Sparta, Georgia, around June 5, 1836: "On reporting myself the next morning to Major Lomax, I ascertained that Dr. Abadie who was despatched [*sic*] from Columbus by Gen. Scott for the purpose, had joined the day previous, and that it would be unnecessary for me to remain with them, when my services may be more needed with other troops" (Motte 1953:2). Abadie's military reports during this time recount the afflictions and fatalities of the Native people as a consequence of fevers, diarrhea, and dysentery (Gillett 1987:54–55).

By December 1837, Abadie was stationed in Florida. He remained there until July 1839. The heaviest fighting of the Second Seminole War occurred during this stretch of time (Bemrose 1966; Mahon 1967; Potter 1836; Sprague 1964). Abadie's correspondence with Morton offers intriguing information about the campaign waged against Seminole groups that resisted migration to Indian Territory. In a letter to Morton on February 3, 1838, Abadie identified his position as the medical director for the Fourth and Sixth Infantries. He also described the various strategies used to collect skulls. In total, Abadie sent Morton nine Seminole skulls. In some instances, he disinterred the recently deceased. Such seems to be the case for the children's skulls recorded as 97-606-728 and 97-606-729, aged three to five and five to nine years old at the time of death, respectively. Support for exhumation is suggested by the detailed information he provided about Seminole graves and their associated goods:

> You no doubt are aware of the manner in which the Seminoles bury their dead, they form 1st on the surface of the ground, a flooring of logs upon which is laid the body enveloped in cow hide with all its trinkets and weapons if a male, also some provisions to carry them, as they believe it, to the end of their journey: they then build around the body a pen dove-tailed at the 4 angles 3 feet high with a roof of logs and raw hides: if the dead had rank they take much pains in the construction of this pen often digging a ditch around it throwing the dirt so as to incline from a level with the flooring. (Abadie 1838)

The absence of any remaining Seminoles in the Tampa area would have made scrutiny of the building materials and stratigraphic levels all the easier. As Abadie (1838) noted, the child's cranium that he collected in the fall of 1837, which Morton later labeled 97-606-729, belonged to the group led by Black Dirt, or Foke Luste Hajo. Morton inked the latter's name across the young decedent's forehead in lettering that has grown faint over the years. Black Dirt led an Alachua band and was one of several leaders who advocated for relocation west of the Mississippi (Covington 1993:61). He and six others had planned to assess the government-allotted lands in October 1832. At the last minute, however, Black Dirt refrained from traveling to Indian Territory (Mahon 1967:79). Site unseen, his band migrated west in 1836. Many perished on the journey, including the Seminole leader's wife and daughter (Lancaster 1994:21). The survivors arrived in Little Rock, Arkansas, on May 5, 1836, and settled near Little River (20, 25). This account reveals an important aspect of relocation. While the early wave of Seminoles appears to have migrated voluntarily, poverty, starvation, racism, and threats of interpersonal violence placed profound constraints on their choices. The untimely deaths of the individuals labeled 97-606-728 and 97-606-729—lives cut short in childhood—and the pathological markers they bear point to malnourishment, chronic infections, and substandard living conditions (Walker et al. 2009). Specifically, slight cribra orbitalia appear active in both the orbital roofs of the older child (97-606-729), and there is porosity around the external auditory meatus's entrance. The younger child (97-606-728) also displays slight cribra orbitalia in the left orbital roof.

In the opinion of the US government, not all Seminoles were as accommodating as Black Dirt and his followers when it came to relocation. Active resistance strengthened alliances between Seminole Indians and Seminole maroons (Micco 2006:122). One of the Second Seminole War's major battles was fought along Lake Okeechobee's northeastern shore on December 25, 1837 (Missall and Missall 2004:142). That morning, Lieutenant Robert Buchanan wrote in his journal: "A Merry Christmas to all of my friends at home, and may they have many happy returns of the season!! Mine I am inclined to think will be more lively, but not so pleasant as theirs." Fighting lasted two and a half hours and ranged over a mile (Carr et al. 1989:209). In total, 25 US soldiers were slain and 111 wounded (Buchanan 1950:148). A month later, Abadie and troops encountered their remains "scattered and bleaching in the sun" (Abadie 1838). They transported the decedents from the battlefield to Colonel Zachary Taylor's camp, where the bodies were placed in graves, later disinterred, and then reinterred at Jefferson Barracks, Missouri (Carr et al. 1989:210). In more recent investigations, archaeologists successfully documented the location of Taylor's camp, but were unable to detect the soldiers' mass grave (Carr et al. 1989).

Such careful mortuary attention contrasts with the treatment of the 12 Seminole warriors who died that day. Mortuary rituals went unperformed and bodies were not buried, providing particularly ripe hunting grounds for skull collection. When he arrived in January 1838, Abadie (1838) sent Morton two of the least "offensive" of these warriors' skulls (97-606-730 and 97-606-732). One (97-606-730) displays no ante- or perimortem trauma, suggesting that a fatal mark was left in the postcranial area. Conversely, the other (97-606-732), a male 35–50 years old at the time of death, displays an unhealed crescent-shaped fracture located centrally on the frontal bone. This individual's left zygomatic and maxillary bones also appear to have been shaved as if a very sharp blade had sliced into the front of the face at a parallel and not perpendicular angle.

EOKLO-EMATHLA

What has struck me as I conduct research on Morton's collection is the great quantity of information I have uncovered about the Euro-American men who procured specimens for him. Biographical documentation on Abadie's family, for example, extends from the present back to a noble heritage in sixteenth-century France (Lippincott 1919; Pittman 1903; Virkus 1925). In contrast, historical sources whisper softly on Seminoles' life stories. Such is the case for the skull numbered 97-606-707. As Morton related in *Crania Americana*, this decedent was a "Seminole warrior, of whose history nothing is known," save his provenience as "12 miles south of the 'Sewannee' River" (1839:168). My examination of the skull offers confirmation. Small and faded lettering, likely penned by Abadie, appears across the right parietal. Indeed, this and other handwritten notations stress the expediency of conceptualizing human remains as yet another type of historic document—the body as text. For my analysis, such a strategy has proved rewarding. Arched across the decedent's frontal bone, Morton inked the word EOKLO-EMATHLA in bold capitals.

Emathla, according to Wickman (2006:46), has several variants—Homarty, *emathlî*, Emarthla, Emarthi, Emarthlee. The term, she explains, was a Maskókî honorific, a "man's civic title," which was translated as a surname by English-speakers. There are many Emathlas discussed in historic texts, the best known being Charley Emathla, a Seminole chief who supported emigration to Indian Territory; in November 1835, Osceola had him executed for this traitorous position (Missall and Missall 2004:92). Research turned up several Emathlas whose names sound phonetically similar to Eoklo, but none seem a likely candidate for the cranium. The Seminole chief Nea-thlocko-Emathla had cooperated with Zachary Taylor (who had been promoted to general), and a May 3, 1839, letter reveals that he was very much alive around the time of *Crania Americana*'s publication (Anonymous 1839:330). Similarly, Echo Emathla, who was originally from the Tallahassee area, had relocated to Indian Territory by the 1840s (Lancaster 1994:58). Histories also contain mention of Oclo Archo-Emathla, a Creek warrior (Drake 1854:436). It is possible that Abadie misidentified Eoklo-Emathla as Seminole. But, given his position as "Surgeon to Emigrating Indians" during the Creek migration, it seems unlikely he would confuse the two cultures.

Skeletal analysis using standards established in Buikstra and Ubelaker (1994) allows for additional inferences about this person's identity. Cranial features, which admittedly are less than ideal when assigning sex, indicate that the decedent was a male who died between 20 and 30 years of age. With regard to sex determination, Eoklo-Emathla's skull is large overall but lightly muscled. Typical male traits include rounded orbital rims, pronounced mastoid processes, zygomatic processes that extend as crests past external auditory meatuses, and a square mandible. More intermediary traits are a moderate nuchal ridge area and supraorbital ridges. Age is indicated by the lack of ecto- or endocranial suture fusion. Additionally, the right and left maxillary third molars have erupted but have no wear, while minimal wear appears on the first and second molars that are present.

Perhaps more intriguing are Eoklo-Emathla's morphological features, which suggest African ancestry. According to Bass's (2005:86–92) standards for the estimation of race, Eoklo-Emathla displays nasal guttering and no nasal sill. Additionally, his facial profile has mild to moderate alveolar prognathism and retreating zygomatic arches. These traits are deemed "Negroid" in Bass's antiquated lingo. Eoklo-Emathla's morphological features are not singular in Morton's collection. The skull of a second individual (97-606-698) also displays moderate alveolar prognathism and retreating zygomatic arches, as well as a slight postbregmatic depression and a pinched nuchal ridge profile. The nasal area, however, displays a double sill and no guttering, which Bass would qualify as "Caucasoid." The latter attribute may be related to fenestrations in the alveolar area, the causes of which are not clear (Janet Monge, pers. comm., 2011).

Similar to Eoklo-Emathla, this second individual, who was 30–40 years of age at the time of death, was also identified as a male warrior (Morton 1849:87). Colonel John James Abert, a topographical engineer for the US government, acquired this decedent's cranium for Morton while marking boundary lines between the Creek and Seminole Confederacies. While Abert might not have engaged in battle, his travels during the 1820s and 1830s would have ranged throughout Florida. Unfortunately, his terse correspondence with Morton provides no additional information about the cranium's provenience or identity. In support of his identification as a Seminole (or possibly Creek) warrior, however, cranial trauma indicates that the individual numbered 97-606-698 died as a result of violent conflict. On the left side of his occipital is a circular and discrete entry wound; it measures 1.82 centimeters in diameter, which is about the size of a musket ball. There is no exit hole, but the shot's internal impact produced a crack that runs the length of the left temporal, sphenoid, and frontal bones.

While "eyeballing" a decedent's ancestry may be a common method of identification for forensic anthropologists, Walsh-Haney and Boys (chapter 7, this volume) recognize that analysts' subjectivity makes it an inherently unreliable one. Therefore, to confirm etic categorizations of ancestry, I have also collected craniometric data based on Howells's (1973, 1989) descriptions of landmark points and measurements. Granted, craniometric study is controversial because Morton's development of it advanced racist agendas. Yet, I do not see a craniometric study as a route to an investigative dead end. At the writing of this chapter, I am in the process of completing my analysis using FORDISC (Ousley and Jantz 2005) and CRANID (Wright 1992). These computer programs estimate ancestry through the discriminant function analysis of standard cranial measurements—29 and 36 required numbers, respectively. Do Eoklo-Emathla and his compatriot 97-606-698, or any "Seminole" decedents for that matter, resemble samples in the FORDISC and CRANID reference databases from sub-Saharan Africa? Confirmation that the Morton collection contains decedents of African ancestry whom collectors initially labeled Seminole Indian should raise questions about a strident commitment to etic categorization, as well as reinforce the need to think about emic identification and hybrid identities, like Black Indians. That is, the use of computer programs like FORDISC and CRANID can offer no definitive assessment of ancestry. Contextualization in place and time is essential, as the complexities of both "black" (or "African") and "Seminole" identities underscore.

SEMINOLE MAROONS

Morton regarded Black Indians with incredulity. In *Crania Americana*, he mentions three "Negroid Indians" among other hyphenated categories (e.g., "Hispano-Peruvians"), "mulattoes," and "mixed races" (Morton 1839). Of one "Negroid Indian," Morton (1839:101) wrote, "Dr. Wilson, who dissected this man, considered him a full-blooded Choctaw, but the skull strongly indicates a mixture of the Negro." The other two individuals in this category included a man identified as "Venezuela Indian and Negro" and a person of African ancestry but undesignated tribal affiliation (i.e., "Indian?") (Morton 1839:101). Clearly, the natural historian was not ignorant of hybrid identities (Morton 1847), but his understanding was shaped by polygenist theories (Gould 1978:503) and sociohistorically bound beliefs about sexuality. Miscegenation, he suggested, may decrease a pure race's fertility rate (Morton 1851).

Anthropologists and historians have begun to tell the stories of Black Indians (e.g., Brooks 2002; Dixon 2007; Katz 1986, 1987; Littlefield 1977; Miles and Holland eds. 2006; Mulroy 2007; TallBear 2003). Their marginalization by and interactions with other Americans (Native and Euro-), scholars note, have been and continue to be complicated. Historical texts, however, cannot quite capture the interpersonal violence and virulent racism that framed these individuals' everyday existence. Though blacks and American Indians tread common ground—shared experiences of forced relocations, military alliances during the United States' nation building—the former's autonomy long remained uncertain.

For individuals of African ancestry who interacted with Seminole communities, there have been multiple referents: Black Seminoles, Seminole Blacks, Seminole Negroes, Seminole Freedmen, freedmans, Afro-Seminoles, Black Muscogulges, and *estelusti*.[3] These designations hint at the dynamism and complexity of identity, whether self-selected or imposed by others. The use of Seminole maroon, for instance, highlights the ethnic group's simultaneous distinctiveness from and relatedness to Seminole Indians (Mulroy 2007), as well as relations that are historically complicated.

Starting in the eighteenth century, Spanish Florida and its sheltering swamps offered a refuge to Africans freed from slavery or escaping from being enslaved. Prior to 1822, when it officially became a US territory, Florida held the promise of emancipation (Missall and Missall 2004:10). Life in colonial Florida—with its mix of European, Native, and African peoples, most of whom were from the Kongo-Angola region (Bateman 2002)—also engendered some strange bedfellows, literally and figuratively (Stojanowski 2005:47–50). Relations between blacks and American Indians were multifaceted (Katz 1987:16–22; Missall and Missall 2004:11; Mulroy 2007:xxvi). Some individuals were brought into the fold of Seminole Indian bands through marriage or adoption (Mulroy 2007:30, 233). Some maroons formed independent communities and acted as tributary allies. Resistance to the US government's land claims, relocation policies, and violent incursions also made for strong military alliances between blacks and Seminole Indians. Indeed, during the Seminole wars, 15 percent of all warriors were black (K. Porter 1996:28). Native and black warriors fought and died together, as many chroniclers remarked. Motte, for instance, offered a firsthand account of the Second Seminole War's Battle of Lake Okeechobee: "The number of Indians engaged were estimated from two to three hundred warriors and there were with them probably as many negroes" (1953:195). Given similar accounts, and by simple mathematics, it is highly likely that at least one of the seven Seminole warriors acquired by Morton would be wholly or partly African in ancestry.

The child whom Abadie collected near Tampa (97-606-728) invites us to think about these entangled and shifting social identities and relations. In a letter to Morton on February 3, 1838, Abadie described the child as having belonged "to the party of Seminoles headed by John Cavallo or Cow-a-gee." The lives of these two individuals, a Seminole maroon and a Seminole Indian, respectively, would become intricately intertwined as a consequence of the Second Seminole War. John Cavallo's mother was black and his father—who may or may not have been her owner, Charles Cavallo (or Imotley)—was Seminole (Dixon 2007:151). Mulroy (2005) suggests that John Cavallo's parents also had hybrid identities. His mother may have been African and Native, and his father native and Spanish. While his identity as a hybrid, or "half-breed" (Buchanan 1950:145), is known, Cavallo's actual name remains in question. Historic chroniclers identify him as Cohia, John Cowaya, John Ca-wai-yie, John Horse, Juan Caballo, Pease Creek John, and Gopher John, among others (Dixon 2007:151–154; Mulroy 2005; Wickman 2006:25, 103). After Charles Cavallo's death, John Cavallo's ownership was transferred to a collective of Seminole leaders. Despite his enslavement, John Cavallo managed to acquire wealth of his own. Prior to the Second Seminole War (ca. 1826), Cavallo was living in a village on Thonotosassa Lake, 12 miles from Fort Brook (Mulroy 2005:271). This location places him in the vicinity of Abadie's later treks. It also situates him at the midpoint of two salient proveniences—Pease Creek and the Oklawaha (or Ocklawaha) River. Abadie identified the former as the collection site for the younger child (97-606-728) in his February 3, 1838, letter to Morton: "On reaching Pease Creek Nov. the 20th [1837] with the 4th and 6th Reg. Infy—to which I was Med. Director, I obtained the skull of another boy belonging to the party of Seminoles headed by John Cavallo or Cow-a-gee." Handwritten across the skull's left frontal and parietal is "Peas Creek." The Oklawaha River might have been geographically connected to the band of maroons that John Cavallo headed, the Oklawaha maroons. He was joined in this endeavor by Kowakochi (Wild Cat, Cowacoochee, or Coacoochee), a Seminole Indian who was the leader of a second Oklawaha band (Mulroy 2007:35–36). Abadie likely phoneticized the latter's name as Cow-a-gee.

Cavallo and Kowakochi fiercely defied the US military during the

Second Seminole War. Both men led groups into battle at Lake Okeechobee. In defeat, they begrudgingly emigrated (Lancaster 1994:37, 84). After his relocation to Indian Territory, Cavallo was emancipated in 1842, his reward for financing the relocation. Kowakochi would later vouch for his freed status when the proper papers could not be located (Mulroy 2007:70). The continued threat of reenslavement is one reason Cavallo led a group of Seminole maroons to Mexico. In 1849, he migrated south, joined by Kowakochi and his band (Sattler 2004:452). Given the bond between John Cavallo and Kowakochi, it is understandable that Abadie would be uncertain about the identity and geographical specifics of the skull labeled 97-606-728. Certainly, the turmoil of the years leading up to and during the Second Seminole War required Seminole Indians and maroons to adopt mobile and intertwined existences.

Cavallo's biography illustrates not only the close relations that developed between some blacks and Natives, but also Seminole Indians' intriguing and distinctive take on enslavement. Mulroy (2007:5–7) contends that slavery changed for the Seminoles once they began enslaving runaway blacks rather than other Natives at the end of the eighteenth century. Prior to this juncture, the Seminoles "associated servitude with capture in warfare," which in time became "associated with prestige, property ownership, and increasingly profit" (Mulroy 2007:7). Yet Seminoles' enslavement of blacks contrasted markedly with its practice by Euro-Americans and neighboring tribes, like the Creek Confederacy. In 1822, William Haynes Simmons, a physician and an explorer of the Florida peninsula, commented, "Another trait in their character, is their great indulgence to their slaves. Though hunger and want be stronger than even the *sacra fumes auri*, the greatest pressure of these evils, never occasions them to impose onerous labours on the Negroes, or to dispose of them, though tempted by high offers, if the latter are unwilling to be sold" (1822:50). No matter how "indulgent" it might have been, this remained slavery. Yet there was a perverse benefit to being the slave of a Seminole Indian. Freed Seminole maroons, as Missall and Missall (2004:11) point out, ran the risk of recapture by slave hunters and renewed bondage.

Seminole and black relations have long been an issue for the US government. The Treaty of Moultrie Creek, for instance, required Seminole Indians to apprehend and return enslaved people seeking refuge in Florida (Missall and Missall 2004:65). They were, however, reluctant to do so. The US government continued to insist, and the issue became quite contentious when relocation to Indian Territory was set in motion. The removal of Seminole Indians was hindered by their refusal to forsake their black allies, who ran the risk of reenslavement by Euro-Americans and Creeks (Missall and Missall 2004:83). General Jesup assessed the situation in a letter to Congress dated December 9, 1836: "This, you may be assured, is a negro, not an Indian war; and if it be not speedily put down, the South will feel the effects of it on their slave population before the end of the next season" (cited in Montgomery 1839:269). Jesup would go on to broker various treaties, starting in March 1837 with the Camp Dade Accord, in support of the westward migration of maroons with Seminole Indians (Mulroy 2007:46–50). The consequences of Jesup's contradictions in these accords—blacks removed to Indian Territory were both "bona fide property" and emancipated—are apparent in descendants' contentious relations.

PRESENT-DAY POLITICS

In 2000, the Seminole Nation of Oklahoma disenrolled its Seminole maroon members. Despite the controversy this action engendered (Micco 2006), other American Indian tribes have increasingly followed suit. Many would agree that the consequences of rescinding the memberships of Black Indians are negative socioeconomically and psychologically (Dao 2011). Disenrollment also raises an ethical quandary for those involved in the repatriation of human remains.

Born of low politics and high emotions about human rights, NAGPRA is now 25 years past its inception. We need to recognize the repatriation process as dynamic and begin to address its identifiable shortcomings, like those surrounding the identification and treatment of mixed-race individuals in historical collections. In the case of crania in the Morton collection labeled "Seminole," for example, the Seminole Tribe of Florida, the Miccosukee Tribe of Indians of Florida, and the Seminole Nation of Oklahoma are all legally entitled to the human remains. And in the fall of 2013, the Seminole Tribe of Florida did submit a repatriation claim. But such repatriation is not straightforward, given tribal politics in the twenty-first century. Moreover, institutions receiving federal funds are only obligated to consult with or repatriate to federally recognized tribes in the United States. Consequently, contemporary Seminole maroon communities, which are currently located in Oklahoma, Texas, Mexico, and the Bahamas (Mock 2010), have no official recourse to repatriate decedents identified as their ancestors.

The basis for disenrollment or, conversely, cultural affiliation should also raise concerns for Native and scholar alike. Analyses of blood and DNA, as Kimberly TallBear (2003:95–98) has noted, have come to trump shared history. Innovative practices, however, do not make for transgressive beliefs. Rather, the preponderance of biological evidence simply replicates hoary scientific logic about classifying "racial" differences. That is, the biologization of race resurrects the scientific racism emergent with Linnaean classification and advanced with Mortonian craniometrics. Native communities run the risk of assimilating those notions, which have historically contributed to their denigration and oppression.

The intent of TallBear's (2003) rejoinder is not to deny that observable biological differences between populations exist and track back to environmental adaptations. But the slope is slippery, as forensic anthropologists in particular have learned. Historically, the forensic analysis of race has utilized the good "commonsense" method (e.g., Gill 1998; Sauer 1992, 1993). Were you to pass an individual on the street, what race would you assign to her? Yet, such logic tells us far more about a priori assumptions and little about identity's self-selection or community significance. With this awareness, Ubelaker (2008:53) has stressed that "forensic analysis also requires broader anthropological interpretation of how an individual with certain skeletal characteristics likely would be regarded (social classification or 'ethnic' identity) by the community in which he or she lived." Such a statement seems to recognize that people from mixed-race backgrounds complicate etic classification and typologization. But in the case of Seminole maroons, where the history is complex, the ethnic designator muddled and mutable, and the contemporary politics contentious, how does one proceed?

Awareness of ambiguity is a viable starting place, as some forensic anthropologists acknowledge. But at best, and collectively, they remain an ambivalent group. Some suggest that race is ambiguous because researchers do a poor job of defining it up front. Ousley and colleagues (2009), for example, contend that qualifying race as either "social race" or "biological race" is sufficient. But, ultimately, they conclude that "a concordance [exists] between social race and cranial morphology, at least in 20th century American blacks and whites," which is attributed to "very low historic gene flow between them in the US" (Ousley et al. 2009:73, 74). For these researchers, the issue is how language structures our thinking about human differences, rather than how context frames human interactions. Others allow for biological admixing. For instance, Alice Brues (1990:6) attributes the racial ambiguity of certain "Negroes" in the Hamann-Todd collection to "appreciable White admixture." Such ambiguity, however, offers no complication to social identity. She still regards these "Negroes" in the Hamann-Todd collection as black, not biracial. The one-drop rule rules. In general, difference remains coded in the language of dichotomy (i.e., black-white), and social interactions—lived experiences, "passing," interracial relationships, illicit assignations, transgressive acts—remain unpondered. I would be interested in hearing these forensic anthropologists' thoughts about structural racism, erotic coupling, and the intertwining of lives that occurred for three centuries in colonial Florida. How would they explain the Seminole maroon "race"?

To bring ambiguity and interaction to the fore, there is a lesson to take from queering the skeletal analysis of sex (Geller 2005, 2008). Like race, the assignment of sex has typically proceeded from an etic (i.e., contemporary Western) understanding of difference as dichotomous: male-female. Though etic categorization exists on a continuum, assignment is predicated upon an analyst's degree of certainty. Physical ambiguity is still unsettling; categories are not regarded as arbitrary but as bounded and static throughout a life course; and the social context that structures interactions is seen as tangential. As a result, inferences drawn about gender are biologically deterministic. As I have pointed out, for anthropological practitioners who purport to grapple with human variability and life course changes, the contradictions are glaring. To address the messiness of life, it is advantageous to contextualize biological data in physical space, historical framework, and sociocultural system. This endeavor is facilitated by an interdisciplinary approach that pulls from pertinent historical sources and associated material conditions. As the above discussion on Seminole maroons has also stressed, such contextualization is similarly advantageous when thinking about race. The emphasis shifts from typology and description to far more humanized emic narrations about individuals' lives, hybridity, ethnogenesis, and the colonial processes connected to nation building.

Admittedly, reconciling a theoretical bent that attends to identities that are ambiguous, fluid, and hybrid with biological data gleaned from skeletal analysis is no easy task, whether analysis focuses on sex or on race/ethnicity/ancestry. And the contemporary identity politics that play out on national stages highlight the sensitive and emotional nature of such work. The task before us is a difficult one. We are poised to move beyond race's biologization to the equally important project of deracializing biology.

CONCLUSIONS

We would be remiss to think of the Samuel G. Morton cranial collection as an archaism of the discipline. The events associated with its assemblage, the scholarship engendered by its study, and the social actions justified by that scholarship are both upsetting and critical to recall. Racism creates and maintains race; it has done so in the past, and it does so in the present. During nineteenth-century nation building, the scientific study of race legitimized state-sanctioned violence against marginalized and indigenous communities. Such physical violence certainly plagues our modern world, as forensic anthropologists' exhumation of mass graves and investigation of human rights violations in varied international locations attest. The bodies of the vanquished and violated will always be a powerful source of evidence that allows us to speak truth to power. Whether power chooses to listen is another matter.

Acknowledging the sustained research potential of the skulls collected by Morton should not be read as an apology. To chalk the natural historian's work up to historical relativity denigrates the concerns expressed by the contemporary descendants whose ancestors comprise the collection. In this regard, Morton's story communicates something about the symbolic violence that scientific inquiry may engender. Though consequences may be unintended, to what degree does racism continue to undergird work conducted on embodied human differences? As Michelle Alexander (2010) has pointed out, virulent racism—both subtle and not so subtle—exists in the ongoing maintenance of US national interests, contoured not by colonialism but by late capitalism in the twenty-first century. Do certain types of genetic or neuroscientific study, those that purport to examine "the biology of culpability" (Rose 2000), justify the disproportionate incarceration in the United States of men of color? If so, the commencement of biology's deracialization should be a disciplinary imperative.

Acknowledgments

I am grateful to Zoë Crossland and Rosemary Joyce for their invitation to participate in the SAR advanced seminar that yielded this edited volume. It has been a pleasure to collaborate with all involved, especially Isaias Rojas-Perez, who provided exceptional feedback on an earlier draft of this chapter. My thanks also to Stacey Espenlaub and Janet Monge of the University of Pennsylvania Museum of Archaeology and Anthropology for their generosity with time and information. Final credit goes to James Brooks and everyone at SAR for providing support and access to a little piece of heaven on earth.

Notes

1. This institution is now known as the Academy of Natural Sciences of Drexel University.

2. Today the collection is located at the National Museum of Health and Medicine of the Armed Forces Institute of Pathology.

3. In Muskogee, *estelusti* means "black man" (Micco 2006:143). An alternative spelling in Creek is *isti-lásti* (Mulroy 2007:xxiii–xxiv).

9

Excavating for Truths

Forensic Anthropology and Bioarchaeology as Ways of Making Meaning from Skeletal Evidence

Debra L. Martin

In AD 1280, in the dark of night, a small farming village sitting high on a fairly isolated mesa in southwest Colorado was ambushed. More than 700 years later, a team of archaeologists would begin to unravel what happened on that night with the gruesome discovery that at least 41 infants, children, teenagers, men, and women were brutally murdered (Kuckelman et al. 2002). The ambush was an act of great violence, since the people were not only killed but also culturally eradicated. Some of the bodies were dismembered and defleshed; the bones were broken, crushed, and heat altered to such a degree that they were almost unrecognizable. Other bodies were left strewn about the village, and those that carnivores could get to were ripped apart. What was found, however, was not all violence and death. It was apparent from the archaeological reconstruction that some time later, surviving village members or relatives returned and ritually closed the abandoned village by pulling down rooftops and burning the structures, an act that is suggestive of the ritual closure of former communities. This was not an isolated event, and similar scenarios played out in neighboring regions during this time. This village and villages throughout the area were abandoned and never reoccupied by the original inhabitants, but it is likely this event remained a part of the oral history and memories of the descendant communities for many generations afterward.

The importance of the event described above is that it was only brought to light because bioarchaeologists and archaeologists worked hard to unravel the larger social context within which this horrific event occurred. Using techniques of excavation, mapping, retrieval, curation, and analysis of the skeletonized remains, the reconstruction of the village in terms of its strategic location and sociopolitical arrangement was similar to the ways that a crime scene or a site of mass murder today would be reconstructed. The biological identity of each individual (age, sex, stature, body size, unusual pathologies, dentition, anomalies) was assessed using the kinds of standard and advanced techniques that are shared by bioarchaeologists (sometimes referred to as paleopathologists or osteologists), forensic anthropologists, and forensic archaeologists.

In this volume, Fondebrider and Rojas-Perez (chapters 2 and 3) both provide examples of horrific scenarios of more recently enacted political massacres and associated violence that are broadly similar to the ancient murders just described. These authors reveal the emotionally charged and psychologically draining aspects of working in contemporary settings where there are not only dead victims to be identified, but also still-living witnesses and, often, the perpetrators. Bioarchaeologists do not go looking for victims of forced disappearance and extrajudicial executions, as do forensic anthropologists such as Fondebrider. As he describes the role in the field, the initial goal is usually to find the bodies of those who went missing, and later to figure out what happened so that the families and communities may find closure, if not resolution. Sometimes the work also involves figuring out who committed the murders. These are aspects of the deathscape that are beyond what bioarchaeologists working with ancient human remains are expected to do or can do.

What follows is written by a bioarchaeologist whose life work has been analyzing violence with a focus on early, nonstate groups. I do not consider myself a forensic anthropologist, and I do not work in contemporary settings with police or coroners, or on humanitarian and human rights projects (as do many of the authors in this book). Hence, I am a bit of an outsider looking in on where forensic anthropology and forensic archaeology are going as subdisciplines and how this body of work articulates with the broader concerns of bioarchaeological and anthropological research.

One theme running throughout this volume involves the ethics of working with the dead. The ethical component of "disturbing bodies" is difficult to discuss because it involves a range of confounding subjective and objective realities. The questions raised by Joyce (chapter 10, this volume) are on the minds of many who work in these areas. Joyce interrogates her own career trajectory and asks how those of us who work intimately with the dead come to rationalize and cope with the fact that we do so largely without consent. The shared intellectual pursuits that crosscut bioarchaeology and forensic anthropology bind researchers together in negotiating the problems and ethical concerns inherent in this kind of work.

In this chapter I emphatically do not aim to provide a detailed history of forensic anthropology or bioarchaeology, nor do I attempt to provide a broad overview of what it is that forensic archaeology encompasses (instead, see Crossland and Joyce, chapter 1, this volume). The thematic glue here is death and violence in its myriad expressions and the theories and methods that permit the collection and interpretation of data from the skeleton and the context within which it is found. I summarize the important ways that the work being done by forensic archaeologists today can enrich and expand the research agenda not only of bioarchaeologists, but also of anthropologists and others who wish to prevent, decrease, and eradicate violence used as a political tool. Here I build on ideas developed in Martin and Anderson (2014), another of the few edited volumes that include both bioarchaeologists and forensic anthropologists, to take an integrated approach to the interpretation of violent events in the past and in the present. The overlapping research goals and techniques of forensic anthropology, forensic archaeology, and bioarchaeology are increasingly being recognized, and the chapters in this volume all speak to the fluidity and porosity at the subdisciplinary boundaries of each.

COMPLEMENTARY APPROACHES AND SHARED AGENDAS

Forensic anthropology is generally considered to be a subdiscipline in biological anthropology. Forensic archaeologists may affiliate more closely with the subdiscipline of archaeology and focus more on the mortuary component, the contextual and artifactual findings that aid in reconstruction. But as outlined by Crossland and Joyce (chapter 1, this volume), there is a fluidity in how each case study is approached and who among the team takes the lead. Forensic anthropology textbooks tend to emphasize techniques for the analysis of human remains in legal settings (e.g., Byers 2010; Komar and Buikstra 2008), while forensic archaeology texts include more detail on the data derived from the crime scene context and grave site through excavation, mapping, and the retrieval of evidence (e.g., Blau and Ubelaker 2009; Connor 2007; Dupras et al. 2012). Bioarchaeology, as the study of human remains in an archaeological context and a subdiscipline in biological anthropology, has come to include a range of methods, theories, and data that are applied to a wide variety of temporal and spatial contexts (Martin et al. 2013).

The intent of this volume as a whole is to highlight the importance of incorporating anthropological perspectives into the work being conducted by forensic archaeologists and to highlight the complexities and interdisciplinarity inherent in working with the dead in the diverse and often murky contexts in which many of these authors work. Training in biological anthropology, the starting point for many forensic anthropologists and bioarchaeologists, has always included a detailed understanding of the form, function, adaptation, and evolution of the human skeleton. Given the nature of biological tissues, the bones and teeth are the most likely to be preserved under many different conditions and far outnumber the instances of ancient, historic, and modern preservation of soft tissue.

The core training in skeletal biology is only the beginning for forensic anthropologists and forensic archaeologists. Because of the nature of their work, forensic archaeologists have had to expand beyond the confines of anthropology. Many of the early physical anthropologists were called upon to use their osteological skills in forensic settings. In 1936, while working at the Smithsonian, Aleš Hrdlička (the founding father of physical anthropology) developed a professional relationship with the Federal Bureau of Investigation during the period when J. Edgar Hoover (1931) was calling for the use of science in criminal investigations. Many others did their work in forensics alongside their more anthropological pursuits, thus always maintaining a connection to anthropology (Snow 1982).

As a consequence of working with human remains in legal settings, forensic work also requires an understanding of issues in criminology, forensic science, law, and clinical pathology, to name a few of the other disciplines necessary (Ubelaker 1999). The importance of understanding these other disciplines has only increased as the identification of skeletonized bodies and body parts associated with warfare, mass disasters, sectarian massacres, and criminal activities continues unabated. And, as Thompson (chapter 4, this volume) notes, forensic archaeology is but a small fraction of the caseload of the larger interdisciplinary teams that include forensic scientists, pathologists, and coroners. Finding long-term and well-paid employment solely as a forensic anthropologist or archaeologist is known to be difficult, but this may change as they become involved in an increasing array of academic arenas and political contexts.

When Clark S. Larsen, Jane E. Buikstra, George J. Armelagos, and others were arguing for the development of bioarchaeology as a more integrated approach to the analysis of ancient and historic skeletal remains, the focus shifted from an individual-based analysis to understanding population-level change and the roles of genetics, culture, and the environment (Martin et al. 2013:7). Forensic archaeologists are often required to identify individuals in a larger collection, and then to identify patterns at the group or population level. The traditional role of forensic archaeologists was to provide as much demographic information on the unidentified victim(s) as possible (e.g., age, sex, height, ancestry), but their work has clearly moved beyond this.

The roles of the researcher in bioarchaeological and forensic settings share many similarities, and the few differences are based mostly on technical expertise that comes from outside of biological anthropology. Despite what is portrayed in popular media, like the novels by Kathy Reichs or the television show, *Bones*, that developed from them (as discussed by Crossland, chapter 6, this volume), the forensic archaeologist is not involved in much of the reconstruction of the scene or in the ongoing investigation of domestic crimes. In international settings, however, where war crimes have been committed, forensic archaeologists may be much more involved in a range of activities surrounding the nature of the deaths. From its conception, the subdiscipline of bioarchaeology has argued that the researcher must likewise be more involved in all aspects of the project in order to more accurately understand what happened at the archaeological site. Given that bioarchaeologists working with ancient and historic human remains often do not have any written records to rely upon, they are forced to look at as many aspects of the archaeological context as possible to be able to discuss patterns in things such as demography, health, diet, activity, subsistence, and trauma.

Historically, the lack of written records and limited contact with living descendants meant that most projects in bioarchaeology placed little emphasis on legal issues, with the exception of obtaining permits to excavate and analyze the human remains. Since the 1990s, with the passage of legislation in the United States and other nations that mandates the inclusion of living descendants in decisions about human remains, this has radically changed. The Native American Graves Protection and Repatriation Act (NAGPRA) in the United States and NAGPRA-like legislation in many other countries mean that bioarchaeologists are often in the position of needing to understand complex county, state, federal, and tribal laws as they pertain to ancient and historic human remains. Forensic archaeologists may have a wide variety of written documents about a genocide or sectarian warfare from historic or contemporary times, but they also have complex legal issues to confront before, during, and after they excavate, retrieve, inventory, and analyze the human remains and their context (see Thompson, chapter 4, and Tuller, chapter 5, this volume).

Bioarchaeology often focuses on reconstructing ancient and historic cultures largely in an academic setting, and the focus may or may not include violence. Forensic anthropologists deal primarily with more recent (and, most times, violent) deaths in local, national, or international arenas, and their work is carried out via a team approach that includes law enforcement, medical examiners, lawyers, and surviving family members. That said, there are many scholars whose work crosses seamlessly from bioarchaeology to forensic anthropology, not least because many forensic anthropology practitioners were originally trained in bioarchaeology. A study that blends aspects of both forensic and bioarchaeological concerns is the chapter by Geller in this volume. Her work with a repository of crania collected in the 1800s raises a range of ethical and methodological issues related to how scientific data are collected and interpreted. The analysis of human remains, her chapter teaches us, is never straightforward and is always shaped by particular scientific and popular points of view.

Another place where bioarchaeology and forensic anthropology share theory, methods, and data is in the detailed reconstruction of individuals using a wide range of skeletal markers of demography, life history, stature, muscularity and size, habitual gait and muscle use, development, disease and trauma (healed, healing, or unhealed), and other changes that can be interpreted with some accuracy. Saul (1967) and Saul and Saul (1987) developed this approach first using an ancient Mayan population, but they also showed the value of these "osteobiographies" for contemporary individuals in the dissection room. These authors applied this method of creating a biography from skeletal remains precisely because they had also worked in forensic settings where single individuals were the focus of a holistic and integrated analysis. Robb (2002) and Stodder and Palkovich (2012) have continued to fine-tune this methodology, and it has since become a common approach to individual skeletons in bioarchaeology. This demonstrates that the flow of ideas from forensic anthropology to bioarchaeology is as important as the flow of method and theory from bioarchaeology to forensic anthropology.

There are many different kinds of forensic archaeologists. The variation is quite broad, with some doing work in academic settings, some working with local police when skeletonized remains are part of a homicide case, some working at mass disasters and other places where large numbers of people have perished, and some working in difficult and even dangerous situations involving massacre and genocide. All of these contexts create the opportunity for important work that provides crucial benefits to law enforcement and to surviving family members. Yet this work has been viewed by academic and practicing bioarchaeologists as merely technical expertise. In full disclosure, I am one of those bioarchaeologists that in the past was critical of forensic work. I saw it solely as a technical exercise and posed the question, where is the anthropology in forensic anthropology? This volume enthusiastically provides an answer. The anthropology is everywhere: in how the research is framed, in how the questions are asked, in how witnesses and family members are interviewed, in how data are contextualized and interpreted, and in the ways that broader issues about human behavior are explicitly addressed. Forensic anthropology is not an atheoretical enterprise, and its centrality to anthropological goals is made explicit by this volume. The work discussed here signals that there is movement toward more hybridity in approaches and goals. For example, forensic archaeology is moving toward an adoption of the notion of "ancestry" (over "race") when providing a biological profile (see Walsh-Haney and Boys, chapter 7, this volume). The chapter by Geller demonstrates another step in the right direction in terms of deconstructing the long legacy of scientific racism that has characterized the history of physical anthropology and thus spilled over into forensic anthropology.

In addition, more bioarchaeologists are becoming interested in the human rights aspects of their work with indigenous populations and in forensic anthropology. As more forensic anthropologists draw on widely accepted theory, methods, and data to help guide and assist with their fieldwork, their ability to interpret deaths within political and social contexts is enhanced. This blurring of goals is breaking down the largely artificial divisions between those who study the ancient dead and those who assist with the more recently dead. There is currently no umbrella term that would subsume the work of both forensic archaeologists and bioarchaeologists, although "forensic bioarchaeology" might be one to consider.

While forensic archaeology and bioarchaeological study rely on anthropological theory, methods, and data, they also both offer much to anthropology. Many of the ethical, legal, and methodological concerns raised in this volume are highly relevant and necessary to consider for everyone working with human remains, be they ancient or modern. Our colleagues working on the front lines of forensic work today help those of us in bioarchaeology to sharpen our focus on what is important and what is at stake. The chapter by Walsh-Haney and Boys (7) is particularly important in this respect since forensic archaeologists can verify how accurate the assignment of sex, age, and ancestry is for individuals who are eventually provided with a full and detailed biography.

Another reason that this is the moment to highlight the shared vision and agendas of bioarchaeology and forensic archaeology is that bioarchaeology itself is emerging in a relatively new configuration (Agarwal and Glencross 2011), an approach to working with human remains that is an important corrective to the narrow focus of human osteology, its use in various historical racial projects (see Geller, chapter 8, this volume), and its decontextualization of human remains. What is emerging is a bioarchaeology that is integrated into broader anthropological agendas of engagement and ethical action. Many bioarchaeologists incorporate theories about human behavior into their work, and this has broadened and deepened the interpretations derived from human remains (Martin et al. 2013).

The forensic archaeologists in this volume make clear the strides that they are making toward engaging with broader anthropological agendas. First and foremost is their recognition of the limitations of the methodologies for reconstruction of identity when trying to address larger questions about violence and human behavior. Forensic archaeologists are confronted with political violence and the larger contexts within which these kinds of activities are initiated and carried out. The work that they do in the field is often in the presence of family members watching and looking for any bits of evidence that can prove to them that a skeletonized body being exhumed is their kin. While scientific methods, including DNA analysis, may help reveal identity, in these complicated arenas of horrific and covert crimes against humanity, Fondebrider (chapter 2, this volume) asks, what does identifying the body really mean in these contexts? The osteological profile or standard biological identity in the sense of a person's lived experience may be much more difficult precisely because in contemporary contexts there is so much more nuance and information to take in than there is for ancient and historic human remains.

Thus, new and previously unimaginable research questions are emerging as many different kinds of anthropologists engage in fieldwork and projects associated with violent death. Bioarchaeologists and forensic anthropologists are fulfilling important roles by providing empirical data to national and international conversations about such deaths and their cultural meanings. In this arena, there are complementary approaches and shared agendas among bioarchaeologists and forensic anthropologists.

BRIDGING SOCIAL THEORY WITH BIOARCHAEOLOGY AND FORENSIC ARCHAEOLOGY

Thompson (chapter 4, this volume) notes the paucity of theoretical work in the field of forensic archaeology. Fondebrider (chapter 2, this volume) makes a singularly compelling case for the ways that theories about cultural and political violence inform the work that forensic archaeologists do. He provides a picture of this new world of violence that we live in, which takes place in larger world arenas and political contexts.

Thus, one of the issues facing forensic archaeology is the need to create a balance between the specialized knowledge embedded in the forensic sciences and training in the other subfields of anthropology (Thompson, chapter 4, this volume). New and previously unimaginable roles are becoming increasingly more common as anthropologists engage in fieldwork associated with death and violence (Tuller, chapter 5, this volume). It is apparent that forensic archaeologists are doing important work in helping to locate, identify, and examine dead and missing bodies. Through interdisciplinary inquiry and engagement across the subfields, anthropology provides different ways to view the violence, warfare, and human rights issues that often result in death, trauma, and social upheaval.

A variety of forms of violence, covert and vicious types of warfare, a broad range of activities of surveillance, and the elimination of human rights have created work for anthropologists that could not have been imagined 50 years ago. Future forensic archaeologists need training not just in the fundamentals of excavation and skeletal analysis. They also need training in all four subfields of anthropology in order to broaden their theoretical and practical approaches to dealing with everyday violence. Forensic archaeology can engage in an interdisciplinary inquiry into the theoretical and empirical issues in the study of violence, warfare, surveillance, and human rights. The strength that anthropology brings to the study of violence is a critical, self-reflective, and nonreductionist perspective that allows for a holistic examination of the dynamics that lead to the wide array of human atrocities committed throughout the world. It is this strength that is needed to keep forensic archaeology from falling into a trap of creating highly specialized technicians who are disconnected from the rest of anthropology.

There is much at stake with forensic archaeology. As Fondebrider and Rojas-Perez demonstrate in their work in this volume (chapters 2 and 3, respectively), forensic archaeologists cannot be neutral. They are implicated from the beginning in particular goals and projects (see Crossland 2013). "Truth making" has much riding on it, with extreme pressure to get it right. As the forensic archaeologists in this volume ably demonstrate, these are very high stakes. Certainly, bioarchaeological work, as demonstrated by Geller (chapter 8, this volume), can have huge political and social outcomes and address past wrongs. The truth is, however, that the pressure to get it right in ancient contexts is not the same as the pressure on those working in highly charged legal and political contexts. There, getting it right is often a matter of life or death, of justice or injustice, of aiding or abetting. The stakes are very high for the families, the international human rights groups, the local lawyers, and the military; that pressure can be a huge strain to work under.

The chapters in this book attest to the complexities of what it means to do forensic archaeology in fraught and often dangerous settings. I am someone who has been critical of forensic archaeology, and these chapters have dramatically shifted my thinking. They represent an important corrective to the perhaps overly technical and dispassionate presentation of forensic cases in many textbooks and case study texts currently available (e.g., Byers 2010; Komar and Buikstra 2008; Steadman 2009). Those texts come nowhere near representing the complex and nuanced methodological issues raised by Thompson (chapter 4, this volume) in his deconstructing of the notion of standardization, or by Tuller (chapter 5, this volume) in his nuanced exploration of the ideal versus actual manner in which projects are carried out.

CONCLUSIONS

Bioarchaeology and forensic archaeology both require extensive and detailed observation of the context of skeletonized human remains. Whether at a crime scene, a mass grave, or a prehistoric tomb, the excavation and the collection of data demand that the surrounding evidence or archaeological context be documented and included in any interpretation. For those bioarchaeologists who have had forensic training, approaching a skeleton in an archaeological context is easier because they have already learned to treat everything as important until it is demonstrated to be irrelevant. This fine attention to detail prevents items related to the human remains from being missed (see Tuller, chapter 5, this volume). At the same time, forensic archaeologists rely on bioarchaeological excavation methods when encountering clandestine graves, and they are a great asset to mapping and producing documentation for prosecutorial and law enforcement activities.

The blending of theories, methods, and data interpretation that comes from being able to draw appropriately from forensic anthropology and bioarchaeology will be more effective in addressing questions about human behavior that would be difficult to address using only one of the fields. Bioarchaeology has the depth and cross-cultural breadth to help understand the profound and complicated ways in which humans think about and use violence and bodies. Bioarchaeologists use human remains as a lens through which to examine cultural processes. The ways that dead bodies are discussed, hidden, and displayed are used as a point of departure for examining the forms of violence that contributed to the deaths under study. Many of the most horrific genocidal events in the last hundred years demonstrate the relationship between violence and the expressive function that such acts and images have as vehicles of human communication. Covert operations are designed with the goal of unraveling culturally constructed webs of trust (Rojas-Perez, chapter 3, this volume). Thus, the bodies of the dead have both real and symbolic properties, as Katherine Verdery (1999) has explored. Bioarchaeology can add time depth and scale, and forensic anthropology can add detailed information from eyewitness accounts of the types of violence inflicted. What connections can be seen through time and cross-culturally in types of violence? A combined bioarchaeological and forensic anthropology approach would be able to get at this. Combining approaches also reveals when types of violence are isolated behaviors or global phenomena with strong patterns.

What I have learned from this book is that it is important for scholars trained in human skeletal analysis to be engaged with local communities. For bioarchaeologists, community involvement may be more related to improving public awareness of archaeological sites and protecting them. It may also include educational activities related to preventing the desecration of human burials, particularly those of Native American communities.

This volume is an excellent guide and an important read for graduate students who wish to follow in the footsteps of anthropologists before them by combining a career in bioarchaeology and forensic anthropology. Graduate students appear to want to be trained in both subdisciplines and to have career opportunities that bridge bioarchaeology with forensic archaeology and forensic anthropology. What this volume makes clear is that the distinctions between ancient and modern investigations of skeletal remains are porous, and many researchers are experts in both ancient and modern contexts of violence. This is a good thing for both forensic anthropology and bioarchaeology.

Yet we must also educate graduate students to be aware that this work is not without its moral and ethical entanglements and implications and its psychic and emotional costs. Galloway (2014:311) has written about the effects of working on the identification of people who died at the hands of others: "the most powerful factor is the sight of the many victims whose bodies we have examined and the opportunity we have to experience, in our minds, their last moments on earth." While this may provide us with some sense of the preciousness of life, it also creates more opportunity to imagine what torture, fear, and agonizingly slow deaths may have been like for others. On many compelling levels, the chapters in this book offer us a chance to grapple with the implications of "disturbing bodies"—but also with the implications of not doing so. The ethical and humanistic aspects of this work are bound to the kinds of expertise and witnessing that come with it. In the end, we investigators are "left trying to reconstruct the unfathomable" (Galloway 2014:315) in order to make life perhaps more fathomable in the present and future.

Joyce (chapter 10, this volume) presents a compelling plea that those of us who work with the dead must be willing to have these risky conversations, which force researchers to confront the multidimensional and intersecting ethical and scientific realms within which they work. This includes questions that range from the relatively mundane (how did this person die?) to the metaphysical (should I be disturbing the dead?). The chapters in this volume are essential reading for all anthropologists interested in how to negotiate the tensions, incongruities, and dialectics ever present in research that looks at violence and death.

Acknowledgments

I thank the editors of this volume for the careful critique and editing suggestions that they provided. Two anonymous reviewers also contributed to the reframing and revising of my commentary, and I am very thankful for their careful consideration.

10

Grave Responsibilities

Encountering Human Remains

Rosemary A. Joyce

In my intervention in this conversation, I deliberately step back to try to focus on the situations that excavating human remains entail and the discursive and experiential dimensions of those situations. My main argument is that despite more than 25 years of discussion, there is still a great need for anthropologists engaged in excavating human remains to find a standpoint from which to articulate why this peculiar practice of ours is not gruesome. I ask with Paul Bahn (1984:220), "Is there any justification for responsible, educated people deliberately disturbing the dead?" (See also Scarre 2003.)

I want to explore how these necessary, unavoidable aspects of our practice can be accomplished without undermining human dignity, and what participation in them does to us as practitioners. I am especially interested in the last point, since it seems to me that there has been too little attention paid to what happens to anthropologists who routinely deal with the passage from life to death. What does this intimate relationship with death do to our way of being in the world? How are we simultaneously estranged from, and connected with, our humanity? What does it even mean to speak of "humanity" in the face of the sometimes disturbing things that human remains tell us?

This chapter does not, obviously, answer these questions fully—and some are raised here precisely because, while they frame my practice, I have not yet found the words to deal with them, here or elsewhere. I hope to provoke a discussion that bridges multiple practices and positions and that might generate an ongoing dialogue in which archaeologists could draw on one of our unacknowledged forms of expertise: we are the only professional academic group that routinely engages in disturbing bodies without the consent of the dead or their relations. That expertise should provide us grounds to comment on many other ambiguous encounters with the embodied dead—if we are willing not to treat it simply as silent background, but acknowledge it as the problematic context that it is.

BONA FIDES

As my opening paragraphs suggest, I am taking a risk here, and asking others to accompany me in a risky conversation. That presumes a degree of mutual trust. I need to establish my bona fides: my good faith, the reason that this conversation is one that you should have with me. So, here is where I speak from: as a field archaeologist with experience excavating burials; as a scholar who has repeatedly chosen to discuss burial populations as a proxy for the social lives I want to understand (Joyce 1999, 2001, 2003a, 2003b, 2011; Joyce et al. 2008); and as a student of comparative experiences of embodiment and the consequences these have for approaches to bodily death.

I began my field career in the archaeology of the nineteenth century in North America, where excavating burials was simply not part of the program. It was not until I began working in Honduras that I personally carried out excavations of human remains. Doing household archaeology, which was my focus at the time, automatically guarantees that you will come across burials, primary and secondary, as well as isolated skeletal elements displaced by remodeling in the past. It was not until the third season I spent in the field in Honduras, though, that I had my first encounter with the bodies of the dead. My first time in the field there, our excavations took place in public architectural zones. When I returned, it was as part of a systematic settlement survey project. I was supposed to be continuing that work when I came back for a second season on the survey project (my third in Honduras); instead, I was immediately assigned to salvage excavations at a professionally looted site in the area where we were slated to complete site recording.

The subsistence diggers had placed their excavation at Campo Pineda on a low rise, the remains of a house or houses inhabited from at least AD 400 to 1000, in the middle of a field of tall, dense stands of mature sugarcane. They had excavated a rectangular pit to more than two meters deep.

A colleague and I were assigned to work on a controlled excavation adjacent to the exposed excavation wall, and almost immediately we encountered skeletal remains. In rereading my field notes from 1980, I am struck by the way I described our process of recognition of these human remains. I was ambivalent, writing about the deposit first as an isolated cranium, noting "some pieces of much decayed bone" near the cranium we initially recognized, and then firmly writing "I don't think it's a burial" in an awkward outbreak of first-person declarative prose in what otherwise reads like a model of distanced, third-person, formal, "scientific" language. For me (for us), "burial" was a category that was reserved for something else. But as the powdery traces of other bones became visible, and especially as the lower limbs, resting at less superficial depths, emerged as identifiable tibiae and a fibula, what we initially treated as a kind of out-of-context artifact became Burial 1.

Since my colleague had some experience, I left it to him to work on the skeletal remains themselves. Our main challenge, as we saw it, was preservation, since the sun beating down rapidly dried out the skeletal elements, reducing them to powdery outlines. In the end, despite my colleague's best efforts, we removed from the excavated unit only the mandible, cranium, and a few partly eroded long bones. Although my role had been reduced to observer, it was I who noticed the two thin fired-clay spools; one was found under the skull, which testified to their likely position as inserted through the earlobes when the person was laid to rest. With the addition of those small things, my notes changed: where before I was ambivalent about whether this was a burial, now I saw a person with "burial goods" who had been deliberately placed along the side of a house floor.

When the US field director arrived, he reassigned us from the excavations that the Honduran field director had started. The last thing I was asked to do was to clean up the messy sidewalls of the looted trench to allow the final drawing of stratigraphic profiles. At one end of that void, as I troweled down the narrow wall, clumps of dirt pulled away from something off-white. I carefully picked at the object with finer tools and soon realized I was looking at a row of teeth in the side of a jaw, part of a body so small that it was obviously a juvenile, curled up as if sleeping. How could I leave this child there, to weather out of the pit wall or, worse, to be torn out carelessly and tossed aside by people searching for the rare carved marble vases that were the biggest payoff for local subsistence diggers? I could not. I spent hours on that last day, long after others had left the field, long enough that my head was reeling from the heat, tracing the pit that contained this small body, talking to it as I did so.

I still have in my notes the improvised label made for the photographing of this second burial. In the field director's neat printing are the site number, the date, and the Spanish words for "North Wall" and "Intrusive in Level II (from Level I)." Underneath, in my own shakier and less-even printing: "skeleton (child)." For me, this was a moment of realization: the personhood of that small body simply could not be left described in the neutral terms used uniformly for every other thing. For me, this was a child.

Shifting how we talk about the dead and their survivors has been my main pursuit in subsequent mortuary analyses (Joyce 2001, 2011). This is part of my broader insistence that how we talk about the past matters (Joyce 2002b). When we talk about the people whose bodies we encounter, often where they were placed deliberately, perhaps even lovingly, as part of the homes that remained occupied for generations, we participate in a different set of relations than when we call these people "human remains" and talk about the "individuals" in "features." I can trace my concerns with the distancing and sanitizing power of language, and its disjunction from my feelings, to that first experience with the exhumation of human remains. I knew what we were doing was necessary; I could see fragments of human bone in the backdirt from the looted part of the site. It was us or the looters: if we left these bones in place, they would be destroyed and tossed aside without producing any information (cf. Bahn 1984). But at the same time, I found myself vacillating, moving back and forth between talking about the skeletal elements as the remains of a person and talking about them as quasi-artifacts.

The rest of that summer I spent finding and mapping sites. The questions raised by my initial experiences fell comfortably back into a zone that was, quite literally, not my problem. My dissertation excavations unearthed no burials: a single stone tomb in one building that might have revived these early experiences had already been emptied long before we came to the site. The stones covering it had been thrown around the gaping pit left behind by the looters, but they mainly served as an annoyance impeding my architectural descriptions. Even when I undertook at the behest of the Honduran Institute of Anthropology and History another salvage excavation in another house site in cane fields, my excavations turned up a pottery kiln, architectural features, and trash, but no mortuary settings.

It was when I decided to try to use published and unpublished burial catalogs to talk about variation by sex and age in an early (ca. 1000–700 BC) central Mexican village, Tlatilco, that I was reminded of my earlier experiences with human remains. Brickworkers digging for clay initially discovered Tlatilco (Piña Chan 1958; M. Porter 1953), and they offered the complete pots and figurines found in some burials for sale. This attracted Mexican art collectors, pre-Columbian specialists, and eventually archaeologists, who documented the contents of burials, if not much about the human bodies that were the focus for the deposit of these things. Professional excavations by meticulous archaeological teams followed, and these produced bioarchaeological assessments of age, sex, and pathologies (García Moll et al. 1991). What attracted my attention was the potential of examining the clusters of burials to identify likely houses and yards from the locations of these features, which were originally placed around houses or under house floors (Joyce 1999).

My entire goal was to see the burials as evidence of social groups acting on the bodies of their own dead relations. In trying to see things that way, I again struggled with the language of mortuary description, which always distanced me from the person whose bodily remains I was contemplating. Though I worked to represent that tension in writing (Joyce 2001, 2002b), what this project taught me was that there was a flattening effect caused by mortuary archaeology's emphasis on variation across a population, on treating burials as a universe or sample and not, as they needed to be seen for my purposes, as kin.

Subsequent experiences in Honduras brought me back to face this dilemma. Unlike sites in the central Maya lowlands to the west, it is uncommon for the dead in the Ulúa valley to be buried with complete pottery vessels or other objects. But it is normal for ear spools or the fragments of ear spools to be recovered in the sediments around human remains. As I focused on these humble yet evocative things in my analyses of deposits dated AD 400–650 from excavations at Puerto Escondido, I noticed that often what was recovered were not simply complete pairs of spools laid on either side of the skull, but fragments from multiple different ear spools embedded in the dirt surrounding the skeletal remains. Statistical analyses demonstrated that ear spool fragments, in addition to complete ear spools, are found more commonly than expected near human remains (Joyce 2011). I have argued that these finds are products of actions by the living who undertook the sequence of practices leading to the burial, people I elsewhere call "the mourning community" (Joyce 2001).

Acknowledging the existence of a mourning community motivated to commemorate the dead through a suite of practices that were mediated in part (but not solely) through bodily remains informed a final problem I faced in my own work: what to make of practices through which skeletal elements, far from being left in the earth, were abstracted, sometimes worked, and at times circulated among the living? In the broader Mesoamerican region that forms one edge of my own research location, the disarticulation of the human body has long been associated by scholars with human sacrifice, cannibalism, and the violence of military victors over the vanquished. More reflectively, both there and in Central America, the region forming the other boundary of my Honduran research site, some analyses have explored how ontologies of personhood have treated bone as a material connecting people across generations, whether left articulated in primary burials, realigned in secondary deposits (often, multiple ossuaries), or represented by selected skeletal elements given ongoing biographies as worked objects (Joyce 1998; Meskell and Joyce 2003; Tiesler and Cucina 2007). How we talk about human remains out of bodily context is, I would argue, indicative of often unexamined assumptions about what kinds of human being merit recognition.

The power of naming to recognize or deny the humanity of the person who in all these cases continues to be represented by bones is perhaps most clear for me in the issues I face in discussing the archaeology of early (800–400 BC) Los Naranjos. There, four contexts excavated decades ago were registered as burials (Baudez and Becquelin 1973:89–98). Specific worked objects were assigned either as primary burial goods associated with an individual articulated body or as shared burial offerings for sets of skeletal elements recomposed in secondary settings, all in the construction fill of a single monumental earthen platform. I struggled, and continue to struggle, to reconcile the original archaeologists' decisions to recognize all these settings as burials and to distinguish them from others recorded as caches. Elements of the human skeleton occur in deposits labeled caches as well as in those labeled burials, and they are understood implicitly as no longer identified persons when they are used in caches. As Marshall Becker (1993) demonstrated, rather than drawing lines between these different forms of deposition in Mexico and Central America, we need to consider them as points on a continuum of practices (see also Tiesler 2007).

In my own work on the long history of Puerto Escondido (1600 BC–AD 650), I have pursued this insight, examining a historical sequence of practices at a household scale, including the disjunction of things into parts, the incorporation of parts into constructed settings, and the acts of commemoration that these settings suggest, practices into which human remains enter but which were not initially created for them (Joyce 2011). Much of my unease about how we think of the completeness or incompleteness of sets of human remains, I have come to realize, revolves around the way that designating one thing a "burial" and another a "cache" or "dedicatory offering" privileges certain kinds of disposal of the bony remains of a person over others, aligning some human remains more firmly with the category of "subject" and others somewhat uneasily with the position of "object."

So, all of that is my proof of good faith. I come here as a fellow traveler, working on the same problems that others in this volume experience, problems that I suggest come in part from unease with the subjectivity of people in the past and from our treatment of the physical traces of people as objects rather than subjects. Geoffrey Scarre (2003:237) framed this within the Kantian philosophical tradition as the demand that we "always treat people as ends in themselves, and never merely as means." My question then is, what can we learn from each other that might advance the cause of rehumanizing the necessary anthropological encounters with the dead?

ENCOUNTERING HUMAN "REMAINS"

Bahn (1984:222) counseled that "any archaeologist with a troubled conscience can turn only to the deliberations of moral philosophers or to the advice of the clergy." I will take at least half of his advice, turning to the work of philosophers as a major foundation for trying to understand our own dilemma. Yet before that, I want to consider a piece of the vocabulary that anthropologists and archaeologists share: that what we deal with are "human remains." Here, I do not turn to ministers or philosophers, but to lawyers for aid. In the United States, "human remains" is a legally defined term. For example, in section 451.005 of the Nevada Revised Statutes, it means "the body of a deceased person…the body in any stage of decomposition and the cremated remains of a body." Or, as the general title for section 451 says more succinctly and bluntly: *Dead Bodies.* What work does it do to substitute the term "human remains" for "dead bodies"? On one level, of course, dead bodies conjure up an image of completeness and integrity that is challenged by actual encounters with traces of the biological human. This is inherent in the extension in this legislative definition of the term "human remains" to cover "any stage of decomposition" and to incorporate even the products of cremation. In bioethics, for example, the question of how to treat human remains routinely extends to parts of the body abstracted from the whole (e.g., Jones et al. 2003).

So we might say that the pluralization of "remains" allows for the potential partibility of the human biological being. This legal definition of human remains helps us understand how exhuming the skeleton of an eighteenth-century Irish "giant" who had a great fear of becoming an object on display after his death was problematic even though "scholars…assumed that he was merely concerned about his *body*, not its bony remnants" (Bahn 1984:221). The integrity implied by the term "body" was understood by the scholars recovering his body as dissolved with the loss of his flesh, but the unity of the plural human remains, even if labeled "remnants," made this still a violation of his explicit desire for his postmortem treatment.

"Remains" derives from the verb "remain," according to the Merriam-Webster dictionary: "to be a part not destroyed, taken, or used up"; "to stay in the same place or with the same person or group" (http://www.merriam-webster.com). The verb "remain" was first recognized in Middle English in the fourteenth century, coming from Latin via French. It shares the Latin root *manere* with the equally old Middle English *mansion*, which originally had the meaning of "to dwell" and "dwelling," not just (as today) an elaborate dwelling. To remain is to continue in place, to continue as part of a collectivity, to dwell. Human remains differ from dead bodies in this uncanny aspect of remaining connected—to place, to group, and above all to person. This connection was anticipated by Heidegger, who wrote that "to remain means: not to disappear, thus, to presence" (quoted in Butchart 2007:161).

Human remains cannot be reduced to the status of mere "material," a point made by Scarre (2003:238) in his discussion of whether we have responsibilities to the dead themselves, separate from those we have to the living who identify themselves as descendants: "interred remains are not simply inanimate matter, like sticks and stones. They are the relics, whether whole, decayed or the skeletal residue, of human beings" (Scarre 2003:243). Scarre consequently disputed the premises of an archaeological article arguing for the capacity of ancient "material" (rather than "remains") "to *contribute* to our understanding of human development and culture" (243, emphasis added). Even when construed as mere "material," human remains maintain a capacity to be effective that troubles the subject-object divide. As Laura Peers (2009:81, emphasis added), writing about the display of human remains at the Pitt Rivers Museum, noted, "One of the central problems in trying to understand the social meanings and *effects* of human remains is that they are not only iconic, but ontologically unstable, and are apt to shift registers of meaning abruptly: human remains lurch between signifying the living and the dead, person and object, specimens and ancestors."

Archaeologists, medical ethicists, and philosophers have, independently and beginning with different questions, repeatedly addressed the capacity of dead bodies to act (contribute, cause effects), in particular to create connections across time and even across space, implicit in the word "remains" (Martin 1998; Weiss-Krejci 2004). To even begin to understand this, we need to think through the implications of the activity of the corporeal body after death.

The definition of human remains as equivalent to the bodies of "deceased persons" presents our first challenge, since it requires a clear determination of the death of the *person*, not merely the end of functioning of the body. A person is not (just) a body. Crossland discussed the seventeenth-century legal mobilization of the dead body of a murdered person as an active witness, concluding that in modern forensic practice the dead are "more than evidence": "revealed in the exhumation of human remains is the usually submerged understanding of dead bodies as things that have agency...constructed as active agents within a network of complex relations that incorporates archaeologists, living relatives, the courts and police, and the person or persons accused of the crime" (2009a:75).

"Things that have agency": the dead body in this formulation recognizably combines the familiarity and unfamiliarity that Freud (2004) defined as "the uncanny": "many people experience the feeling in the highest degree in relation to death and dead bodies, to the return of the dead, and to spirits and ghosts.... Dismembered limbs, a severed head, a hand cut off at the wrist, feet which dance by themselves—all these have something peculiarly uncanny about them, especially when, as in the last instance, they prove able to move of themselves" (2004:91, 92). A dead body is troubling because, as human *remains*, it represents the lingering or renewed presence of a person, and yet at the same time it appears to be a nonperson, a thing. Human remains are in some sense dead and not-dead at the same time.

Devettere, discussing the contemporary question of the determination of death in bodies that continue to function after neocortical functions cease, proposed a useful distinction between *concepts* and *criteria* of death: "Concepts reveal what we mean by 'death' and 'dead'; criteria tell us how to determine that someone is actually dead" (1990:96). He further distinguished between theoretical concepts of death and concepts that arise from experience, noting that the latter "are meaningful for those who share the experience" and may conflict with theoretical concepts of death. His purpose was to lay out arguments against adopting neocortical death as a criterion of death, in part because it violates experiential concepts. Devettere's propositions also provide us with useful ways to think about the problem of dead bodies that "remain" human. Medical criteria may say the person is dead, but if that person's remains have a capacity to act, they may still violate community concepts of what death means.

Ariss (2004:33, emphasis added), arguing in a similar vein, considered the way that modern British common-law tradition privileges remembering as a "moral practice" in relation to "dead bodies *requiring* respectful treatment." Citing anthropological discussions of memory, Ariss noted that in practice "to remember is never solely to recount the past, but to put forward one's relation to it [as] a validation of continuity (or caring) and discontinuity (mourning) that each person experiences in relations with others" (2004:36). Among the examples she gave are a US legal case citing the Native American Graves Protection and Repatriation Act, which was brought against the Bishop Museum by the Hawaiian Native group Hui Malama. The court accepted Hui Malama as plaintiffs because the living are *required* to care for the dead. Ariss argued that this established a legal recognition for the connection of the living to the dead as maintained in memory and through acts of commemoration.

The anthropological exhumation of human remains should be related to broader debates about the ways in which human remains may be at issue in the contemporary world, including questions raised by organ donation. Paul Bahn (1984:215) drew a connection between ancient Egyptian concerns with bodily integrity and "modern fears of donating organs after death." Yet the alignment he suggested is not universal: Ariss (2004:39, emphasis added) noted that "in North America and Britain many organ donor families have constructed the donation of body parts as a way to ease their grief, *allowing their loved one, in death to remain connected to the world of the living*." Scarre (2003:237) argued that the dead are not automatically wronged when "we utilise their physical remains for our own purposes" in the specific case of willed organ donation: "some people carry donor-cards permitting their organs to be used posthumously for transplant surgery, while others bequeath their bodies to medical research." For Scarre, these instances of postmortem participation by human remains in routes of circulation, authorized before death, are consistent with the continuity of subjectivity, which is a consequence of the unstable nature of the dead body as human remains.

As a notable boundary case, consider the popular traveling exhibitions *Body Worlds*. Medical ethicist Michael Barilan (2006:1) writes that "an attitude of respect and not regarding human remains as mere raw material are non-alienable substantial duties" of *Body Worlds*. By "substantial duties" Barilan means actions that are required due to the meanings they are ascribed: "the acts in question are taken solely with the intention of honouring and benefiting the deceased" (2006:239). His discussion of the ethics of this use of modern human remains in what at times verges on sheer spectacle underlines the conclusion: human remains remain human.

INDIVIDUALS, SELVES, OTHERS

If we conceive of our encounters with human remains as experiences that connect us with living beings through what does not disappear and thus remains to presence the person, then we enter into a different set of discussions. These require us to understand the variety of forms of personhood that may be involved, starting with those current in Europe and its colonial offspring that are our half, if you will, of the circuit of personhood involved.

Scarre (2003:239) described what he views as a common archaeological stance on the status of the dead body, in which "either they think that death is extinction, or, if they believe in an afterlife, they do not suppose that the spirits of the dead can be harmed by events that happen to their mortal dust." Such attitudes, to the extent that they accurately characterize anthropologists participating in studies of the dead (which I think is an open empirical question), would be rooted in a particular understanding of personhood. That vision of personhood, including what Devettere (1990:96) called "concepts" of death, is of course not by definition shared with the person with whose remains we engage. Nor is it immediately clear that this really is the attitude toward people and their bodies in contemporary societies in Europe or North America (the targets of Scarre's analysis). Scarre (2003:240) said, "if we take death to mark the end of the subject, then we must regard the dead as being beyond all good and evil," but "this view runs up against the widely held conviction that postmortem states and events can, somehow, be bad for us."

Archaeologists have in some cases undertaken the work of theorizing the personhood of those whose human remains are under discussion. Gillespie (2003) described the Classic Maya practice of burying the dead in the houses of the living in terms of a goal on the part of the remaining group to "keep the spirits in place." She argued that the specific ways of interacting with human remains that archaeologists have described for the Classic Maya were underwritten by relational and distributed forms of personhood (Gillespie 2001). The Classic Maya dead were of public interest, connected to a wider network of people, places, and things. Gillespie (2003:67) argued that Classic Maya mortuary treatment involved "the proper disposition of the nontangible components of deceased persons along with their physical remains." She demonstrated that the person was composed not only of corporeal stuff, but also of such incorporeal things as names and souls, which circulated between generations, connecting the buried group members to those still active in the flesh.

Discussing NAGPRA, Ariss (2004:46, emphasis added) noted that it originally did not define "human remains," but proposed to include bodies under the term "cultural items." Following criticism, the latter term was replaced with a definition of human remains notably different from the broader legal one cited above: "the physical remains of a human body of a *person*." Where a dead body is a material thing that we can hope to define empirically, what constitutes a person is something more, as Vizenor (1986:320) noted: "concern over the soul, and the spiritual return of souls, is pertinent" when we turn to the impact on Native American *persons* of the collection and holding of the physical remains that were or are parts of persons. In contrast, Ariss (2004:39) argued that in contemporary North America, death is "sequestered from public space" and understood as fundamentally private, lacking what she called "a communally-accepted framework" for dealing with death. While her comments were primarily about the experience of the dying, they are founded in an analysis of the modern idealized individual. They serve equally well to describe the position occupied by those who professionally engage in exhumation of the dead, whether deceased in relatively recent and violent circumstances or having died in ancient times and (sometimes) more peaceful ways.

Now we are coming to the point that concerns me most. If we acknowledge that human remains (in place of mere "dead bodies") have continuing human presence and that the perception of that human presence is predicated on the understanding by the living of their own personhood, then it seems that participation in exhumation is a form of ethical self-making. We are shaped by our encounters with the dead because they are not securely in the past, but are remains, and remains not just of biological matter, but also of a human being.

What kind of ethical person is being produced by these encounters? Scarre (2003:238) described archaeologists who have "developed 'a property of easiness' in dealing with the dead," questioning whether "this moral complacency is warranted." We can consider as similar the common, if uncommonly discussed, habit of field excavators giving nicknames to the bodies they encounter in otherwise unmarked graves. Bahn (1984:216) wrote that "even archaeologists can feel uncomfortable about exposing or removing [human skeletons], and their frequent practice of giving the skeletons nicknames might well be interpreted by a psychologist as an attempt to assuage their own slight uneasiness."

Crossland (2009a:75), in her discussion of forensics, argued that the capacity of presence and agency that are attributed to human remains "transfers the feelings and emotions denied to the forensic observer to the corpse." Barilan (2006:244) concluded that the originators of the *Body*

Worlds exhibitions have a "substantial duty" to the dead that stems from the requirement to "never regard the human body as a natural resource in need of utilization," implying a necessity to recognize the humanity of remains that persists and, indeed, is stronger than any knowledge to be gained from analysis. He wrote: "If we accept the concept of human dignity with regard to dead bodies, we have to reject any use of human remains *as a goal in itself*.... We object to *using* human remains whenever a reasonable alternative to achieve the goal in mind is available.... We harbour a *substantial duty* not to utilize dead bodies unless we have good enough reasons to do so" (Barilan 2006:245, original emphases).

QUESTIONS OF REPRESENTATION

I will end by proposing that all the preceding has implications as well for our representations of the dead whose human remains create a bond of personhood with us. This is, of course, not at all unfamiliar in one sense: it has become standard to make disclaimers before projecting images of human remains, even in scholarly venues. Most of us are sensitized enough that we would shy away from placing recognizable images of human remains on the cover of a book. Many of us, myself included, have experimented with other ways to visually presence what we lose in argument if we do not represent burials: orientation, for example, can be indicated by drawings with generalized symbols.

There are some confusions in all these instances that are worth discussion. For example, one well-meaning archaeologist reader of a book that carried as a cover image a historic photograph of Dorothy Popenoe, an early twentieth-century archaeologist about whom I wrote, took the press to task for this selection because her keen eyes had detected what neither the editor nor I had: on the ground where Popenoe squatted, there were visible not only pots, but also some skeletal elements. Are we to censor all images that, even glancingly, incorporate human remains? Would it have been enough to crop the photo (cutting off the body of the woman in question, which could be even more disturbing)? Or must we conceal any iconography acknowledging that archaeologists have historically communed with the dead? At the other end of a spectrum of practice, when a lecturer announces the inclusion of images of human remains in a talk, who is being warned? Only descendant communities? People from particular groups whose religious beliefs preclude exposure to the dead? Or everyone?

There is clearly a lot to be discussed here. But my concern with "representation" should not be taken simply as a concern for *visual* representation and cannot be satisfied simply by omitting visual information from some accounts or by warning prospective viewers of what is coming. Instead, I am concerned with "representation" defined as what we do routinely in our texts (written and oral). This is terrain famously addressed by Native American scholar Gerald Vizenor (1986) in his scorching critique "Bone Courts: The Rights and Narrative Representation of Tribal Bones." Vizenor (1986:319) wrote about the "rights of human remains, sovereign tribal bones, to be their own narrators." Like the implied continuity contained in the phrase "human remains," codified in laws that refer to the dead body as inviolate "in any state of decomposition," the rights of self-narration Vizenor referenced do not end with death. He linked the treatment of organs at death with the treatment of the rest of the bodily remains, the "tribal bones" whose ability to narrate "their time and place on the earth" he wanted to reclaim (1986:320).

From the perspective of 25 years' experience with NAGPRA, it is now possible to see a set of claims in Vizenor's radical proposal that speak less about repatriation and reburial than about the recognition of the continuing personhood of human remains and the responsibilities that recognition demands. In Vizenor's words, under his called-for model of treating human remains as legal persons, academic interests would not disappear; rather, "archaeologists, osteologists, anthropologists, and others, would answer to the rights of tribal bones; the rights and interests of bones would be represented and narrated" (1986:325). His proposition—that bones have the right to tell their own stories—continues to be a challenge that we have to address directly. I suggest that we embrace the responsibility that comes from being part of the apparatus through which bones speak. That would mean an acknowledgment of our haunting by the uncanny, by the loss of the speaking voice that we are replacing. In place of a *right of* narration, we would see a *responsibility for* narration.

In my own attempt to think through the competing claims that arose during the framing and implementation of NAGPRA, I resorted to a related shift, from the language of a right to research as embodied in the concept of academic freedom, to the concept of research as a privilege (Joyce 2002a). More broadly, I have advocated for treating archaeological practice as always generating a set of responsibilities, given the fact that we are narrating for others who can no longer speak for themselves and have no way to object to our speech about them (Joyce 2002b, 2008; cf. Scarre 2003).

Vizenor (1986:327) vigorously objected to the dominant mode of narration of Native American remains as he perceived it: "neocolonial tropes to power...causal methodologies, reductive expiries, but not an agonistic discourse on *anthropos* or humans and their *real* narrative remains." Citing Manfred Stanley, he mourned the loss of "knowledge based upon sensuous relations of human beings to a perceived object world" (Vizenor 1986:328).

This call—to narrate the sensuous experience of knowing—echoes the words of ethnographer and archaeologist Susan Kus (1992), who called for us to attend to the sensory experience of death when we talk about the exhumed archaeological body. In her view, we have to take on the responsibility for representing the past in ways that convey the lived reality of "sensuous human practice" so that we do honor to the past. Drawing on a framework based on concepts indigenous to Madagascar, she wrote that "history is not just a series of unrelated incidents to be recited out of order and out of context; these pearls must be strung with care to do justice and honor to history. Those who know how to listen to and to tell history will understand this 'sense'; those who do not will do it dishonor" (Kus 1997:211).

While proceeding from a different source—ethnographic engagement in place of philosophical speculation—Kus made a point not unlike the view of Scarre (2003:241), who suggested that spreading falsehoods after a person is deceased (essentially, dishonoring history) does damage after death to the once-living person. Citing a philosophical tradition extending from Kant forward, Scarre (2003) argued that things can happen to human beings as subjects outside the boundaries of their lives (cf. Barilan 2006:236–237). The principle that the living and the dead should be treated symmetrically—that what would be wrong to do to a living person is also wrong to do to a dead one—frames a substantially more complicated position for those of us who must, in the course of our work, take part in the removal of the dead body from its resting place. "The evaluation of a life, or a phase of it, not uncommonly turns on the posthumous fate of its key projects or interests" (Scarre 2003:241).

To the extent that we mediate the persistence of specific human projects or interests after death, we have the potential to be the means to realize interests of the dead. Scarre (2003:247) argued that scholars engaged in exhumation do one thing that is relatively clearly in the interests of the dead: bear historical witness to their lives. While he accepted that archaeologists "may be little interested in their subjects as individuals," logically his argument would require us to evince that level of care: to treat each person with whose life we intersect after the animation of the body comes to an end as a subject with his or her own history. And we must recognize in that history the weight we bear, sometimes as the only person situated to mourn the loss or celebrate the life.

CONCLUSION

Where all this leaves me is in a position little different from the naïve one I described at the outset of this chapter: facing the skeletal traces of what I must—and do—recognize were persons in the past, remains that persist not only as indirect testimony of past lives, but as agential subjects in the present (see Barad 1999). Among the powerful productive capacities of human remains that I encounter in my work is that they do not just demand representation and rebuke badly articulated narratives: the dead also have the power to shape my own personhood. Treated properly, they convert the distanced and distancing practices through which archaeology objectively renders a site as evidence for others into intersubjective experiences. It matters when I recognize articulated skeletal elements as the remains of a child, or a man, or a woman. It matters that I worry about whether disarticulated skeletal elements continued to be seen in the past as traces of personhood, and if so, what kinds of persons these were. It matters that I view the worked and recirculated skeletal elements as potentially still presencing a known and named person, not simply serving as raw material or as a trophy, "human grave goods," or another form of object.

This leads me to several conclusions, some bearing on the responsibility of representation, some on the nature of being an archaeologist engaged in mortuary analysis. As the person privileged to revoice something of the life of a person who once lived, I feel a responsibility to the form of personhood that was entailed in that person's life: to thinking about and talking about their daily experiences, and how these situated the person in society. Aggregate statistics are useful for some purposes, but it is only when we attend to the personhood of the dead that we can hope to see the evidence of the unique experiences whose final witness we may be. Where that leaves us, I think, is in need of the services, not of a minister, philosopher, or lawyer, but of another professional, the undertaker, with whom we share the experience of walking the line that separates the living and the dead. We need to approach the process we administer with a similar degree of solemnity. We need to acknowledge that, at least in the world today, our intimate experience with the dead marks us. We are not everyday; we are uncanny, and we should ask what that does to us, and how we should act in light of it.

References

Abadie, Eugene H.

1838 Letter to Samuel G. Morton, February 3. Samuel George Morton Papers, American Philosophical Society.

Abu El-Haj, Nadia

2001 Facts on the Ground: Archaeological Practice and Territorial Self-Fashioning in Israeli Society. Chicago: University of Chicago Press.

2007 The Genetic Reinscription of Race. Annual Review of Anthropology 36:283–300.

Agamben, Giorgio

1999 Remnants of Auschwitz: The Witness and the Archive. New York: Zone.

Agarwal, Sabrina C., and Bonnie A. Glencross, eds.

2011 Social Bioarchaeology. Malden, MA: Wiley-Blackwell.

Albanese, John, and Shelley R. Saunders

2006 Is It Possible to Escape Racial Typology in Forensic Identification? *In* Forensic Anthropology and Medicine: Complementary Sciences from Recovery to Cause of Death. Aurore Schmitt, Eugénia Cunha, and João Pinheiro, eds. Pp. 281–316. Totowa, NJ: Humana.

Alexander, Michelle

2010 The New Jim Crow: Mass Incarceration in the Age of Colorblindness. New York: New Press.

Anderson, Bruce E.

2008 Identifying the Dead: Method Utilized by the Pima County (Arizona) Office of the Medical Examiner for the Undocumented Border Crossers: 2001–2006. Journal of Forensic Sciences 53(1):8–15.

Anderson, Bruce E., Walter H. Birkby, and Todd W. Fenton

2008 Identifying Southwest Hispanics Using Nonmetric Traits and the Cultural Profile. Journal of Forensic Sciences 53(1):29–33.

Anonymous

1839 Domestic Intelligence: Florida War, 23 May 1839. Army and Navy Chronicle 13(21):321–336.

1874 Obituary: Surgeon Eugene H. Abadie. New York Tribune, December 23.

Appadurai, Arjun

1998 Dead Certainty: Ethnic Violence in the Era of Globalization. Public Culture 10(2):225–247.

REFERENCES

Aptheker, Herbert

2003 The Event. *In* Nat Turner: A Slave Rebellion in History and Memory. K. S. Greenberg, ed. Pp. 45–57. Oxford: Oxford University Press.

Ariss, Rachel

2004 "Bring Out Your Dead": Law, Human Remains, and Memory. Canadian Journal of Law and Society 19:33–54.

Asociación de las Madres de Plaza de Mayo

1995 Historia de las Madres de Plaza de Mayo. Buenos Aires: Asociación de las Madres de Plaza de Mayo.

Babener, Liahna Klenman

1988 The Shadow's Shadow: The Motif of the Double in Edgar Allan Poe's "The Purloined Letter." *In* The Purloined Poe: Lacan, Derrida, and Psychoanalytic Reading. John P. Muller and William J. Richardson, eds. Pp. 21–32. Baltimore, MD: Johns Hopkins University Press.

Bahn, Paul

1984 Do Not Disturb? Archaeology and the Rights of the Dead. Journal of Applied Philosophy 1(2):213–225.

Ballbé, Ermengol Gassiot, and Dawnie Wolfe Steadman

2008 The Political, Social, and Scientific Contexts of Archaeological Investigations of Mass Graves in Spain. Archaeologies: Journal of the World Archaeological Congress 4(3):429–444.

Baptist, Edward E.

2002 Creating an Old South: Middle Florida's Plantation Frontier Before the Civil War. Chapel Hill: University of North Carolina Press.

Barad, Karen

1999 Agential Realism: Feminist Interventions in Understanding Scientific Practices. *In* The Science Studies Reader. Mario Biagioli, ed. Pp. 1–11. New York: Routledge.

Baraybar, Jose-Pablo, Valerie Brasey, and Andrew Zadel

2007 The Need for a Centralized and Humanitarian-Based Approach to Missing Persons in Iraq. International Journal of Human Rights 11(3):265–274.

Barilan, Y. Michael

2006 *Bodyworlds* and the Ethics of Using Human Remains: A Preliminary Discussion. Bioethics 20(5):233–247.

Barnes, Joseph K.

1867–1868 Circular No. 2. Medical Record: A Semi-Monthly Journal of Medicine and Surgery 2:167.

Bass, Jefferson

2006 Carved in Bone: A Body Farm Novel. New York: Harper.

Bass, William M.

1971 Human Osteology: A Laboratory and Field Manual of the Human Skeleton. Columbia: Missouri Archaeological Society.

2005 Human Osteology: A Laboratory and Field Manual. 5th edition. Columbia: Missouri Archaeological Society.

Bass, William, and Jon Jefferson
2003 Death's Acre: Inside the Legendary Forensic Lab the Body Farm, Where the Dead Do Tell Tales. New York: Penguin.

2007 Beyond the Body Farm: A Legendary Bone Detective Explores Murders, Mysteries, and the Revolution in Forensic Science. New York: Morrow.

Bateman, Rebecca B.
2002 Naming Patterns in Black Seminole Ethnogenesis. Ethnohistory 49(2):227–257.

Baudez, Claude, and Pierre Becquelin
1973 Archéologie de los Naranjos, Honduras. Etudes Mesoaméricaines 2. México DF: Mission Archeologique et Ethnologique Française au Mexique.

Becker, Marshall
1993 Earth Offerings Among the Classic Maya: Burials and Caches as Ritual Deposits. *In* Perspectivas Antropológicas en el Mundo Maya. María Josefa Iglesias and Francesc Ligorred, eds. Pp. 45–74. Madrid: Sociedad Española de Estudios Mayas.

Bemrose, John K.
1966 Reminiscences of the Second Seminole War. J. K. Mahon, ed. Gainesville: University Press of Florida.

Bensaude-Vincent, Bernadette
2001 A Genealogy of the Increasing Gap Between Science and the Public. Public Understanding of Science 10(1):99–113.

Bernadi, Patricia, and Luis Fondebrider
2007 Forensic Archaeology and the Scientific Documentation of Human Rights Violations: An Argentine Example from the Early 1980s. *In* Forensic Archaeology and Human Rights Violations. Roxana Ferllini, ed. Pp. 205–232. Springfield, IL: Charles C. Thomas.

Bertolli, Jeanne, Lisa M. Lee, and Patrick S. Sullivan
2007 Racial Misidentification of American Indians/Alaska Natives in the HIV/AIDS Reporting Systems of Five States and One Urban Health Jurisdiction, US, 1984–2002. Public Health Reports 122(3):382–392.

Binford, Leigh
1996 The El Mozote Massacre: Anthropology and Human Rights. Tucson: University of Arizona Press.

Blaauw, Margriet, and Virpi Lahteenmäki
2002 "Denial and Silence" or "Acknowledgement and Disclosure." International Review of the Red Cross 84(848):767–783.

Black, Sue M.
2003 Forensic Anthropology: Regulation in the United Kingdom. Science and Justice 43(4):187–192.

References

Blakely, Robert L., and Judith M. Harrington, eds.

1997 Bones in the Basement: Postmortem Racism in Nineteeth-Century Medical Training. Washington, DC: Smithsonian Institution Press.

Blau, Soren

2004 Forensic Archaeology in Australia: Current Situations, Future Possibilities. Australian Archaeology 58:11–14.

Blau, Soren, and Mark Skinner

2005 The Use of Forensic Archaeology in the Investigation of Human Rights Abuse: Unearthing the Past in East Timor. International Journal of Human Rights 9(4):449–463.

Blau, Soren, and Douglas Ubelaker, eds.

2009 Handbook of Forensic Anthropology and Archaeology. Walnut Creek, CA: Left Coast.

Blumenfeld, Jodi

2011 Racial Identification in the Skull and Teeth. Totem: The University of Western Ontario Journal of Anthropology 8(1):4.

Bourdieu, Pierre

1987 The Force of Law: Toward a Sociology of the Juridical Field. Hastings Journal of Law 38:805–853.

Bousquet, Jean-Pierre

1984 Las Locas de la Plaza de Mayo. Córdoba: Fundación para la Democracia en Argentina.

Bray, Tamara L., ed.

2001 The Future of the Past: Archaeologists, Native Americans, and Repatriation. New York: Garland.

Brickley, Megan B., and Roxana Ferllini

2007 Forensic Anthropology: Developments in Two Continents. *In* Forensic Anthropology: Case Studies from Europe. Megan B. Brickley and Roxana Ferllini, eds. Pp. 3–18. Springfield, IL: Charles C. Thomas.

Brkic, Courtney Angela

2003 Stillness and Other Stories. New York: Farrar, Straus and Giroux.

2004 The Stone Fields. New York: Farrar, Straus and Giroux.

Brooks, James F., ed.

2002 Confounding the Color Line: The Indian-Black Experience in North America. Lincoln: University of Nebraska Press.

Brooks, Sheilagh, and Judy M. Suchey

1990 Skeletal Age Determination Based on the *Os Pubis*: The Comparison of the Acsádi-Nemeskéri and Suchey-Brooks Methods. Human Evolution 5(3):227–238.

Brothwell, Don R.

1981 Digging Up Bones: The Excavation, Treatment, and Study of Human Skeletal Remains. Ithaca, NY: Cornell University Press.

Brues, Alice

1990 The Once and Future Diagnosis of Race. *In* Skeletal Attribution of Race: Methods for Forensic Anthropology. George W. Gill and Stanley Rhine, eds. Pp. 1–8. Albuquerque, NM: Maxwell Museum of Anthropology.

1993 The Objective View of Race. NAPA Bulletin 13(1):74–78.

Buchanan, Robert C.

1950 A Journal of Lt. Robert C. Buchanan During the Seminole War. Florida Historical Quarterly 29(2):132–552.

Buchli, Victor, and Gavin Lucas

2001 Archaeologies of the Contemporary Past. London: Routledge.

Buikstra, Jane E., and Douglas H. Ubelaker, eds.

1994 Standards for Data Collection from Human Skeletal Remains: Proceedings of a Seminar at the Field Museum of Natural History. Fayetteville: Arkansas Archaeological Survey.

Burns, Karen Ramsey

1999 Forensic Anthropology Training Manual. Upper Saddle River, NJ: Prentice Hall International.

Burt, Jo Marie

2009 Guilty as Charged: The Trial of Former Peruvian President Alberto Fujimori. International Journal of Transitional Justice 3(3):384–405.

Butchart, Garnet C.

2007 On the Void: The Fascinating Object of Evil in "Human Remains." *In* The Changing Face of Evil in Film and Television. Martin Norden, ed. Pp. 159–175. New York: Rodopi.

Byers, Steven N.

2005 Introduction to Forensic Anthropology. London: Pearson.

2010 Introduction to Forensic Anthropology. 4th edition. Upper Saddle River, NJ: Pearson.

Callon, Michel, and Vololona Rabeharisoa

2003 Research "in the Wild" and the Shaping of New Social Identities. Technology in Society 25(2):193–204.

Calsamiglia, Helena, and Carmen Lopez Ferrero

2003 Role and Position of Scientific Voices: Reported Speech in the Media. Discourse Studies 5(2):147–173.

Carr, Robert, Marilyn Masson, and Willard Steele

1989 Archaeological Investigations at the Okeechobee Battlefield. Florida Anthropologist 42(3):205–236.

References

Carrescia, Olivia, dir.

2008 Sacred Soil. OLC Productions, New York. Distributed by Icarus Films, Brooklyn, NY.

Cartmill, Matt

1998 The Status of the Race Concept in Physical Anthropology. American Anthropologist 100(3):651–660.

Casallas, Diego A., and Juliana Padilla Piedrahita

2004 Antropología Forense en el Conflicto Armado en el Contexto Latino-americano: Estudio Comparativo Argentina, Guatemala, Perú y Colombia. Maguaré 18:293–310.

Caspari, Rachel

2003 From Types to Populations: A Century of Race, Physical Anthropology, and the American Anthropological Association. American Anthropologist 105(1):65–76.

2009 1918: Three Perspectives on Race and Human Variation. American Journal of Physical Anthropology 139(1):5–15.

Cattaneo, Cristina

2007 Forensic Anthropology: Developments of a Classical Discipline in the New Millennium. Forensic Science International 165(2):185–193.

Cattaneo, Cristina, D. Porta, Danilo De Angelis, Daniele Gibelli, Pasquale Poppa, and Marco Grandi

2010 Unidentified Bodies and Human Remains: An Italian Glimpse Through a European Problem. Forensic Science International 195:167.e1–167.e6.

Catterberg, Edgardo R.

1991 Argentina Confronts Politics: Political Culture and Public Opinion in the Argentine Transition to Democracy. Boulder, CO: Lynne Rienner.

Cavell, Stanley

1994 A Pitch of Philosophy: Autobiographical Exercises. Cambridge, MA: Harvard University Press.

Caveney, Angela F., Melinda A. Smith, Lewis B. Morgenstern, and Lynda D. Lisabeth

2006 Use of Death Certificates to Study Ethnic-Specific Mortality. Public Health Reports 121(3):275–281.

Christensen, Angi M.

2004 Testing the Reliability of Frontal Sinuses in Positive Identification. Journal of Forensic Sciences 50(1):18–22.

2014 Anthropology. American Academy of Forensic Sciences News 44(2):55–56.

Christensen, Angi M., and Christian M. Crowder

2009 Evidentiary Standards for Forensic Anthropology. Journal of Forensic Sciences 54(6):1211–1216.

Clemens, Elisabeth S.

1986 Of Asteroids and Dinosaurs: The Role of the Press in the Shaping of Scientific Debate. Social Studies of Science 16(3):421–456.

Cohen, Daniel, Nick Sevdalis, David Taylor, Karen Kerr, Mick Heys, Keith Willett, Nicola Batrick, and Ara Darzi

2012 Emergency Preparedness in the 21st Century: Training and Preparation Modules in Virtual Environments. Resuscitation 84(1):78–84.

Cole, Simon A.

2001 Suspect Identities: A History of Fingerprinting and Criminal Identification. Cambridge, MA: Harvard University Press.

Cole, Simon A., and Rachel Dioso-Villa

2007 *CSI* and Its Effects: Media, Juries, and the Burden of Proof. New England Law Review 41(3):435–469.

2009 Investigating the "*CSI* Effect" Effect: Media and Litigation Crisis in Criminal Law. Stanford Law Review 61(6):1335–1374.

Committee on Missing Persons in Cyprus

1981 Terms of Reference and Mandate. http://www.cmp-cyprus.org/about-the-cmp/terms-of-reference-and-mandate (accessed May 5, 2014).

Conan Doyle, Arthur

1986[1893] The Complete Sherlock Holmes. Garden City, NY: Doubleday.

Congram, Derek, and Ariana Fernández

2010 Uncovering Trauma: The Exhumation and Repatriation of Spanish Civil War Dead. Anthropology News 51(3):23–24.

Congram, Derek, and Dawnie Wolfe Steadman

2008 Distinguished Guests or Agents of *Ingérence*: Foreign Participation in Spanish Civil War Grave Excavations. Complutum 19(2):161–173.

Congram, Derek, and Jon Sterenberg

2009 Grave Challenges in Iraq. *In* Handbook of Forensic Anthropology and Archaeology. Soren Blau and Douglas H. Ubelaker, eds. Pp. 441–454. Walnut Creek, CA: Left Coast.

Connor, Melissa

2007 Forensic Methods: Excavation for the Archaeologist and Investigator. Lanham, MD: AltaMira.

Connor, Melissa, and Douglas D. Scott

2001 Paradigms and Perspectives. Historical Archaeology 35(1):1–6.

Cordner, Stephen

2005 The Missing: Action to Resolve the Problem of Those Unaccounted for as a Result of Armed Conflict or Internal Violence, and to Assist Their Families. Victorian Institute of Forensic Medicine Review 3(1):2–6.

References

Cordner, Stephen, and Helen McKelvie

2002 Developing Standards in International Forensic Work to Identify Missing Persons. International Review of the Red Cross 48(848):867–884.

Cornwell, Patricia

1994 The Body Farm. New York: Scribner's.

2003 Foreword: The Mayor of the Body Farm. *In* Death's Acre: Inside the Legendary Forensic Lab the Body Farm, Where the Dead Do Tell Tales by William Bass and Jon Jefferson. Pp. ix–xii. New York: Penguin.

Covington, James W.

1993 The Seminoles of Florida. Gainesville: University Press of Florida.

Cox, Katharine, Nancy G. Tayles, and Hallie R. Buckley

2006 Forensic Identification of "Race": The Issues in New Zealand. Current Anthropology 47(5):869–874.

Cox, Margaret

2001 Forensic Archaeology in the UK: Questions of Socio-Intellectual Context and Socio-Political Responsibility. *In* Archaeologies of the Contemporary Past. Victor Buchli and Gavin Lucas, eds. Pp. 145–157. London: Routledge.

2003 A Multidisciplinary Approach to the Investigation of Crimes Against Humanity, War Crimes, and Genocide: The Inforce Foundation. Science and Justice 43(4):225–227.

2009 Forensic Anthropology and Archaeology: Past and Present—A United Kingdom Perspective. *In* Handbook of Forensic Anthropology and Archaeology. Soren Blau and Douglas H. Ubelaker, eds. Pp. 29–41. Walnut Creek, CA: Left Coast.

Crist, Thomas A. J.

2001 Bad to the Bone? Historical Archaeologists in the Practice of Forensic Science. Historical Archaeology 35(1):39–56.

Crossland, Zoë

2000 Buried Lives: Forensic Archaeology and the Disappeared in Argentina. Archaeological Dialogues 7(2):146–159.

2002 Violent Spaces: Conflict over the Reappearance of Argentina's Disappeared. *In* Matériel Culture: The Archaeology of Twentieth-Century Conflict. John Schofield, William G. Johnson, and Colleen M. Beck, eds. Pp. 115–131. London: Routledge.

2009a Of Clues and Signs: The Dead Body and Its Evidential Traces. American Anthropologist 111(1):69–80.

2009b Acts of Estrangement: The Making of Self and Other Through Exhumation. Archaeological Dialogues 16(1):102–125.

2011 The Archaeology of Contemporary Conflict. *In* The Oxford Handbook of the Archaeology of Ritual and Religion. Tim Insoll, ed. Pp. 285–306. Oxford: Oxford University Press.

2013 Evidential Regimes of Forensic Archaeology. Annual Review of Anthropology 42:121–137.

Dao, James

2011 In California, Indian Tribes with Casino Money Cast Off Members. New York Times, December 12.

Das, Veena

1995 Critical Events: An Anthropological Perspective on Contemporary India. New York: Oxford University Press.

Das, Veena, Arthur Kleinman, Margaret Lock, Mamphela Ramphele, and Pamela Reynolds, eds.

2001 Remaking a World: Violence, Social Suffering, and Recovery. Berkeley: University of California Press.

Daston, Lorraine, and Peter Galison

2007 Objectivity. Boston: Zone.

Davenport, Anna, and Karl Harrison

2011 Swinging the Blue Lamp: The Forensic Archaeology of Contemporary Child and Animal Burial in the UK. Mortality 16(2):176–190.

Dawes, James

2007 That the World May Know. Cambridge, MA: Harvard University Press.

De Baets, Antoon

2004 A Declaration of the Responsibilities of Present Generations Toward Past Generations. History and Theory 43:130–164.

Degregori, Carlos Iván

1991 Ayacucho 1980–1983: Jóvenes y Campesinos ante la Violencia Política. *In* Poder y Violencia en los Andes. Henrique Urbano, ed. Pp. 395–417. Cusco: Bartolome de las Casas.

1998 Harvesting Storms: Peasant Rondas and the Defeat of Sendero Luminoso in Ayacucho. *In* Shining and the Other Paths: War and Society in Peru, 1980–1995. Steve Stern, ed. Pp. 128–157. Durham, NC: Duke University Press.

Degregori, Carlos Iván, José Coronel, Ponciano del Pino, and Orin Starn

1996 Las Rondas Campesinas y la Derrota de Sendero Luminoso. Lima, Peru: Instituto de Estudios Peruanos.

De León, Jason

2012 "Better to Be Hot than Caught": Excavating the Conflicting Roles of Migrant Material Culture. American Anthropologist 114(3):477–495.

Derrida, Jacques

1990 The Force of Law: The "Mystical Foundation of Authority." Cardozo Law Review 11(5–6):919–973.

References

Deter, Christina A.

2009 Gradients of Occlusal Wear in Hunter-Gatherers and Agriculturalists. American Journal of Physical Anthropology 138(3):247–254.

Devettere, Raymond J.

1990 Neocortical Death and Human Death. Journal of Law, Medicine, and Ethics 18(1-2):96–104.

Dirkmaat, Dennis C.

2012 A Companion to Forensic Anthropology. Oxford: Blackwell.

Dirkmaat, Dennis C., and James M. Adovasio

1997 The Role of Archaeology in the Recovery and Interpretation of Human Remains from an Outdoor Forensic Setting. *In* Forensic Taphonomy: The Postmortem Fate of Human Remains. William D. Haglund and Marcella H. Sorg, eds. Pp. 39–64. Boca Raton, FL: CRC.

Dirkmaat, Dennis C., and Luis L. Cabo

2012 Forensic Anthropology: Embracing the New Paradigm. *In* A Companion to Forensic Anthropology. Dennis C. Dirkmaat, ed. Pp. 3–39. Oxford: Blackwell.

Dirkmaat, Dennis C., Luis L. Cabo, James M. Adovasio, and Vincente C. Rozas

2005 Mass Graves, Human Rights and Commingled Remains: Considering the Benefits of Forensic Archaeology. Proceedings of the American Academy of Forensic Sciences 11:316.

Dirkmaat, Dennis C., Luis Cabo, Stephen D. Ousley, and Steven A. Symes

2008 New Perspectives in Forensic Anthropology. Yearbook of Physical Anthropology 137(S47):33–52.

Dixon, Anthony E.

2007 Black Seminole Involvement and Leadership During the Second Seminole War, 1835–1842. PhD thesis, Department of History, Indiana University, Bloomington.

Doretti, Mercedes, and Luis Fondebrider

2001 Science and Human Rights: Truth, Justice, Reparation and Reconciliation, a Long Way in Third World Countries. *In* Archaeologies of the Contemporary Past. Victor Buchli and Gavin Lucas, eds. Pp. 138–144. London: Routledge.

Doretti, Mercedes, and Clyde C. Snow

2003 Forensic Anthropology and Human Rights: The Argentine Experience. *In* Hard Evidence: Case Studies in Forensic Anthropology. Dawnie Wolfe Steadman, ed. Pp. 290–310. Upper Saddle River, NJ: Prentice Hall.

Drake, Samuel G.

1854 The Aboriginal Races of North America. Boston: Higgins and Bradley.

Duhig, Corinne, and Nicola Martinsen

2007 Many Layers of Taphonomy: Dismemberment and Other Body Processing. *In* Forensic Anthropology: Case Studies from Europe. Megan B. Brickley and Roxana Ferllini, eds. Pp. 86–89. Springfield, IL: Charles C. Thomas.

Dupras, Tosha L., John J. Schultz, Sandra M. Wheeler, and Lana J. Williams
2012 Forensic Recovery of Human Remains: Archaeological Approaches. 2nd edition. Boca Raton, FL: CRC.

Duray, Stephen M., H. B. Morter, and F. J. Smith
1999 Morphological Variation in Cervical Spinous Processes: Potential Applications in the Forensic Identification of Race from the Skeleton. Journal of Forensic Sciences 44(5):937–944.

EAAF
2001 Annual Report. Buenos Aires: Argentine Forensic Anthropology Team.

2002 Annual Report. Buenos Aires: Argentine Forensic Anthropology Team.

Edgeworth, Matthew, ed.
2006 Ethnographies of Archaeological Practice: Cultural Encounters, Material Transformations. Lanham, MD: AltaMira.

Elkins, Aaron
1982 Fellowship of Fear. New York: Penguin.

Ellison, George, Andrew Smart, Richard Tutton, Simon M. Outram, Richard Ashcroft, and Paul Martin
2007 Racial Categories in Medicine: A Failure of Evidence-Based Practice. PLOSMed 4(9)a:e287.

Emanovsky, Paul D., and William R. Belcher
2012 The Many Hats of a Recovery Leader: Perspectives on Planning and Executing Worldwide Forensic Investigations and Recoveries at the JPAC Central Identification Library. *In* A Companion to Forensic Anthropology. Dennis C. Dirkmaat, ed. Pp. 567–592. Oxford: Blackwell.

EPAF
N.d. Desaparición Forzada en el Perú: El Aporte de la Investigación Anthropológica Forense en la Obtención de Evidencia Probatoria y la Construcción de un Paraguas Humanitario. Lima, Peru: Equipo Peruano de Antropología Forense.

Epstein, Steven
2008 The Rise of "Recruitmentology": Clinical Research, Racial Knowledge, and the Politics of Inclusion and Difference. Social Studies of Science 38(5):801–832.

Etxeberría, Francisco, ed.
2012 Prólogo. Antropología Forense de la Guerra Civil Española. Special issue of Boletín Galego de Medicina Legal e Forense 18(9):9.

Fabian, Ann
2003 The Curious Cabinet of Dr. Morton. *In* Acts of Possession: Collecting in America. L. Dilworth, ed. Pp. 112–137. New Brunswick, NJ: Rutgers University Press.

2010 The Skull Collectors. Chicago: University of Chicago Press.

References

Fahnestock, Jeanne

1986 Accommodating Science: The Rhetorical Life of Scientific Facts. Written Communication 3(3):275–296.

FAME

2010 Practice and Guidelines for Florida Medical Examiners. http://www.fdle.state.fl.us/Content/CJST/Documents/Medical-Examiners-Commission-%28MEC%29/MEC-Publications-and-Forms/Practice-Guidelines-2009-Adopted.aspx (accessed September 30, 2014).

Ferllini, Roxana

1999 The Role of Forensic Anthropology in Human Rights Issues. *In* Forensic Osteological Analysis: A Book of Case Studies. Scott I. Fairgrieve, ed. Pp. 287–302. Springfield, IL: Charles C. Thomas.

2007 Bone Scatter on Chalk: The Importance of Osteological Knowledge and Environmental Assessment. *In* Forensic Anthropology: Case Studies from Europe. Megan B. Brickley and Roxana Ferllini, eds. Pp. 216–231. Springfield, IL: Charles C. Thomas.

Ferllini, Roxana, ed.

2007 Forensic Archaeology and Human Rights Violations. Springfield, IL: Charles C. Thomas.

Ferrándiz, Francisco

2006 The Return of Civil War Ghosts: The Ethnography of Exhumations in Contemporary Spain. Anthropology Today 22:7–12.

2008 Cries and Whispers: Exhuming and Narrating Defeat in Spain Today. Journal of Spanish Cultural Studies 9(2):177–192.

2009 Fosas Comunes, Paisajes Del Terror. Revista de Dialectología y Tradiciones Populares 64(1):61–94.

2013 Exhuming the Defeated: Civil War Mass Graves in 21st-Century Spain. American Ethnologist 40(1):38–54.

Ferrara, Santo Davide, Thomas Bajanowski, Rossanna Cecchi, Rossella Snenghi, Colette Case, and Guido Viel

2010 Bio-Medicolegal Guidelines and Protocols: Survey and Future Perspectives in Europe. International Journal of Legal Medicine 124(4):345–350.

Ferrara, Santo Davide, and Heidi Pfeiffer

2010 Unitariness, Evidence and Quality in Bio-Medicolegal Sciences. International Journal of Legal Medicine 124(4):343–344.

Fforde, Cressida, Jane Hubert, and Paul Turnbull

2002 The Dead and Their Possessions: Repatriation in Principle, Policy, and Practice. London: Routledge.

Fiorato, Veronica, Anthea Boylston, and Christopher Knüsel

2000 Blood Red Roses: The Archaeology of a Mass Grave from the Battle of Towton AD 1461. Oxford: Oxbow.

Fisher, Jo
1989 Mothers of the Disappeared. London: Zed.

Flavel, Ambika, and Caroline Barker
2009 Forensic Anthropology and Archaeology in Guatemala. *In* Handbook of Forensic Anthropology and Archaeology. Soren Blau and Douglas H. Ubelaker, eds. Pp. 426–440. Walnut Creek, CA: Left Coast.

Fondebrider, Luis
2002 Reflections on the Scientific Documentation of Human Rights Violations. International Review of the Red Cross 84(848):885–891.

2004 Uncovering Evidence: The Forensic Sciences in Human Rights. Minneapolis, MN: Center for Victims of Torture, New Tactics in Human Rights Projects.

2009 The Application of Forensic Anthropology to the Investigation of Political Violence: Perspectives from South America. *In* Handbook of Forensic Anthropology and Archaeology. Soren Blau and Douglas Ubelaker, eds. Pp. 67–75. Walnut Creek, CA: Left Coast.

2012 The Application of Forensic Anthropology to the Investigation of Cases of Political Violence. *In* A Companion to Forensic Anthropology. Dennis C. Dirkmaat, ed. Pp. 639–648. Oxford: Blackwell.

France, Diane L., Tom J. Griffin, Jack G. Swanburg, John W. Lindemann, G. Clark Davenport, Vickey Trammell, Cecilia T. Travis, Boris Kondratieff, Al Nelson, Kim Castellano, Dick Hopkins, and Tom Adair
1992 A Multidisciplinary Approach to the Detection of Clandestine Graves. Journal of Forensic Sciences 37(6):1445–1458.

Freud, Sigmund
2004[1919] The Uncanny. *In* Fantastic Literature: A Critical Reader. David Sandner, ed. Pp. 74–101. Westport, CT: Praeger.

Froidevaux, Sylvain
2002 L'Humanitaire, le Religieux et la Mort. International Review of the Red Cross 48(848):785–799.

Fuentes, Agustin
2012 Race, Monogamy, and Other Lies They Told You: Busting Myths About Human Nature. Berkeley: University of California Press.

Fuentes, Miguel, Jairo Sepúlveda, and Alexander San Francisco
2009 Espacios de Represión, Lugar de Memoria: El Estadio Víctor Jara Como Campo de Detención de la Dictadura en Chile. Revista Atlántica-Mediterránea de Prehistoria y Arqueología Social 11:137–169.

Funari, Pedro Paulo A., Andrés Zarankin, and Melissa A. Salerno
2009 Memories from Darkness: Archaeology of Repression and Resistance in Latin America. New York: Springer.

References

Galloway, Alison

2014 Living on the Sidelines of Death: Anthropologists and Violence. *In* Bioarchaeological and Forensic Perspectives on Violence. Debra L. Martin and Cheryl P. Anderson, eds. Pp. 311–320. Cambridge: Cambridge University Press.

Galloway, Alison, and Tal L. Simmons

1997 Education in Forensic Anthropology: Appraisal and Outlook. Journal of Forensic Sciences 42(5):796–801.

Garbarino, Merwyn S.

1989 The Seminoles. New York: Chelsea House.

García Moll, Roberto, Daniel Juáres Cossio, Carmen Pijoan Aguade, María Elena Salas Cuesta, and Marcela Salas Cuesta

1991 Catálogo de Entierros de San Luis Tlatilco, México, Temporada IV. México DF: Instituto Nacional de Antropologia e Historia.

Garrido Varas, Claudia, and Marisol Intriago Leiva

2012 Managing Commingled Remains from Mass Graves: Considerations, Implications and Recommendations from a Human Rights Case in Chile. Forensic Science International 219(1–3):e19–e24.

Garvin, Heather M., and Nicholas V. Passalacqua

2012 Current Practices by Forensic Anthropologists in Adult Skeletal Age Estimation. Journal of Forensic Sciences 57(2):427–433.

Geller, Pamela L.

2005 Skeletal Analysis and Theoretical Complications. World Archaeology 37(4):597–609.

2008 Conceiving Sex: Fomenting a Feminist Bioarchaeology. Journal of Social Archaeology 8(1):113–138.

2009 Bodyscapes, Biology, and Heteronormativity. American Anthropologist 111(4):504–516.

Gieryn, Thomas F.

1983 Boundary-Work and the Demarcation of Science from Non-Science: Strains and Interests in Professional Ideologies of Scientists. American Sociological Review 48(6):781–795.

Giles, Eugene, and Orville Elliot

1963 Sex Determination by Discriminant Function Analysis of Crania. American Journal of Physical Anthropology 21(1):53–68.

Gill, George W.

1990 Skeletal Attribution of Race. Albuquerque, NM: Maxwell Museum of Anthropology.

1998 Craniofacial Criteria in the Skeletal Attribution of Race. *In* Forensic Osteology: Advances in the Identification of Human Remains. K. J. Reichs, ed. Pp. 293–317. Springfield, IL: Charles C. Thomas.

Gill, George W., and Stanley Rhine, eds.
2004 Skeletal Attribution of Race: Methods in Forensic Anthropology. Albuquerque, NM: Maxwell Museum of Anthropology.

Gillespie, Susan D.
2001 Personhood, Agency, and Mortuary Ritual: A Case Study from the Ancient Maya. Journal of Anthropological Archaeology 20(1):73–112.

2003 Body and Soul Among the Maya: Keeping the Spirits in Place. *In* The Space and Place of Death. Helaine Silverman and David Small, eds. Pp. 67–78. Archaeological Papers of the American Anthropological Association. Arlington, VA: American Anthropological Association.

Gillett, Mary C.
1987 The Army Medical Department 1818–1865. Washington, DC: US Government Printing Office.

Gill-King, Harrell
2005 Determination of Ancestry and Skeletal Age in Forensic Anthropology. Journal of the Federation of American Societies for Experimental Biology 19(4):A226.

Ginzburg, Carlo
1989 Clues, Myths, and the Historical Method. Baltimore, MD: Johns Hopkins University Press.

Girdwoyn, Piotr A., and Tadeusz J. Tomaszewski
2009 New Method Underlying Forensic Education. Forensic Science Policy and Management 1(1):62–64.

Gómez López, Ana María, and Andrés Patiño Umaña
2007 Who Is Missing? Problems in the Application of Forensic Archaeology and Anthropology in Colombia's Conflict. *In* Forensic Archaeology and Human Rights Violations. Roxana Ferllini, ed. Pp. 170–204. Springfield, IL: Charles C. Thomas.

González-Ruibal, Alfredo
2007 Making Things Public: Archaeologies of the Spanish Civil War. Public Archaeology 6(4):203–226.

2011 The Archaeology of Internment in Francoist Spain (1936–1952). *In* Archaeologies of Internment. Adrian Myers and Gabriel Moshenska, eds. Pp. 53–73. New York: Springer.

Good, Byron
1994 Medicine, Rationality, and Experience: An Anthropological Perspective. Cambridge: Cambridge University Press.

Goodman, Alan H.
1997 Bred in the Bone? Sciences 37(2):20–25.

Goodman, Alan H., and George J. Armelagos, eds.
1996 The Resurrection of Race: The Concept of Race in Physical Anthropology in the 1990s. Dix Hills, NY: General Hall.

References

Gorriti, Gustavo

1990 The Shining Path: A History of the Millenarian War in Peru. Chapel Hill: University of North Carolina Press.

Gould, Stephen Jay

1978 Morton's Ranking of Races by Cranial Capacity: Unconscious Manipulation of Data May Be a Scientific Norm. Science 200(5):503–509.

1981 The Mismeasure of Man. New York: Norton.

Gowland, Rebecca, and Tim Thompson

2013 Human Identity and Identification. Cambridge: Cambridge University Press.

Grandin, Greg

2005 The Instruction of Great Catastrophe: Truth Commissions, National History, and State Formation in Argentina, Chile, and Guatemala. American Historical Review 110(1). http://www.historycooperative.org/journals/ahr/110.1/grandin.html, accessed June 12, 2006.

Graves Brown, Paul

2011 Touching from a Distance: Alienation, Abjection, Estrangement, and Archaeology. Norwegian Archaeological Review 44(2):131–144.

Gravlee, Clarence C.

2009 How Race Becomes Biology: Embodiment of Social Inequality. American Journal of Physical Anthropology 139(1):47–57.

Green, Linda

1999 Fear as a Way of Life: Mayan Widows in Rural Guatemala. New York: Columbia University Press.

Greenslade, William M.

1994 Degeneration, Culture, and the Novel: 1880–1940. Cambridge: Cambridge University Press.

Gregory, Jane, and Steven Miller

1998 Science in Public: Communication, Culture, and Credibility. New York: Plenum.

Grivas, Christopher R., and Debra Komar

2008 *Kumho, Daubert,* and the Nature of Scientific Inquiry: Implications for Forensic Anthropology. Journal of Forensic Sciences 53(4):771–776.

Guzman Bouvard, Marguerite

1994 Revolutionizing Motherhood: The Mothers of the Plaza de Mayo. Wilmington, DE: Scholarly Resources.

Haglund, William D.

2001 Archaeology and Forensic Death Investigations. Historical Archaeology 35(1):26–34.

Haglund, William D., Melissa Connor, and Douglas D. Scott
2001 The Archaeology of Contemporary Mass Graves. Historical Archaeology 35(1):57–69.

Hamilakis, Yannis, and Aris Anagnostopoulos
2009 Archaeological Ethnographies. London: Maney.

Hanby, Laura J., and Craig Bennell
2008 The *CSI* Effect: An Examination of the Source of Biases Toward Forensic Science. *In* Proceedings of the 2007 North American Correctional and Criminal Justice Psychology Conference. Guy Bourgon, R. Karl Hanson, Joanna D. Pozzulo, Kelly E. Morton Bourgon, and Carrie L. Tanasichuk, eds. Pp. 85–93. Ottawa, ON: Public Safety Canada.

Harding, Vanessa
1989 "And One More May Be Laid There": The Location of Burials in Early Modern London. London Journal 14(2):112–129.

1992 Burial Choice and Burial Location in Later Medieval London. *In* Death in Towns: Urban Responses to the Dying and the Dead, 100–1600. Steven R. Bassett, ed. Pp. 119–135. Leicester: Leicester University Press.

Hefner, Joseph T.
2009 Cranial Nonmetric Variation and Estimating Ancestry. Journal of Forensic Sciences 54(5):985–995.

Hefner, Joseph, Stephen D. Ousley, and Dennis C. Dirkmaat
2012 Morphoscopic Traits and the Assessment of Ancestry. *In* A Companion to Forensic Anthropology. Dennis C. Dirkmaat, ed. Pp. 287–310. Oxford: Blackwell.

Heller, Kevin Jon
2012 The Nuremberg Military Tribunals and the Origins of International Criminal Law. Oxford: Oxford University Press.

Hilgartner, Stephen
1990 The Dominant View of Popularization: Conceptual Problems, Political Uses. Social Studies of Science 20(3):519–539.

Hinkes, Madeleline, ed.
1990 Shovel-Shaped Incisors in Human Identification. Albuquerque, NM: Maxwell Museum of Anthropology.

Hinton, Alexander Laban
2002 A Head for an Eye: Revenge in the Cambodian Genocide. *In* Genocide: An Anthropological Reader. Alexander Laban Hinton, ed. Pp. 254–285. Oxford: Blackwell.

Hinton, Alexander Laban, and Kevin Lewis O'Neill, eds.
2009 Genocide: Truth, Memory, and Representation. Durham, NC: Duke University Press.

References

Holland, Thomas

2006 One Drop of Blood. New York: Simon and Schuster.

Holland, Thomas, John Byrd, and Vincent Sava

2008 Joint POW/MIA Accounting Command's Central Identification Laboratory. *In* The Forensic Anthropology Laboratory. Michael W. Warren, Heather A. Walsh-Haney, and Laurel Freas, eds. Pp. 47–64. Boca Raton, FL: Taylor and Francis.

Holobinko, Anastasia

2012 Forensic Human Identification in the United States and Canada: A Review of the Law, Admissible Techniques, and the Legal Implications of Their Application in Forensic Cases. Forensic Science International 222(1–3):394.e1–394.e13.

Hoover, J. Edgar

1931 Criminal Identification. American Journal of Police Science 2(1):8–19.

Hoshower, Lisa M.

1998 Forensic Archaeology and the Need for Flexible Excavation Strategies: A Case Study. Journal of Forensic Sciences 43(1):53–56.

Howells, William W.

1973 Cranial Variation in Man: A Study by Multivariate Analysis of Patterns of Difference Among Recent Human Populations. Papers of the Peabody Museum of Archaeology and Ethnology 67. Cambridge, MA: Peabody Museum Press.

1989 Skull Shapes and the Map: Craniometric Analyses in the Dispersion of Modern Homo. Papers of the Peabody Museum of Archaeology and Ethnology 79. Cambridge, MA: Peabody Museum Press.

Huffine, Edwin, John Crews, Brenda Kennedy, Kathryne Bomberger, and Asta Zinbo

2001 Mass Identification of Persons Missing from the Break-Up of the Former Yugoslavia: Structure, Function, and the Role of the International Commission on Missing Persons. Croatian Medical Journal 42(3):271–275.

Hughes, Cris E., Chelsea Juarez, Taylor L. Hughes, Alison Galloway, Gillian Fowler, and Shirley Chacon

2011 A Simulation for Exploring the Effects of the "Trait List" Method's Subjectivity on Consistency and Accuracy of Ancestry Estimations. Journal of Forensic Sciences 56(5):1094–1106.

Hunnisett, R. F.

1961 The Medieval Coroner. Cambridge: Cambridge University Press.

Hunter, John

1999 The Excavation of Modern Murder. *In* The Loved Body's Corruption: Archaeological Contributions to the Study of Human Mortality. Jane Downes and Tony Pollard, eds. Pp. 209–223. Glasgow: Cruithne.

Hunter, John R., Charlotte A. Roberts, Carol Heron, Rob C. Janaway, Anthony L. Martin, and Mark Pollard
1994 Forensic Archaeology in Britain. Antiquity 68(261):758–769.

Hunter, John R., and Barrie Simpson
2007 Preparing the Ground: Archaeology in a War Zone. *In* Forensic Archaeology and Human Rights Violations. Roxana Ferllini, ed. Pp. 266–292. Springfield, IL: Charles C. Thomas.

Hurst, Carolyn V.
2012 Morphoscopic Trait Expressions Used to Identify Southwest Hispanics. Journal of Forensic Sciences 57(4):859–865.

Ignatiev, Noel
1995 How the Irish Became White. London: Routledge.

İşcan, Mehmet Yaşar, and Horacio Elbio Solla Olivera
2000 Forensic Anthropology in Latin America. Forensic Science International 109(1):15–30.

Jagose, Annamarie
1996 Queer Theory: An Introduction. Melbourne, Australia: Melbourne University Press.

Jantz, Richard, and Stephen Ousley
2010 FORDISC 3.1. Knoxville: University of Tennessee Press.

Jones, D. Gareth, R. Gear, and Kerry A. Galvin
2003 Stored Human Tissue: An Ethical Perspective on the Fate of Anonymous, Archival Material. Journal of Medical Ethics 29(6):343–347.

Jorde, Lynn B., and Stephen P. Wooding
2006 Genetic Variation, Classification, and "Race." Nature Genetics (Suppl.) 36(11):S28–S33.

Joyce, Rosemary A.
1998 Performing the Body in Prehispanic Central America. Res: Anthropology and Aesthetics 33:147–165.

1999 Social Dimensions of Pre-Classic Burials. *In* Social Patterns in Pre-Classic Mesoamerica. David C. Grove and Rosemary A. Joyce, eds. Pp. 15–47. Washington, DC: Dumbarton Oaks.

2001 Burying the Dead at Tlatilco: Social Memory and Social Identities. *In* New Perspectives on Mortuary Analysis. Meredith Chesson, ed. Pp. 12–26. Archaeological Papers of the American Anthropological Association. Arlington, VA: American Anthropological Association.

2002a Academic Freedom, Stewardship, and Cultural Heritage: Weighing the Interests of Stakeholders in Crafting Repatriation Approaches. *In* The Dead and Their Possessions: Repatriation in Principle, Policy, and Practice. Cressida Fforde, Jane Hubert, and Paul Turnbull, eds. Pp. 99–107. London: Routledge.

2002b The Languages of Archaeology: Dialogue, Narrative, and Writing. Oxford: Blackwell.

2003a Las Raíces de la Tradición Funeraria Maya en Prácticas Mesoamericanas del Período Formativo. *In* Antropología de la Eternidad: La Muerte en la Cultura Maya. Andrés Ciudad Ruiz, Mario Humberto Ruz Sosa, and Maria Josefa Iglesias Ponce de León, eds. Pp. 7–34. Madrid: Sociedad Española de Estudios Mayas.

2003b Making Something of Herself: Embodiment in Life and Death at Playa de los Muertos, Honduras. Cambridge Archaeological Journal 13(2):248–261.

2008 Speaking for Absent Subjects: Responsibility in Archaeological Discourse. *In* Mixtec Writing and Society/Escritura de Nuu Dzaui. Maarten E. R. G. N. Jansen and Laura N. K. van Broekhoven, eds. Pp. 15–26. Amsterdam: Royal Netherlands Academy of Arts and Sciences.

2011 In the Beginning: The Experience of Residential Burial in Prehispanic Honduras. *In* Residential Burial: A Multiregional Exploration. Ron L. Adams and Stacie King, eds. Pp. 33–43. Archaeological Papers of the American Anthropological Association. Arlington, VA: American Anthropological Association.

Joyce, Rosemary A., Julia A. Hendon, and Russell N. Sheptak

2008 Una Nueva Evaluación de Playa de los Muertos: Exploraciones en el Periodo Formativo Medio en Honduras. *In* Ideología Politica y Sociedad en el Periodo Formativo: Ensayos en Homenaje al Doctor David C. Grove. Ann Cyphers and Kenneth G. Hirth, eds. Pp. 283–310. México DF: Instituto de Investigaciones Antropológicas, Universidad Nacional Autonoma de México.

Juhl, Kirsten, and Odd Einar Olsen

2006 Societal Safety, Archaeology and the Investigation of Contemporary Mass Graves. Journal of Genocide Research 8(4):411–435.

Kallenberger, Lauren, and Varsha Pilbrow

2012 Using CRANID to Test the Population Affinity of Known Crania. Journal of Anatomy 221(5):459–464.

Kaplan, Erin

2003 Black Like I Thought I Was. LA Weekly, October 6.

Katz, William

1986 Black Indians. New York: Macmillan.

1987 The Black West. Garden City, NY: Anchor.

Kemkes-Grottenthaler, Ariane

2001 The Reliability of Forensic Osteology: A Case in Point. Forensic Science International 117(1–2):65–72.

Kershaw, Alan

2001 Expressing a Standard. Science and Justice 41(3):226–228.

Kirschner, Robert H., and Kari E. Hannibal

1994 The Application of the Forensic Sciences to Human Rights Investigations. Medicine and Law 13(5–6):451–460.

Klonowski, Eva-Elvira

2007a Exhumations in Bosnia and Herzegovina: Caves as Mass Graves, from Recovery to Identification. *In* Forensic Anthropology: Case Studies from Europe. Megan B. Brickley and Roxana Ferllini, eds. Pp. 183–202. Springfield, IL: Charles C. Thomas.

2007b Forensic Anthropology in Bosnia and Herzegovina: Theory and Practice Amidst Politics and Egos. *In* Forensic Archaeology and Human Rights Violations. Roxana Ferllini, ed. Pp. 148–169. Springfield, IL: Charles C. Thomas.

Koff, Clea

2004 The Bone Woman: A Forensic Anthropologist's Search for Truth in the Mass Graves of Rwanda, Bosnia, Croatia, and Kosovo. New York: Random House.

2011 Freezing. Sutton, England: Severn House.

Komar, Debra A.

2003 Lessons from Srebrenica: The Contributions and Limitations of Physical Anthropology in Identifying Victims of War Crimes. Journal of Forensic Sciences 48(4):713–716.

2008a Patterns of Mortuary Practice Associated with Genocide: Implications for Archaeological Research. Current Anthropology 49(1):123–133.

2008b Variables Influencing Victim Selection in Genocide. Journal of Forensic Sciences 53(1):172–177.

Komar, Debra A., and Jane E. Buikstra

2008 Forensic Anthropology: Contemporary Theory and Practice. Oxford: Oxford University Press.

Kristeva, Julia

1982 Powers of Horror: An Essay on Abjection. New York: Columbia University Press.

Krogman, Wilton Marion, and Mehmet Yaşar İşcan,

1986 The Human Skeleton in Forensic Medicine. Springfield, IL: Charles C. Thomas.

Kuckelman, Kristin A., Ricky R. Lightfoot, and Debra L. Martin

2002 The Bioarchaeology and Taphonomy of Violence at Castle Rock and Sand Canyon Pueblos, Southwestern Colorado. American Antiquity 67(3):486–513.

Kus, Susan

1992 Toward an Archaeology of Body and Soul. *In* Representations in Archaeology. Jean-Claude Gardin and Christopher S. Peebles, eds. Pp. 168–177. Bloomington: Indiana University Press.

1997 Archaeologist as Anthropologist: Much Ado About Something After All? Journal of Archaeological Method and Theory 4(3-4):199–213.

References

Kwon, Heonik

2008 Ghosts of War in Vietnam. Cambridge: Cambridge University Press.

L'Abbé, Ericka, and Maryna Steyn

2012 The Establishment and Advancement of Forensic Anthropology in South Africa. *In* A Companion to Forensic Anthropology. Dennis C. Dirkmaat, ed. Pp. 626–638. Oxford: Blackwell.

Lancaster, Jane

1994 Removal Aftershock: The Seminoles' Struggle to Survive in the West. Knoxville: University of Tennessee Press.

Latour, Bruno

1987 Science in Action: How to Follow Scientists and Engineers Through Society. Cambridge, MA: Harvard University Press.

2000 When Things Strike Back: A Possible Contribution of "Science Studies" to the Social Sciences. British Journal of Sociology 51(1):107–123.

Lefebvre, Alexander

2008 The Image of Law: Deleuze, Bergson, Spinoza. Stanford, CA: Stanford University Press.

Lentini, John J.

2009 Forensic Science Standards: Where They Come From and How They Are Used. Forensic Science Policy and Management 1(1):10–16.

Lewenstein, Bruce

1995 Science and the Media. *In* Handbook of Science and Technology Studies. Sheila Jasanoff, Gerald E. Markle, James C. Petersen, and Trevor Pinch, eds. Pp. 343–360. London: Sage.

Lewis, Jason, David DeGusta, Marc Meyer, Janet Monge, Alan Mann, and Ralph Holloway

2011 The Mismeasure of Science: Stephen Jay Gould versus Samuel George Morton on Skulls and Bias. PLOS Biology 9(6):1–6.

Lewontin, Richard C.

1972 The Apportionment of Human Diversity. Evolutionary Biology 6:381–398.

Lieberman, Leonard, Rodney C. Kirk, and Alice Littlefield

2003 Perishing Paradigm: Race: 1931–99. American Anthropologist 105(1):110–113.

Lippincott, Horace Mather

1919 The University of Pennsylvania, Franklin's College. Philadelphia: Lippincott.

Littlefield, Daniel F., Jr.

1977 Africans and Seminoles: From Removal to Emancipation. Westport, CT: Greenwood.

Lõugas, Vello

1991 The Archaeology of Terror: Archaeological Excavation of Mass-Murder Sites in the Soviet Union. Fennoscandia Archaeologica 8:77–84.

Lovejoy, C. Owen, Richard S. Meindl, Thomas R. Pryzbeck, and R. P. Mensforth

1985 Chronological Metamorphosis of the Auricular Surface of the Ilium: A New Method for Determination of Age at Death. American Journal of Physical Anthropology 68(1):15–28.

Luhmann, Niklas

1989 Law as a Social System. Northwestern University Law Review 83(1–2):136–150.

Mahon, John K.

1967 History of the Second Seminole War, 1835–1842. Gainesville: University Press of Florida.

Malkoc, Ekrem, and Wim Neuteboom

2007 The Current Status of Forensic Science Laboratory Accreditation in Europe. Forensic Science International 167(2):121–126.

Manhein, Mary H.

1999 The Bone Lady: Life as a Forensic Anthropologist. Baton Rouge: Louisiana State University Press.

2005 Trail of Bones: More Cases from the Files of a Forensic Anthropologist. Baton Rouge: Louisiana State University Press.

2012 Floating Souls: The Canal Murders. Donaldsonville, LA: Margaret Media.

2013 Bone Remains: Cold Cases in Forensic Anthropology. Baton Rouge: Louisiana State University Press.

Mann, Robert, and Miryam Ehrlich Williamson

2006 Forensic Detective: How I Cracked the World's Toughest Cases. New York: Ballantine.

Manrique, Nelson

2002 El Tiempo del Miedo: La Violencia Política en el Perú 1980–1996. Lima: Congreso del Perú.

Mant, Arthur Keith

1987 Knowledge Acquired from Post-War Exhumations. *In* Death, Decay, and Reconstruction: Approaches to Archaeology and Forensic Science. Andrew Boddington, A. Neil Garland, and Robert C. Janaway, eds. Pp. 65–78. Manchester, England: Manchester University Press.

Maples, William R., and Michael Browning

1994 Dead Men Do Tell Tales: The Strange and Fascinating Cases of a Forensic Anthropologist. Garden City, NY: Doubleday.

Márquez-Grant, Nicholas, Stephen Litherland, and Julie Roberts

2012 European Perspectives and the Role of the Forensic Archaeologist in the UK. *In* A Companion to Forensic Anthropology. Dennis C. Dirkmaat, ed. Pp. 598–625. Oxford: Blackwell.

References

Martin, Debra L.

1998 Historical Trends, Missed Opportunities, and New Directions in the Study of Human Remains. *In* Building a New Biocultural Synthesis: Political-Economic Perspectives on Human Biology. Alan Goodman and Thomas Leatherman, eds. Pp. 171–190. Ann Arbor: University of Michigan Press.

Martin, Debra L., and Cheryl P. Anderson, eds.

2014 Bioarchaeological and Forensic Perspectives on Violence. Cambridge: Cambridge University Press.

Martin, Debra L., Ryan P. Harrod, and Ventura R. Pérez

2013 Bioarchaeology: An Integrated Approach to Working with Human Remains. New York: Springer.

Martin, Sophie

2002 The Missing. International Review of the Red Cross 48(848):723–726.

McGuire, Randall H.

1989 The Sanctity of the Grave: White Concepts and American Indian Burials. *In* Conflict in the Archaeology of Living Traditions. Robert Layton, ed. Pp. 167–181. Winchester, MA: Unwin Hyman.

Meierhenrich, Jens

2009 The Transformation of Lieux de Mémoire: The Nyabarongo River in Rwanda, 1992–2009. Anthropology Today 25(5):13–19.

Meigs, Charles D.

1851 A Memoir of Samuel George Morton, M.D.: Late President of the Academy of Natural Sciences of Philadelphia. Philadelphia: T. K. and P. G. Collins.

Meigs, J. Aitken

1857 Catalogue of Human Crania in the Collection of the Academy of Natural Sciences of Philadelphia: Based upon the Third Edition of Dr. Morton's "Catalogue of Skulls," &c. Philadelphia: Lippincott.

Meindl, Richard S., and C. Owen Lovejoy

1985 Ectocranial Suture Closure: A Revised Method for the Determination of Skeletal Age at Death Based on the Lateral-Anterior Sutures. American Journal of Physical Anthropology 68(1):57–66.

Meskell, Lynn M., and Rosemary A. Joyce

2003 Embodied Lives: Figuring Ancient Egypt and the Classic Maya. London: Routledge.

Micco, Melinda

2006 "Blood and Money": The Case of Seminole Freedmen and Seminole Indians in Oklahoma. *In* Crossing Waters, Crossing Worlds: The African Diaspora in Indian Country. Tiya Miles and Sharon Patricia Holland, eds. Pp. 121–144. Durham, NC: Duke University Press.

Michael, John S.

1988 A New Look at Morton's Craniological Research. Current Anthropology 29(2):349–354.

Miles, Tiya, and Sharon P. Holland, eds.

2006 Crossing Waters, Crossing Worlds: The African Diaspora in Indian Country. Durham, NC: Duke University Press.

Minow, Martha

1998 Between Vengeance and Forgiveness: Facing History After Genocide and Mass Violence. Boston: Beacon.

Missall, John, and Mary Lou Missall

2004 The Seminole Wars: America's Longest Indian Conflict. Gainesville: University Press of Florida.

Mitrović, Slobodan

2008 Fresh Scars on the Body of Archaeology: Excavating Mass Graves at Batajnica, Serbia. *In* Past Bodies: Body-Centered Research in Archaeology. Dušan Borić and John Robb, eds. Pp. 79–88. Oxford: Oxbow.

Mock, Shirley

2010 Dreaming with the Ancestors: Black Seminole Women in Texas and Mexico. Norman: University of Oklahoma Press.

Montgomery, William

1839 Remarks of Mr. Montgomery of North Carolina. *In* The Congressional Globe, Containing Sketches of the Debates and Proceedings of the Twenty-Fifth Congress, Third Session. Volume 7. F. P. Blair and J. C. Rives, eds. Pp. 268–270. Washington, DC: Globe Office.

Moore-Jansen, Peer H., Stephen D. Ousley, and Richard L. Jantz

1994 Data Collection Procedures for Forensic Skeletal Material. Knoxville: Forensic Anthropology Center, Department of Anthropology, University of Tennessee.

Mopas, Michael

2007 Examining the "*CSI* Effect" Through an ANT lens. Crime, Media, Culture 3(1):110–117.

Morris, Alan G.

2011 Missing and Murdered: A Personal Adventure in Forensic Anthropology. Cape Town, South Africa: Zebra.

Morton, Samuel G.

1839 Crania Americana. Philadelphia: Penington.

1847 Hybridity in Animals, Considered in Reference to the Question of the Unity of the Human Species. American Journal of Science and Arts 3(Jan):39–50, (Mar):203–212.

1849 Catalogue of Skulls of Man and the Inferior Animals. 3rd edition. Philadelphia: Merrihew and Thompson, Printers.

1851 April 22nd. Proceedings of the Academy of Natural Sciences 5:173–175.

References

Moscoso Möller, Fernando

1995 Antropología Forense: Resultados de su Aplicación en Guatemala. *In* VIII Simposio de Investigaciones Arqueológicas en Guatemala, 1994. Juan Pedro Laporte and Hector Escobedo, eds. Pp. 327–337. Guatemala City: Museo Nacional de Arqueología y Etnología.

Motte, Jacob Rhett

1953 Journey into Wilderness: An Army Surgeon's Account of Life in Camp and Field During the Creek and Seminole Wars 1836–1838. J. F. Sunderman, ed. Gainesville: University of Florida Press.

Mulroy, Kevin

2005 Horse, John. *In* American National Biography: Supplement 2. M. C. Carnes, ed. Pp. 270–273. Oxford: Oxford University Press.

2007 The Seminole Freedmen: A History. Norman: University of Oklahoma Press.

Mundorf, Amy Zelson

2003 Urban Anthropology: Case Studies from the New York City Medical Examiner's Office. *In* Hard Evidence: Case Studies in Forensic Archaeology. Dawnie Wolfe Steadman, ed. Pp. 52–62. Upper Saddle River, NJ: Prentice Hall.

2011 Integrating Forensic Anthropology into Disaster Victim Identification. Forensic Science, Medicine, and Pathology 8(2):131–139.

Myers, Greg

2003 Discourse Studies of Scientific Popularization: Questioning the Boundaries. Discourse Studies 5(2):265–279.

Nakhaeizadeh, Sherry, Itiel E. Dror, and Ruth M. Morgan

2013 Cognitive Bias in Forensic Anthropology: Visual Assessment of Skeletal Remains Is Susceptible to Confirmation Bias. Science and Justice 54(3):208–214.

Nakhaeizadeh, Sherry, Ian Hanson, and Nathalie Dozzi

2014 The Power of Contextual Effects in Forensic Anthropology: A Study of Biasability in the Visual Interpretations of Trauma Analysis on Skeletal Remains. Journal of Forensic Sciences 59(5):1177–1183.

National Research Council, Committee on Identifying the Needs of the Forensic Sciences Community

2009 Strengthening Forensic Science in the United States: A Path Forward. Washington, DC: National Academy of Sciences.

Needham, T. H.

1817 The Complete Sportsman. London: Simpkin and Marshall.

Novak, Shannon A., and Derinna Kopp

2003 To Feed a Tree in Zion: Osteological Analysis of the 1857 Mountain Meadows Massacre. Historical Archaeology 37(2):85–108.

Olivier, Laurent
2011 The Dark Abyss of Time: Archaeology and Memory. Lanham, MD: AltaMira.

Olmo, Darío, ed.
2005 Cemeterio de San Vicente: Informe 2003. Córdoba, Argentina: Ferreyra.

Ortner, Donald J.
2003 Identification of Pathological Conditions in Human Skeletal Remains. New York: Academic.

Ossorio, Pilar, and Troy Duster
2005 Race and Genetics: Controversies in Biomedical, Behavioral, and Forensic Sciences. American Psychologist 60(1):115–128.

Ost, François
2005 El Tiempo del Derecho. Buenos Aires: Siglo XXI Editores Argentina.

Ousley, Stephen D., and Richard L. Jantz
2005 FORDISC 3.0: Personal Computer Forensic Discriminant Functions. Knoxville: University of Tennessee Press.

Ousley, Stephen D., Richard L. Jantz, and Donna Freid
2009 Understanding Race and Human Variation: Why Forensic Anthropologists Are Good at Identifying Race. American Journal of Physical Anthropology 139(1):68–76.

Owen, David
2000 Hidden Evidence: Forty True Crimes and How Forensic Science Helped Solve Them. Buffalo, NY: Firefly.

Page, Mark, Jane Taylor, and Matt Blenkin
2011 Forensic Identification Science Evidence Since *Daubert*: Part 1-a Quantitative Analysis of the Exclusion of Forensic Identification Science Evidence. Journal of Forensic Sciences 56(5):1180–1184.

Paperno, Irina
2001 Exhuming the Bodies of Soviet Terror. Representations 75(Summer):89–118.

Patry, Marc W., and Steven M. Smith
2008 Blurring the Line Between Fact and Fiction: Expert Opinions About Forensic Investigation Tools Represented on *CSI*. *In* Proceedings of the 2007 North American Correctional and Criminal Justice Psychology Conference. Guy Bourgon, R. Karl Hanson, Joanna D. Pozzulo, Kelly E. Morton Bourgon, and Carrie L. Tanasichuk, eds. Pp. 94–97. Ottawa, ON: Public Safety Canada.

Patterson, Henry S.
1854 Memoir of the Life and Scientific Labors of Samuel George Morton. Philadelphia: Lippincott, Grambo.

Paul, Danette
2004 Spreading Chaos: The Role of Popularizations in the Diffusion of Scientific Ideas. Written Communication 21(1):32–68.

References

Paule, Stephanie

2013 Determination of Ancestry Based on the Measurement of the Intercondylar Shelf Angle of the Distal Femur. Fort Myers: Florida Gulf Coast University.

Pearl, Matthew, ed.

2006 The Murders in the Rue Morgue: The Dupin Tales by Edgar Allan Poe. New York: Modern Library.

Pearson, Michael, and Michael Shanks

2001 Theatre/Archaeology. London: Routledge.

Peccerelli, Fredy

2007 Investigaciones Antropológico-Forenses en América Latina. *In* Resistencias Contra el Olvido: Trabajo Psicosocial en Procesos de Exhumaciones. Pau Pérez-Sales and Susana Navarro García, eds. Pp. 25–28. Barcelona: Gedisa.

Peers, Laura

2009 On the Treatment of Dead Enemies: Indigenous Human Remains in Britain in the Early Twenty-First Century. *In* Social Bodies. Helen Lambert and Maryon McDonald, eds. Pp. 77–99. Oxford: Berghahn.

Peirce, Charles Sanders

1955 Logic as Semiotic: The Theory of Signs. *In* Philosophical Writings of Peirce. Justus Buchler, ed. Pp. 98–119. New York: Dover.

Perdue, Theda, and Michael D. Green

2001 The Columbia Guide to American Indians of the Southeast. New York: Columbia University Press.

Pérez-Sales, Pau, and Susana Navarro García, eds.

2007 Resistencias Contra el Olvido: Trabajo Psicosocial en Procesos de Exhumaciones. Barcelona: Gedisa.

Peters, Bernard C.

1997 Indian-Grave Robbing at Sault Ste. Marie, 1826. Michigan Historical Review 23(2):49–80.

Petit, Michel

1999 La Fiction à Substrat Professionnel: Une Autre Voie d'Accès à l'Anglais de Spécialité. ASp: La Revue du GERAS 23–26:57–81.

2000 Le Paratexte dans la Fiction à Substrat Professionnel. Bulletin de la Société de Stylistique Anglaise 21:173–195.

Petrović-Šteger, Maja

2009 Anatomizing Conflict, Accommodating Human Remains. *In* Social Bodies. Helen Lambert and Maryon McDonald, eds. Pp. 47–76. New York: Berghahn.

Piña Chan, Román

1958 Tlatilco. Serie Investigaciones 1–2. México DF: Instituto Nacional de Antropologia e Historia.

Pittman, Hannah D.
1903 Americans of Gentle Birth and Their Ancestors. Volume 1. St. Louis, MO: Buxton and Skinner.

Pluciennik, Mark
1999 Archaeological Narratives and Other Ways of Telling. Current Anthropology 40(5):653–678.

Pollack, Craig Evan
2003 Burial at Srebrenica: Linking Place and Trauma. Social Science and Medicine 56(4):793–801.

Poole, Deborah, ed.
1994 Unruly Order: Violence, Power, and Cultural Identity in the High Provinces of Southern Peru. Boulder, CO: Westview.

Poole, Deborah, and Gerardo Rénique
1992 Peru: Time of Fear. London: Latin America Bureau.

Porter, Kenneth W.
1996 The Black Seminoles: History of a Freedom-Seeking People. Alcione M. Amos and Thomas P. Senter, eds. Gainesville: University of Florida Press.

Porter, Muriel N.
1953 Tlatilco and the Preclassic Cultures of the New World. Publications in Anthropology 19. New York: Viking Fund.

Potter, Woodburne
1836 The War in Florida: Being an Exposition of Its Causes, and an Accurate History of the Campaigns of Generals Clinch, Gaines, and Scott. Baltimore, MD: Lewis and Coleman.

Presley, Lawrence A., Michael Haas, and Lawrence Quarino
2009 The Forensic Science Assessment Test (FSAT): A Potential Tool for the Academic Assessment of Forensic Science Programs. Forensic Science Policy and Management 1(2):74–84.

Preucel, Robert W.
2006 Archaeological Semiotics. Malden, MA: Blackwell.

Primorac, Dragan, Simun Andelinovic, Marija Definis-Gojanovic, Irena Drmic, Bojac Rezic, Michael M. Baden, Mitchell A. Kennedy, Moses S. Schanfield, Stephen B. Skakel, and Henry C. Lee
1996 Identification of War Victims from Mass Graves in Croatia, Bosnia, and Herzegovina by the Use of Standard Forensic Methods and DNA Typing. Journal of Forensic Sciences 41(5):891–894.

Quintyn, Conrad B.
2010 The Existence or Non-Existence of Race? Forensic Anthropology, Population Admixture, and the Future of Racial Classification in the U.S. Youngstown, NY: Teneo.

References

Rabinow, Paul
1999 French DNA: Trouble in Purgatory. Chicago: University of Chicago Press.

Rainio, Juha, Kaisa Lalu, Helena Ranta, Kari Takamaa, and Antti Penttilä
2001 Practical and Legal Aspects of Forensic Autopsy Expert Team Operations. Legal Medicine 3(4):220–232.

Rainwater, Christopher W., Christian Crowder, Kirsten M. Hartnett, Jeannette S. Fridie, Benjamin J. Figura, Jennifer Godbold, Scott C. Marnasch, and Bradley J. Adams
2012 Forensic Anthropology at the New York City Office of Chief Medical Examiner. *In* A Companion to Forensic Anthropology. Dennis C. Dirkmaat, ed. Pp. 549–566. Oxford: Blackwell.

Rankin, Brian W. J., Gillian Taylor, and Timothy J. U. Thompson
2012 Should Higher Education Respond to Recent Changes in the Forensic Science Marketplace? New Directions 8:27–32.

Reichs, Kathleen, J.
1998 Déjà Dead. New York: Pocket Star.

Reichs, Kathleen, J., ed.
1998 Forensic Osteology: Advances in the Identification of Human Remains. Springfield, IL: Charles C. Thomas.

Relethford, John H.
2009 Race and Global Patterns of Phenotypic Variation. American Journal of Physical Anthropology 139(1):16–22.

Renschler, Emily
2007 An Osteobiography of an African Diasporic Skeletal Sample: Integrating Skeletal and Historical Information. PhD thesis, Department of Anthropology, University of Pennsylvania, Philadelphia.

Renschler, Emily, and Janet Monge
2008 The Samuel George Morton Cranial Collection: Historical Significance and New Research. Expedition 50(3):30–38.

Renshaw, Layla
2007 The Iconography of Exhumation: Representations of Mass Graves from the Spanish Civil War. *In* Archaeology and the Media. Tim Clack and Marcus Brittain, eds. Pp. 237–251. Walnut Creek, CA: Left Coast.

2011 Exhuming Loss: Memory, Materiality, and Mass Graves of the Spanish Civil War. Walnut Creek, CA: Left Coast.

Rév, István
2005 Retroactive Justice: Prehistory of Post-Communism. Stanford, CA: Stanford University Press.

Rhine, Stanley
1990 Non-Metric Skull Racing. *In* Skeletal Attribution of Race: Methods for Forensic Anthropology. George W. Gill and Stanley Rhine, eds. Pp 9–20. Albuquerque NM: Maxwell Museum of Anthropology, Anthropological Papers No. 4.

1998 Bone Voyage: A Journey in Forensic Anthropology. Albuquerque: University of New Mexico Press.

Robb, John

2002 Time and Biography: Osteobiography of the Italian Neolithic Lifespan. *In* Thinking Through the Body: Archaeologies of Corporeality. Yannis Hamilakis, Mark Pluciennik, and Sarah Tarlow, eds. Pp. 153–171. New York: Springer.

Robben, Antonius C. G. M.

2000 State Terror in the Netherworld: Disappearance and Reburial in Argentina. *In* Death Squad: The Anthropology of State Terror. Jeffrey A. Sluka, ed. Pp. 91–113. Philadelphia: University of Pennsylvania Press.

Rogers, Tracey L.

2005 Recognition of Cemetery Remains in a Forensic Context. Journal of Forensic Sciences 50(1):5–11.

Rojas-Perez, Isaias

2008 Writing the Aftermath: Anthropology and "Post Conflict." *In* A Companion to Latin American Anthropology. Deborah Poole, ed. Pp. 254–275. Malden, MA: Blackwell.

2010 Fragments of Soul: Law, Transitional Justice, and Mourning in Post War Peru. PhD dissertation, Department of Anthropology, Johns Hopkins University.

2013 Inhabiting Unfinished Pasts: Law, Transitional Justice, and Mourning in Post War Peru. Humanity: An International Journal of Human Rights, Humanitarianism, and Development 4(1):149–170.

Rose, Nikolas

2000 The Biology of Culpability: Pathological Identity and Crime Control in a Biological Culture. Theoretical Criminology 4(1):5–34.

Rosenblatt, Adam

2010 International Forensic Investigations and the Human Rights of the Dead. Human Rights Quarterly 32(4):922–951.

Ross, Ann H., Dennis E. Slice, Douglas H. Ubelaker, and Anthony B. Falsetti

2004 Population Affinities of 19th Century Cuban Crania: Implications for Identification Criteria in South Florida Cuban Americans. Journal of Forensic Sciences 49(1):1–5.

Sanford, Victoria

2003a Buried Secrets: Truth and Human Rights in Guatemala. New York: Palgrave Macmillan.

2003b The "Grey Zone" of Justice: NGOs and Rule of Law in Postwar Guatemala. Journal of Human Rights 2(3):303–405.

2009 Excavations of the Heart: Healing Fragmented Communities. *In* Human Rights: An Anthropological Reader. Mark Goodale, ed. Pp. 135–166. Oxford: Blackwell.

References

Sant Cassia, Paul

2005 Bodies of Evidence: Burial, Memory, and the Recovery of Missing Persons in Cyprus. Oxford: Berghahn.

2006 Recognition and Emotion: Exhumations of Missing Persons in Cyprus. *In* Divided Cyprus: Modernity, History, and an Island in Conflict. Yiannis Papadakis, Nicos Peristianis, and Gisela Welz, eds. Pp. 194–214. Bloomington: Indiana University Press.

Sassòli, Marco, and Marie-Louise Tougas

2002 The ICRC and the Missing. International Review of the Red Cross 48(848):727–750.

Sattler, Richard

2004 Seminole in the West. *In* Handbook of North American Indians, vol. 14: Southeast. Raymond Fogelson, ed. Pp. 450–464. Washington, DC: Smithsonian Institution.

Sauer, Norman J.

1992 Forensic Anthropology and the Concept of Race: If Races Don't Exist, Why Are Forensic Anthropologists So Good at Identifying Them? Social Science and Medicine 34(2):107–111.

1993 Applied Anthropology and the Concept of Race: A Legacy of Linnaeus. NAPA Bulletin 13(1):79–84.

Sauer, Norm J., and Jane C. Wankmiller

2009 The Assessment of Ancestry and the Concept of Race. *In* Handbook of Forensic Anthropology and Archaeology. Soren Blau and Douglas H. Ubelaker, eds. Pp. 187–200. Walnut Creek, CA: Left Coast.

Saul, Frank. P.

1967 Osteobiography of Lowland Maya of Altar de Sacrificios Guatemala [abstract]. American Journal of Physical Anthropology 27(2):237.

Saul, Frank P., and Julie M. Saul

1987 An Osteobiographic Analysis of an Early Dissecting Room Population. Anatomical Record 218(1):1–120A.

Saunders, Rebecca

2002 Tell the Truth: The Archaeology of Human Rights Abuses in Guatemala and the Former Yugoslavia. *In* Matériel Culture: The Archaeology of Twentieth-Century Conflict. John Schofield, William Gray Johnson, and Colleen M. Beck, eds. Pp. 103–114. London: Routledge.

Savelsberg, Joachim J., and Ryan D. King

2007 Law and Collective Memory. Annual Review of Law Social Science 3:189–211.

Scarre, Geoffrey

2003 Archaeology and Respect for the Dead. Journal of Applied Philosophy 20(3):237–249.

2006 Can Archaeology Harm the Dead? *In* The Ethics of Archaeology:

Philosophical Perspectives on Archaeological Practice. Chris Scarre and Geoffrey Scarre, eds. Pp. 181–198. Cambridge: Cambridge University Press.

Scheper-Hughes, Nancy, and Margaret M. Lock
1987 The Mindful Body: A Prolegomenon to Future Work in Medical Anthropology. Medical Anthropology Quarterly 1(1):6–41.

Schmitt, Stefan
2002 Mass Graves and the Collection of Forensic Evidence: Genocide, War Crimes, and Crimes Against Humanity. *In* Advances in Forensic Taphonomy: Method, Theory, and Archaeological Perspectives. William D. Haglund and Marcella H. Sorg, eds. Pp. 277–292. Boca Raton, FL: CRC.

Schweitzer, Nicholas J., and Michael J. Saks
2007 The *CSI* Effect: Popular Fiction About Forensic Science Affects the Public's Expectations About Real Forensic Science. Jurimetrics 47(Spring):357–364.

Simmons, Tal, and William D. Haglund
2005 Anthropology in a Forensic Context. *In* Forensic Archaeology: Advances in Theory and Practice. John Hunter and Margaret Cox, eds. Pp. 159–176. London: Routledge.

Simmons, William Haynes
1822 Notices of East Florida, with an Account of the Seminole Nation of Indians. Charleston, SC: A. E. Miller.

Skinner, Mark F.
1987 Planning the Archaeological Recovery of Evidence from Recent Mass Graves. Forensic Science International 34(4):267–287.

2007 Hapless in Afghanistan: Forensic Archaeology in a Political Maelstrom. *In* Forensic Archaeology and Human Rights Violations. Roxana Ferllini, ed. Pp. 233–265. Springfield, IL: Charles C. Thomas.

Skinner, Mark, Djordje Alempijevic, and M. Djuric-Srejic
2003 Guidelines for International Forensic Bio-Archaeology Monitors of Mass Grave Exhumations. Forensic Science International 134(2):81–92.

Skinner, Mark F., Heather P. York, and Melissa A. Connor
2002 Postburial Disturbance of Graves in Bosnia-Herzegovina. *In* Advances in Forensic Taphonomy: Method, Theory, and Archaeological Perspectives. William D. Haglund and Marcella H. Sorg, eds. Pp. 293–308. Boca Raton, FL: CRC.

Sledzik, Paul S.
2012 Forensic Anthropology in Mass Disasters. *In* Forensic Anthropology: An Introduction. Maria Teresa A. Tersigni-Tarrant and Natalie R. Shirley, eds. Pp. 439–450. Boca Raton, FL: CRC.

Smay, Diana, and George Armelagos
2000 Galileo Wept: A Critical Assessment of the Use of Race in Forensic Anthropology. Transforming Anthropology 9(2):19–29.

Smith, Steven M., Marc W. Patry, and Veronica Stinson
2008 Exploring the *CSI* Effect: Is It Real? If So, What Is It? *In* Proceedings of the 2007 North American Correctional and Criminal Justice Psychology Conference. Guy Bourgon, R. Karl Hanson, Joanna D. Pozzulo, Kelly E. Morton Bourgon, and Carrie L. Tanasichuk, eds. Pp. 81–84. Ottawa, ON: Public Safety Canada.

Snow, Clyde Collins
1982 Forensic Anthropology. Annual Review of Anthropology 11:97–131.

Snow, Clyde C., Lowell J. Levine, Leslie Lukash, Luke G. Tedeschi, Cristian Orrego, and Eric Stover
1984 The Investigation of the Human Remains of the "Disappeared" in Argentina. American Journal of Forensic Medicine and Pathology 5(4):297–299.

Sommer, Peter
2010 Forensic Science Standards in Fast-Changing Environments. Science and Justice 50(1):12–17.

Spradley, M. Katherine, Richard L. Jantz, A. Robinson, and Fredy Peccerelli
2008 Demographic Change and Forensic Identification: Problems in Metric Identification of Hispanic Skeletons. Journal of Forensic Sciences 53(1):21–28.

Sprague, John T.
1964[1847] The Origins, Progress, and Conclusion of the Florida War. Gainesville: University of Florida Press.

Steadman, Dawnie W.
2003 Hard Evidence: Case Studies in Forensic Anthropology. Upper Saddle River, NJ: Prentice Hall.

2009 Hard Evidence: Case Studies in Forensic Anthropology. 2nd edition. Upper Saddle River, NJ: Pearson.

Steadman, Dawnie L. Wolfe, William Basler, Michael J. Hochrein, Dennis Klein, and Julia Goodin
2009 Domestic Homicide Investigations: An Example from the United States. *In* Handbook of Forensic Anthropology and Archaeology. Soren Blau and Douglas H. Ubelaker, eds. Pp. 351–362. Walnut Creek, CA: Left Coast.

Steadman, Dawnie L. Wolfe, and William D. Haglund
2005 The Scope of Anthropological Contributions to Human Rights Investigations. Journal of Forensic Sciences 50(1):1–8.

Steele, Caroline
2008 Archaeology and the Forensic Investigation of Recent Mass Graves: Ethical Issues for a New Practice of Archaeology. Archaeologies: Journal of the World Archaeological Congress 4(3):414–428.

Stern, Steve, ed.
1998 Shining and the Other Paths: War and Society in Peru, 1980–1995. Durham, NC: Duke University Press.

Stewart, T. Dale

1978 George A. Dorsey's Role in the Luetgert Case: A Significant Episode in the History of Forensic Anthropology. Journal of Forensic Sciences 23(4):786–791.

1982 Background of American Forensic Anthropology. Criminal Justice Review 7(1):4–7.

Stewart, Thomas Dale, and Ellis R. Kerley

1979 Essentials of Forensic Anthropology, Especially as Developed in the United States. Springfield, IL: Charles C. Thomas.

Stodder, Ann L.W., and Anne Palkovich, eds.

2012 Bioarchaeology of Individuals. Gainesville: University Press of Florida.

Stoerr, Michelle

2011 Introducing Forensic Science FASP: Towards a Characterization of the Substrat Scientifique. Les Cahiers de l'APLIUT 30(2):82–95.

Stojanowski, Christopher

2005 Biocultural Histories in La Florida: A Bioarchaeological Perspective. Tuscaloosa: University of Alabama Press.

Stone, Paul

2011 Legacy of Excellence: The Armed Forces Institute of Pathology, 1862–2011. Fort Detrick, MD: Borden Institute, US Army Medical Department.

Stover, Eric

1997 The Grave at Vukovar. Smithsonian 27(12):40–51.

Stover, Eric, William D. Haglund, and Margaret Samuels

2003 Exhumation of Mass Graves in Iraq: Considerations for Forensic Investigations, Humanitarian Needs, and the Demands of Justice. Journal of the American Medical Association 290(5):663–666.

Stover, Eric, and Gilles Peress

1998 The Graves: Srebrenica and Vukovar. Zurich: Scalo.

Stover, Eric, and Rachel Shigekane

2002 The Missing in the Aftermath of War: When Do the Needs of Victims' Families and International War Crimes Tribunals Clash? International Review of the Red Cross 84(848):845–866.

2004 Exhumation of Mass Graves: Balancing Legal and Humanitarian Needs. *In* My Neighbor, My Enemy: Justice and Community in the Aftermath of Mass Atrocity. Eric Stover and Harvey M. Weinstein, eds. Pp. 85–103. Cambridge: Cambridge University Press.

Sturtevant, William C., and Jessica R. Cattelino

2004 Florida Seminole and Miccosukee. *In* Handbook of North American Indians, vol. 14: Southeast. Raymond Fogelson, ed. Pp. 429–449. Washington, DC: Smithsonian Institution.

References

Ta'ala, Sabrina C., Gregory E. Berg, and Kathryn Haden

2006 Blunt Force Cranial Trauma in the Cambodian Killing Fields. Journal of Forensic Sciences 51(5):996–1001.

TallBear, Kimberly

2003 DNA, Blood, and Racializing the Tribe. Wicazo Sa Review 18(1):81–107.

Taussig, Michael T.

1993 Mimesis and Alterity: A Particular History of the Senses. New York: Routledge.

Tepper, Michael H., ed.

1986 Passenger Arrivals at the Port of Philadelphia, 1800–1819: The Philadelphia Baggage Lists. E. P. Bentley, trans. Baltimore, MD: Genealogical Publishing.

Thomas, Andrew P.

2006 The CSI Effect: Fact or Fiction. Yale Law Journal, Pocket Part 115:70–72. http://www.thepocketpart.org/2006/02/thomas.html, accessed February 12, 2012.

Thomas, David Hurst

2002 Skull Wars: Kennewick Man, Archaeology, and the Battle for Native American Identity. New York: Basic.

Thomas, Ronald R.

1999 Detective Fiction and the Rise of Forensic Science. Cambridge: Cambridge University Press.

Thompson, Tim J. U.

2003 Supply and Demand: The Shifting Expectations of Forensic Anthropology in the United Kingdom. Science and Justice 43(4):183–186.

2008 The Role of the Photograph in the Application of Forensic Anthropology and the Interpretation of Clandestine Scenes of Crime. Photography and Culture 1(2):163–182.

2013a Forensic Anthropology and Its Progress. Interfaces 75:8–9.

2013b Forensic Anthropology Component Standards in a Global Market. Interfaces 76:14–15.

Tidball-Binz, Morris

2006 Forensic Investigations into the Missing: Recommendations and Operational Best Practices. *In* Forensic Anthropology and Medicine: Complementary Sciences from Recovery to Cause of Death. Aurore Schmitt, Eugénia Cunha, and João Pinheiro, eds. Pp. 383–407. Totowa, NJ: Humana.

Tiesler, Vera

2007 Funerary or Nonfunerary? New References in Identifying Ancient Maya Sacrificial and Postsacrificial Behaviors from Human Assemblages. *In* New Perspectives on Human Sacrifice and Ritual Body Treatments in Ancient Maya Society. Vera Tiesler and Andrea Cucina, eds. Pp. 14–44. New York: Springer.

Tiesler, Vera, and Andrea Cucina, eds.

2007 New Perspectives on Human Sacrifice and Ritual Body Treatments in Ancient Maya Society. New York: Springer.

Trouillot, Michel-Rolph

1995 Silencing the Past: Power and the Production of History. Boston: Beacon.

Tuller, Hugh

2012 Mass Graves and Human Rights: Latest Developments. *In* A Companion to Forensic Anthropology. Dennis Dirkmaat, ed. Pp. 157–174. Oxford: Blackwell.

Turner, Trudy R., ed.

2005 Biological Anthropology and Ethics: From Repatriation to Genetic Identity. Albany: State University of New York Press.

Turney, Jon

1998 Frankenstein's Footsteps: Science, Genetics and Popular Culture. New Haven, CT: Yale University Press.

Twain, Mark

1883 Life on the Mississippi. Boston: J. R. Osgood.

1894 The Tragedy of Pudd'nhead Wilson, and the Comedy of Those Extraordinary Twins. Hartford, CT: American Publishing.

Ubelaker, Douglas H.

1999 Aleš Hrdlička's Role in the History of Forensic Anthropology. Journal of Forensic Sciences 44(4):724–730.

2008 Forensic Anthropology: Methodology and Diversity of Applications. *In* Biological Anthropology of the Human Skeleton. 2nd edition. M. Anne Katzenberg and Shelley R. Saunders, eds. Pp. 41–69. Hoboken, NJ: Wiley.

2009 Historical Development of Forensic Anthropology: Perspectives from the United States. *In* Handbook of Forensic Anthropology and Archaeology. Soren Blau and Douglas H. Ubelaker, eds. Pp. 76–86. Walnut Creek, CA: Left Coast.

Ubelaker, Douglas H., and Henry Scammell

1992 Bones: A Forensic Detective's Casebook. New York: HarperCollins.

Uceda, Ricardo

2004 Muerte en el Pentagonito: Los Cementerios Secretos del Ejército Peruano. Bogotá: Planeta Colombiana.

Uribe, Maria Victoria

2004 Dismembering and Expelling: Semantics of Political Terror in Colombia. Public Culture 16(1):79–95.

US Census Bureau

2014 1890 Overview—History—U.S. Census Bureau. https://www.census.gov/history/www/through_the_decades/overview/1890.html, accessed December 22, 2014.

Valverde, Mariana

2003 Law's Dream of Common Knowledge. Princeton, NJ: Princeton University Press.

Vanezis, Peter

1999 Investigation of Clandestine Graves Resulting from Human Rights Abuses. Journal of Clinical Forensic Medicine 6(4):238–242.

Verdery, Katherine

1999 The Political Lives of Dead Bodies: Reburial and Postsocialist Change. New York: Columbia University Press.

Virkus, Frederick A., ed.

1925 Abridged Compendium of American Genealogy: The Standard Genealogical Encyclopedia of the First Families of America. Volume 1. Chicago, IL: Virkus.

Vizenor, Gerald

1986 Bone Courts: The Rights and Narrative Representation of Tribal Bones. American Indian Quarterly 10(4):319–331.

Wagner, Sarah E.

2008 To Know Where He Lies: DNA Technology and the Search for Srebrenica's Missing. Berkeley: University of California Press.

Walker, Phillip, Rhonda Bathurst, Rebecca Richman, Thor Gjerdrum, and Valerie Andrushko

2009 The Causes of Porotic Hyperostosis and Cribra Orbitalia: A Reappraisal of the Iron-Deficiency-Anemia Hypothesis. American Journal of Physical Anthropology 139(2):109–125.

Walsh-Haney, Heather

2011 Can Grave Secrets Be Revealed Via Analysis of Bare Bones? How Kathy Reichs's Fiction Novels Feed the Public Perception of Forensic Anthropology. American Anthropologist 113(4):650–652.

Wärmländer, Sebastian K. T. S., and Sabrina B. Sholts

2011 Sampling and Statistical Considerations for the Suchey-Brooks Method for Pubic Bone Age Estimation: Implications for Regional Comparisons. Science and Justice 51(3):131–134.

Warren, Michael W., Traci Van Deest, and Kristina Ballard

2011 Quality Assurance as Pedagogy for Academic Forensic Anthropology Laboratories. Forensic Science Policy and Management 2(2):70–74.

Warren, Michael W., Heather A. Walsh-Haney, and Laurel Freas, eds.

2008 The Forensic Anthropology Laboratory. Boca Raton, FL: Taylor and Francis.

Watkins, Joe

2001 Yours, Mine, or Ours? Conflicts Between Archaeologists and Ethnic Groups. *In* The Future of the Past: Archaeologists, Native Americans and Repatriation. Tamara Bray, ed. Pp. 57–68. New York: Garland.

Weisberg, Michael
2014 Remeasuring Man. Evolution and Development 16(3):166–178.

Weisman, Brent Richards
1989 Like Beads on a String: A Culture History of the Seminole Indians in North Peninsular Florida. Tuscaloosa: University of Alabama Press.

1999 Unconquered People: Florida's Seminole and Miccosukee Indians. Gainesville: University Press of Florida.

Weiss, Lindsay M.
2010 Terra Incognita: The Material World in International Criminal Courts. *In* Archaeology and Memory. Dusan Boric, ed. Pp. 185–195. Oxford: Oxbow.

Weiss-Krejci, Estella
2004 Mortuary Representations of the Noble House: A Cross-Cultural Comparison Between Collective Tombs of the Ancient Maya and Dynastic Europe. Journal of Social Anthropology 4(3):368–404.

Welsh, Charles, and Marc Hannis
2011 Are UK Undergraduate Forensic Science Degrees Fit for Purpose? Science and Justice 51(3):139–142.

Wickman, Patricia Riles
2006 Osceola's Legacy. Tuscaloosa: University of Alabama Press.

Wilson, Richard A.
2003 Anthropological Studies of National Reconciliation Processes. Anthropological Theory 3(3):367–387.

Wood, George B.
1853 A Biographical Memoir of Samuel George Morton, M.D. Philadelphia: T. K. and P. G. Collins.

Wright, Richard V. S.
1992 Correlation Between Cranial Form and Geography in Homo Sapiens: CRANID—A Computer Program for Forensic and Other Applications. Archaeology in Oceania 27(3):128–134.

1995 Investigating War Crimes: The Archaeological Evidence. Sydney Papers 7(3):39–44.

Youngers, Coletta, and Jo Marie Burt
2009 Human Rights Tribunals in Latin America. Washington, DC: George Mason University, WOLA, and Instituto de Defensa Legal.

Zarankin, Andrés, and Pedro Paulo A. Funari
2008 "Eternal Sunshine of the Spotless Mind": Archaeology and Construction of Memory of Military Repression in South America (1960–1980). Archaeologies: Journal of the World Archaeological Congress 4(2):310–327.

Index

Index

School for Advanced Research Advanced Seminar Series

Published by SAR Press

Chaco & Hohokam: Prehistoric Regional Systems in the American Southwest
Patricia L. Crown & W. James Judge, eds.

Recapturing Anthropology: Working in the Present
Richard G. Fox, ed.

War in the Tribal Zone: Expanding States and Indigenous Warfare
R. Brian Ferguson & Neil L. Whitehead, eds.

Ideology and Pre-Columbian Civilizations
Arthur A. Demarest & Geoffrey W. Conrad, eds.

Dreaming: Anthropological and Psychological Interpretations
Barbara Tedlock, ed.

Historical Ecology: Cultural Knowledge and Changing Landscapes
Carole L. Crumley, ed.

Themes in Southwest Prehistory
George J. Gumerman, ed.

Memory, History, and Opposition under State Socialism
Rubie S. Watson, ed.

Other Intentions: Cultural Contexts and the Attribution of Inner States
Lawrence Rosen, ed.

Last Hunters–First Farmers: New Perspectives on the Prehistoric Transition to Agriculture
T. Douglas Price & Anne Birgitte Gebauer, eds.

Making Alternative Histories: The Practice of Archaeology and History in Non-Western Settings
Peter R. Schmidt & Thomas C. Patterson, eds.

Cyborgs & Citadels: Anthropological Interventions in Emerging Sciences and Technologies
Gary Lee Downey & Joseph Dumit, eds.

Senses of Place
Steven Feld & Keith H. Basso, eds.

The Origins of Language: What Nonhuman Primates Can Tell Us
Barbara J. King, ed.

Critical Anthropology Now: Unexpected Contexts, Shifting Constituencies, Changing Agendas
George E. Marcus, ed.

Archaic States
Gary M. Feinman & Joyce Marcus, eds.

Regimes of Language: Ideologies, Polities, and Identities
Paul V. Kroskrity, ed.

Biology, Brains, and Behavior: The Evolution of Human Development
Sue Taylor Parker, Jonas Langer, & Michael L. McKinney, eds.

Women & Men in the Prehispanic Southwest: Labor, Power, & Prestige
Patricia L. Crown, ed.

History in Person: Enduring Struggles, Contentious Practice, Intimate Identities
Dorothy Holland & Jean Lave, eds.

The Empire of Things: Regimes of Value and Material Culture
Fred R. Myers, ed.

Catastrophe & Culture: The Anthropology of Disaster
Susanna M. Hoffman & Anthony Oliver-Smith, eds.

Uruk Mesopotamia & Its Neighbors: Cross-Cultural Interactions in the Era of State Formation
Mitchell S. Rothman, ed.

Remaking Life & Death: Toward an Anthropology of the Biosciences
Sarah Franklin & Margaret Lock, eds.

Tikal: Dynasties, Foreigners, & Affairs of State: Advancing Maya Archaeology
Jeremy A. Sabloff, ed.

Published by SAR Press

Gray Areas: Ethnographic Encounters with Nursing Home Culture
Philip B. Stafford, ed.

Pluralizing Ethnography: Comparison and Representation in Maya Cultures, Histories, and Identities
John M. Watanabe & Edward F. Fischer, eds.

American Arrivals: Anthropology Engages the New Immigration
Nancy Foner, ed.

Violence
Neil L. Whitehead, ed.

Law & Empire in the Pacific: Fiji and Hawai'i
Sally Engle Merry & Donald Brenneis, eds.

Anthropology in the Margins of the State
Veena Das & Deborah Poole, eds.

The Archaeology of Colonial Encounters: Comparative Perspectives
Gil J. Stein, ed.

Globalization, Water, & Health: Resource Management in Times of Scarcity
Linda Whiteford & Scott Whiteford, eds.

A Catalyst for Ideas: Anthropological Archaeology and the Legacy of Douglas W. Schwartz
Vernon L. Scarborough, ed.

The Archaeology of Chaco Canyon: An Eleventh-Century Pueblo Regional Center
Stephen H. Lekson, ed.

Community Building in the Twenty-First Century
Stanley E. Hyland, ed.

Afro-Atlantic Dialogues: Anthropology in the Diaspora
Kevin A. Yelvington, ed.

Copán: The History of an Ancient Maya Kingdom
E. Wyllys Andrews & William L. Fash, eds.

The Seductions of Community: Emancipations, Oppressions, Quandaries
Gerald W. Creed, ed.

The Evolution of Human Life History
Kristen Hawkes & Richard R. Paine, eds.

The Gender of Globalization: Women Navigating Cultural and Economic Marginalities
Nandini Gunewardena & Ann Kingsolver, eds.

New Landscapes of Inequality: Neoliberalism and the Erosion of Democracy in America
Jane L. Collins, Micaela di Leonardo, & Brett Williams, eds.

Imperial Formations
Ann Laura Stoler, Carole McGranahan, & Peter C. Perdue, eds.

Opening Archaeology: Repatriation's Impact on Contemporary Research and Practice
Thomas W. Killion, ed.

Small Worlds: Method, Meaning, & Narrative in Microhistory
James F. Brooks, Christopher R. N. DeCorse, & John Walton, eds.

Memory Work: Archaeologies of Material Practices
Barbara J. Mills & William H. Walker, eds.

Figuring the Future: Globalization and the Temporalities of Children and Youth
Jennifer Cole & Deborah Durham, eds.

Timely Assets: The Politics of Resources and Their Temporalities
Elizabeth Emma Ferry & Mandana E. Limbert, eds.

Democracy: Anthropological Approaches
Julia Paley, ed.

Confronting Cancer: Metaphors, Inequality, and Advocacy
Juliet McMullin & Diane Weiner, eds.

Development & Dispossession: The Crisis of Forced Displacement and Resettlement
Anthony Oliver-Smith, ed.

Global Health in Times of Violence
Barbara Rylko-Bauer, Linda Whiteford, & Paul Farmer, eds.

Published by SAR Press

The Evolution of Leadership: Transitions in Decision Making from Small-Scale to Middle-Range Societies
Kevin J. Vaughn, Jelmer W. Eerkins, & John Kantner, eds.

Archaeology & Cultural Resource Management: Visions for the Future
Lynne Sebastian & William D. Lipe, eds.

Archaic State Interaction: The Eastern Mediterranean in the Bronze Age
William A. Parkinson & Michael L. Galaty, eds.

Indians & Energy: Exploitation and Opportunity in the American Southwest
Sherry L. Smith & Brian Frehner, eds.

Roots of Conflict: Soils, Agriculture, and Sociopolitical Complexity in Ancient Hawai'i
Patrick V. Kirch, ed.

Pharmaceutical Self: The Global Shaping of Experience in an Age of Psychopharmacology
Janis Jenkins, ed.

Forces of Compassion: Humanitarianism between Ethics and Politics
Erica Bornstein & Peter Redfield, eds.

The Shape of Script: How and Why Writing Systems Change
Stephen D. Houston, ed.

Enduring Conquests: Rethinking the Archaeology of Resistance to Spanish Colonialism in the Americas
Matthew Liebmann & Melissa S. Murphy, eds.

Dangerous Liaisons: Anthropologists and the National Security State
Laura A. McNamara & Robert A. Rubinstein, eds.

Breathing New Life into the Evidence of Death: Contemporary Approaches to Bioarchaeology
Aubrey Baadsgaard, Alexis T. Boutin, & Jane E. Buikstra, eds.

Nature, Science, and Religion: Intersections Shaping Society and the Environment
Catherine M. Tucker, ed.

The Global Middle Classes: Theorizing Through Ethnography
Rachel Heiman, Carla Freeman, & Mark Liechty, eds.

Keystone Nations: Indigenous Peoples and Salmon across the North Pacific
Benedict J. Colombi & James F. Brooks, eds.

Big Histories, Human Lives: Tackling Problems of Scale in Archaeology
John Robb & Timothy R. Pauketat, eds.

Reassembling the Collection: Ethnographic Museums and Indigenous Agency
Rodney Harrison, Sarah Byrne, & Anne Clarke, eds.

Images That Move
Patricia Spyer & Mary Margaret Steedly, eds.

Vital Relations: Modernity and the Persistent Life of Kinship
Susan McKinnon & Fenella Cannell, eds.

Anthropology of Race: Genes, Biology, and Culture
John Hartigan, ed.

Street Economies in the Urban Global South
Karen Tranberg Hansen, Walter E. Little, & B. Lynne Milgram, eds.

Cash on the Table: Markets, Values, and Moral Economies
Edward F. Fischer, ed.

(Mis)Managing Migration: Guestworkers' Experiences with North American Labor Markets
David Griffith, ed.

Katherine Dunham: Recovering an Anthropological Legacy, Choreographing Ethnographic Futures
Elizabeth Chin, ed.

Bio*In*secutrity and Vulnerability
Nancy N. Chen & Lesley A. Sharp, eds.

Artisans and Advocacy in the Global Market: Walking the Heart Path
Jeanne Simonelli, Katherine O'Donnell, & June Nash, eds.

TIMELESS CLASSICS FROM SAR PRESS

THE ANASAZI IN A CHANGING ENVIRONMENT
George J. Gumerman, ed.

ANCIENT CIVILIZATION AND TRADE
Jeremy A. Sabloff & C. C. Lamberg-Karlovsky, eds.

THE ANTHROPOLOGY OF WAR
Jonathan Haas, ed.

THE ARCHAEOLOGY OF LOWER CENTRAL AMERICA
Frederick W. Lange & Doris Z. Stone, eds.

CHAN CHAN: ANDEAN DESERT CITY
Michael E. Moseley & Kent C. Day, eds.

THE CHEMISTRY OF PREHISTORIC HUMAN BONE
T. Douglas Price, ed.

CHIEFDOMS: POWER, ECONOMY, AND IDEOLOGY
Timothy Earle, ed.

THE CLASSIC MAYA COLLAPSE
T. Patrick Culbert, ed.

CLASSIC MAYA POLITICAL HISTORY: HIEROGLYPHIC AND ARCHAEOLOGICAL EVIDENCE
T. Patrick Culbert, ed.

DEMOGRAPHIC ANTHROPOLOGY: QUANTITATIVE APPROACHES
Ezra B. W. Zubrow, ed.

THE DYING COMMUNITY
Art Gallaher Jr. & Harlan Padfield, eds.

ELITES: ETHNOGRAPHIC ISSUES
George E. Marcus, ed.

THE EMERGENCE OF MODERN HUMANS: BIOCULTURAL ADAPTATIONS IN THE LATER PLEISTOCENE
Erik Trinkaus, ed.

ENTREPRENEURS IN CULTURAL CONTEXT
Sidney M. Greenfield, Arnold Strickon, & Robert T. Aubey, eds.

THE EVOLUTION OF POLITICAL SYSTEMS
Steadman Upham, ed.

EXPLANATION OF PREHISTORIC CHANGE
James N. Hill, ed.

EXPLORATIONS IN ETHNOARCHAEOLOGY
Richard A. Gould, ed.

LATE LOWLAND MAYA CIVILIZATION: CLASSIC TO POSTCLASSIC
Jeremy A. Sabloff & E. Wyllys Andrews V, eds.

LOWLAND MAYA SETTLEMENT PATTERNS
Wendy Ashmore, ed.

MEANING IN ANTHROPOLOGY
Keith H. Basso & Henry A. Selby, eds.

METHODS AND THEORIES OF ANTHROPOLOGICAL GENETICS
M. H. Crawford & P. L. Workman, eds.

MORLEYANA: A COLLECTION OF WRITINGS IN MEMORIAM, SYLVANUS GRISWOLD MORLEY—1883–1948

NEW PERSPECTIVES ON THE PUEBLOS
Alfonso Ortiz, ed.

THE ORIGINS OF MAYA CIVILIZATION
Richard E. W. Adams, ed.

PHOTOGRAPHY IN ARCHAEOLOGICAL RESEARCH
Elmer Harp, Jr., ed.

RECONSTRUCTING PREHISTORIC PUEBLO SOCIETIES
William A. Longacre, ed.

REGIONAL PERSPECTIVES ON THE OLMEC
Robert J. Sharer & David C. Grove, eds.

SHIPWRECK ANTHROPOLOGY
Richard A. Gould, ed.

SIMULATIONS IN ARCHAEOLOGY
Jeremy A. Sabloff, ed.

STRUCTURE AND PROCESS IN LATIN AMERICA
Arnold Strickon & Sidney M. Greenfield, eds.

TURKO-PERSIA IN HISTORICAL PERSPECTIVE
Robert L. Canfield, ed.

THE VALLEY OF MEXICO: STUDIES IN PRE-HISPANIC ECOLOGY AND SOCIETY
Eric R. Wolf, ed.

Published by University of California Press

Writing Culture: The Poetics and Politics of Ethnography
James Clifford & George E. Marcus, eds.

Published by University of Arizona Press

The Collapse of Ancient States and Civilizations
Norman Yoffee & George L. Cowgill, eds.

Published by University of New Mexico Press

Sixteenth-Century Mexico: The Work of Sahagun
Munro S. Edmonson, ed.

Southwestern Indian Ritual Drama
Charlotte J. Frisbie, ed.

Participants in the School for Advanced Research advanced seminar "Disturbing Bodies: A Relational Exploration of Forensic Archaeological Practice" co-chaired by Zoë Crossland and Rosemary A. Joyce, March 25–29, 2012. *Standing, from left:* Pamela L. Geller, Tim Thompson, Heather Walsh-Haney, Victoria Sanford, Isaias Rojas-Perez, Debra L. Martin, Luis Fondebrider; *seated, from left:* Rosemary A. Joyce, Zoë Crossland, Hugh Tuller.